Cronies

ALSO BY ROBERT BRYCE

Pipe Dreams: Greed, Ego, and the Death of Enron

CRONIES

Oil, the Bushes, and the Rise of Texas, America's Superstate

ROBERT BRYCE

PublicAffairs *New York*

Published in the United States by PublicAffairs™,
a member of the Perseus Books Group.

Book design by Mark McGarry, Texas Type & Book Works
Set in Dante

Library of Congress Cataloging-in-Publication Data
Bryce, Robert.
Cronies: Oil, the Bushes, and the Rise of Texas, America's Superstate / Robert Bryce.
p. cm.
Includes bibliographical references and index.
ISBN 1-58648-188-6
1. Texas—Politics and government—1951– . 2. Texas—Biography.
3. Bush family. 4. Petroleum industry and trade—Political aspects—Texas.
5. Business and politics—Texas. 6. Political culture—Texas. 7. Petroleum industry
and trade—Political aspects—United States. 8. Business and politics—United States.
9. Political culture—United States. 10. United States—Political and government—1989– .
I. Title.
F391.2.B795 2004
976.4'063—dc22
2003070694

FIRST EDITION
10 9 8 7 6 5 4 3 2 1

For Lorin

The good Lord didn't see fit to put oil and gas only where there are democratically elected regimes friendly to the United States.

—Richard B. Cheney, "Defending Liberty in a Global Economy,"
speech at the Cato Institute, June 23, 1998

Texas is a state of mind. Texas is an obsession. Above all, Texas is a nation in every sense of the word.

—John Steinbeck, *Travels with Charley,* 1962

It may not be a wholesome thing to say, but the oil industry today is in complete control of the state government and state politics.

—Robert Calvert, chairman,
Texas Democratic State Executive Committee, 1947
(quoted in Anthony Champagne, *Congressman Sam Rayburn*)

Contents

CONTENTS

THE TEXAS CRONY WEB

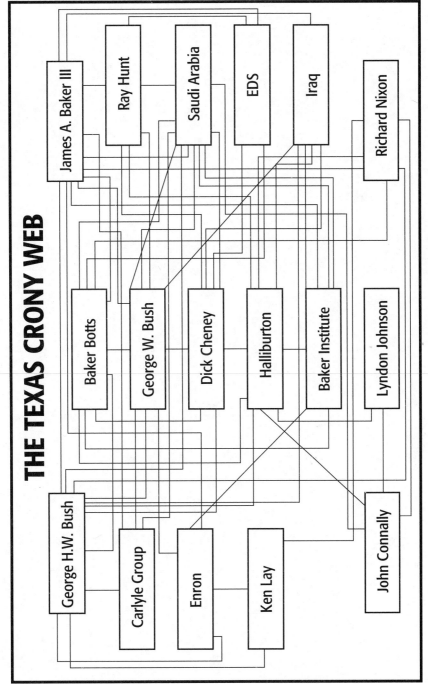

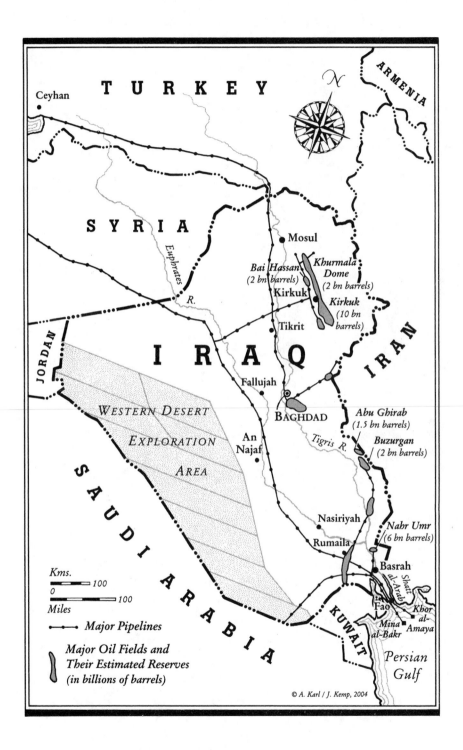

Ceyhan

TURKEY

ARMENIA

SYRIA

Mosul

Euphrates R.

Bai Hassan
(2 bn barrels)

Khurmala
Dome
(2 bn barrels)

Kirkuk

Kirkuk
(10 bn
barrels)

Tikrit

IRAQ

IRAN

Fallujah

BAGHDAD

Abu Ghirab
(1.5 bn barrels)

JORDAN

WESTERN DESERT

EXPLORATION

AREA

An
Najaf

Tigris R.

Buzurgan
(2 bn barrels)

SAUDI ARABIA

Nasiriyah

Rumaila

Nahr Umr
(6 bn barrels)

Basrah

Kms.

0   100

100

Miles

Fao

Shatt al-Arab

Khor
al-
Amaya

KUWAIT

Mina
al-Bakr

Persian
Gulf

•—•— Major Pipelines

Major Oil Fields and
Their Estimated Reserves
(in billions of barrels)

© A. Karl / J. Kemp, 2004

Author's Note

The thesis of this book grew out of research I did for my first book, *Pipe Dreams: Greed, Ego, and the Death of Enron*. Enron was a classic example of a hugely influential Texas energy company that set out to change the world. Its leaders, like its CEO, Ken Lay, were members of the Texas crony network. Enron's political power, market power, and media power were indicative of something deeper that I wanted to explore: the roots of Texas power and how it has grown to dominate America.

Of all the elements that have contributed to Texas' power, one factor stands out: oil. Oil is money. Money is power. Texas has oil. Therefore, Texas has power. But there's more to the story of Texas power than just energy. The more I looked, the more it became clear that it was the relationships among a few key players that helped propel Texas to prominence. The cronies who ran Texas in the past—and who run Texas today—have been able to convert those relationships into political power, market power, and incredible wealth. And as they have done so, the lines between their personal business and government have become nearly indistinguishable. This book is not meant to be an attack on business or an attack on government. I'm all for business. I'm all for government. I just don't want them to be the same thing.

In the course of my research, it didn't take long to realize that the people I really needed to talk with were people like James A. Baker III and George H. W. Bush. Alas, they didn't want to talk to me. No one at Baker's law firm, Baker Botts, would talk. James A. Baker III's secretary responded to my request for a formal interview by saying that he was "unable to commit to an interview due to prior commitments. He appreciates your request." Ray Hunt, the head of Hunt Oil, also refused to answer any questions, saying, "That's one of the advantages of being a private company." The press office at Halliburton, the biggest oilfield service–construction company in America, refused to answer questions. George H. W. Bush's office in Houston did not respond to my request for an interview with the former president.

Furthermore, I found the archival material for this book to be less extensive than I'd have liked. The records managers at the George Bush Presidential Library at Texas A&M in College Station informed me that none of the papers from George H. W. Bush's tenure as vice president are available to the public. A similar situation holds true for the papers of James A. Baker III. Baker himself gives permission to researchers wanting to view his papers, which are now at Princeton University. Librarians at Princeton indicated that Baker has not yet permitted anyone to view his papers, which are also still being catalogued.

The most maddening efforts to obtain material for this book came in dealing with the White House. The Kremlin under Leonid Brezhnev was surely an easier institution to deal with.

Perhaps this lack of access, this lack of public dialogue, is to be expected. The powerful don't want to discuss the power they wield.

Even though a handful of people avoided me, many more were interested and helpful. Thanks to Peter O'Donnell, George Bayoud, Bill Clements, Jim Wright, Robert Strauss, Charles Matthews, and several others for their cooperation and insights. I'm certain some of the conclusions in this book don't match theirs, but I appreciate their willingness to talk to me.

Thanks also to Bill Lee, Arlie Sherman, George Strong, Jim Moore,

Lou Dubose, Bill Black, Ron and Violet Cauthon, Mauro Renteria, Farris Rookstool, Ben Barnes, Don Carleton, Kurt Holmes, Art Smith, Molly Ivans, Tom Sommers, Barry Silverman, Lisa Stewart, Mike Stewart, Robb Walsh, Turk Pipkin, John S. Herold Inc., Wayne Slater, Pete Slover, Jim Tanner, Michael Economides, Paul Hobby, Bobby Ray Inman, Jim Akins, Sissy Farenthold, David Berg, Jim Norman, John Olson, Jim Runzheimer, Ruhi Ramazani, Ray Close, Mike Ameen, Lyn Nofziger, Bill Rosch, Babe Schwarz, Tom Pauken, Raymond Plank, Ken McNeil, the staff at the Center for American History, the staff at the George Bush Presidential Library, Madeline Jowdy, Elizabeth Allen, John MacCormack, Jim Barth, Andrew Wheat, members of the organization Texans for Public Justice, Dan Green, and Simon Green. Special thanks to the remarkable people at PublicAffairs, including my editor, Lisa Kaufman, as well as Martha Deery, Robert Kimzey, Gene Taft, Nina D'Amario, David Patterson, and the publisher, Peter Osnos.

Particular thanks to Bob Elder for his encouragement and critiques, and to my older, smarter, and better-looking brother, Wally Bryce. Thanks also to Ann Bryce, R. J. Bryce, Eileen Bryce, Patti Bryce, and Mary Fox for their unflagging love and support. Thanks, too, to Leslie McLain, Amy Smith, Peter Voskamp, and Pokey Anderson for their research work; to Mimi Bardagjy for her punctilious fact checking; and to Kate Scott, who copyedited the manuscript and provided many helpful changes and clarifications.

Finally, thanks to Lorin, Mary, Michael, and Jacob. I still love you more than chocolate.

Robert Bryce
Austin, Texas
February 2004

Cronies

Chapter 1

From Mina al-Bakr to Houston

S ome of the soldiers carried shotguns, others carried Heckler & Koch MP5 submachine guns. A few carried crowbars to be used for breaking open doors. All of the men wore green jumpsuits, body armor packed with ammunition, and black balaclavas to cover their faces. Within a minute or so of boarding their 82-foot-long Mark V jet-boats, the four platoons of Navy SEALs were zipping across the uppermost end of the Persian Gulf at nearly 60 miles per hour. Speed was critical. They had to get from their land base in Kuwait to the target as quickly as possible to avoid detection and to assure the element of surprise. It was March 20, 2003. George W. Bush's ultimatum to Saddam Hussein had expired only a few hours earlier.

The SEALs were heading into the very first battle of the Second Iraq War. Their mission was the capture of Iraq's most valuable asset: its oil spigot.

During the First Iraq War, the generals at the Pentagon hadn't paid attention to details. When U.S. planes began bombing Iraqi targets in January 1991, Saddam Hussein's henchmen responded by opening the valves at various oil terminals, dumping enormous quantities of crude oil into the Persian Gulf. American ground forces began their invasion several weeks later, but by that time, the Persian Gulf was awash in oil. Several million barrels of crude oil were killing fish, sea birds, and anything else it touched. Hundreds of miles of beach were coated in oil and a Saudi Arabian desalinization plant located at Jubail was nearly forced to shut down because of the contamination. The effects of the massive spill lingered throughout the Persian Gulf for years afterward. After that fiasco, the soldiers were going to make sure that this time, they seized Saddam Hussein's financial arteries right at the get-go.

Within a few minutes of leaving Kuwaiti waters, the SEALs' jet-boats were within range of their targets: Mina al-Bakr, Iraq's main oil export terminal, a sprawling metal spider of pipes, pumps, and pilings; and a smaller terminal located five miles northeast, called Khor al-Amaya. Together, the two terminals—located a few miles southeast of the mouth of the Shatt al-Arab, the river that separates Iraq and Iran—were capable of loading about two million barrels of oil per day onto supertankers in the Persian Gulf. That capacity made the terminals into the equivalent of a cash machine, a machine backed by a nearly inexhaustible supply of liquid money redeemable at dozens of thirsty refineries around the world.

Saddam Hussein's military didn't have a chance.

In addition to the platoons of SEALs on the jet-boats, the Navy had backup SEAL teams flying aboard a flock of UH–60 Sea Hawk helicopters hovering nearby. Snipers aboard the choppers had their rifles at the ready, scanning the oil terminals for signs of trouble. Five miles away, the USS *Valley Forge,* a Ticonderoga-class guided missile cruiser, monitored the action. The ship's control room was crammed with people watching huge monitors showing a live video feed that was beamed to the ship from a camera mounted on one of the helicopters.

When the jet-boats reached Mina al-Bakr, the SEALs quietly crept up the ladders, their weapons at the ready. When they got to the main level, they stormed through the doorways and into the terminal's control room and cramped living quarters. Instead of a gunfight, all they got was a bunch of sleepy Iraqis eager to surrender. The battle for Mina al-Bakr lasted about two minutes. "I think they were actually relieved to have the place taken over," said one SEAL after the raid.[1]

The takeover of Mina al-Bakr won't be recalled alongside Gettysburg, D-Day, or Khe Sahn in the annals of American military history. But it has more than passing significance. By taking Mina al-Bakr, the American military prevented Iraq from repeating the ecoterrorism-by-intentional-oil-spill of 1991. It further assured that the upper section of the Persian Gulf near the mouth of the Shatt al-Arab was secure and that oil tankers, Navy vessels, and freighters would not be threatened by Iraqi boats.

Mina al-Bakr is significant for another reason: it's a Texas outpost in the heart of the Persian Gulf.

The terminal may be owned by the Iraqi government, but it was built by the quintessential Texas company: Brown & Root. That's the same Brown & Root that helped put Lyndon Johnson in power. That's the same Brown & Root that's part of Halliburton, the world's second-largest oilfield services firm. That's the same Halliburton that, until the summer of 2000, employed a former defense secretary named Dick Cheney. It's the same firm that gave Cheney a going-away present worth tens of millions of dollars for all of his hard work as Halliburton's CEO. It's the same firm that, in 2001 and 2002, *while Cheney was vice president of the United States*, paid him more than $367,000 in deferred compensation. It's the same firm that has garnered federal contracts worth $11 billion to rebuild Iraq's oilfields and civil infrastructure. As soon as Baghdad was captured, one of Halliburton's first tasks was to assure that Mina al-Bakr was open and ready for business.

Halliburton's privileged role in Iraq has been controversial—but it's hardly a new phenomenon. Since the 1960s, the United States has been involved in four major fights to extend its military and commercial interests in the Persian Gulf and the Far East: Vietnam, Iran, the First Iraq War, and now, the Second Iraq War. And in each of those gambits, Texas politicians and Texas corporations have had starring roles. Whether the locale was Saigon, Tehran, Kuwait City, or Baghdad, Texas companies like Halliburton have been planting the Lone Star flag right next to Old Glory and they've been making big profits by doing so. All this action has led to the creation of the slogan "When cannons shoot, call Brown & Root."

The Second Iraq War is just the latest example of Texas politicos' and Texas corporations' taking lead roles in America's foreign policy and energy policy. Ever since 1973, when the Organization of the Petroleum Exporting Countries threw the world into turmoil with the first in a series of price hikes, American politicians, working hand in glove with oil producers from Texas and other states, have been trying to regain some control over the world's oil supply—and therefore world oil prices.

George W. Bush and his supporters have repeatedly said the war against Iraq was not about oil. They've told us it's about stopping terrorism; it's about weapons of mass destruction; it's about spreading democracy in the Middle East; it's about preserving human rights. Whatever the stated reason for the war, the facts of the military action are unassailable: the very first target of the Second Iraq War was an oil facility. And while the SEALs were storming the terminals, American and British troops were seizing Iraq's oilfields. Special Operations forces raced into the oilfields around Kirkuk in northern Iraq. In southern Iraq, 20,000 U.S. Marines and 4,000 British Royal Marines hurried into the prolific oilfields of Rumaila and Basra.

The United States' fundamental and overriding interest in Iraq—and the rest of the Persian Gulf—is oil. By gaining control of Mina al-Bakr and the oil fields, the U.S. sent a message to OPEC that said, in effect, *we're here and we're not leaving any time soon.*

By securing the oil targets first, the United States immediately gained effective control of the second-largest oil deposits on earth. A cynic might think there's something malicious or untoward about fighting a war over oil, but it is hardly a new phenomenon. Oil has long been a strategic asset. Indeed, the Second Iraq War is markedly similar to the decision made in 1931 by a Texas governor, a fellow who also happened to be an oilman-turned-politician. That year, Governor Ross Sterling—who had served as the first president of Humble Oil & Refining, a company now known as Exxon Mobil—sent more than a thousand troops from the Texas National Guard into the enormously rich oilfields of East Texas to force oil producers there to bow to controls on their production volume. Sterling was forced to act, he claimed, because the oil producers in that region were "in a state of insurrection" and their actions "openly, flagrantly and rebelliously violate the laws."

The problem for Sterling in 1931—and the problem today—is that oil production is difficult to control. The entire history of the oil business has been marked by swings between too much production, which leads to low prices, and too little production, which leads to high prices. Some critics may think that the oil industry always wants high prices. That isn't necessarily true. The best price for the oil industry is a stable midlevel price, one that assures oil consumers, oil producers, and oil refiners that they won't be hit with a shortage or a surplus.

Managing the supply of the world's most precious commodity is not easily done. It requires collaboration or coercion. Collaboration— or perhaps, more precisely, *price fixing*—works. But price fixing has a rather unsavory history.

Sometimes coercion is the only option. It's doubtful that the Chinese leader Mao Tse-tung ever drilled an oil well. But his line—"Political power grows out of the barrel of a gun"—also applies to the oilfield. Ultimately, the only way to control oil supplies is through the barrel of a gun. That fact has been understood in Texas for seven decades. Now it's being played out once again in the Persian Gulf. And it's being played out by a former Texas oilman-turned-politician, George W. Bush, and his vice president, Dick Cheney, a politician-turned-Texas-energy-man-turned-politician.

Bush and Cheney are part of a small group of powerful, Big Rich Texans who through their connections to the energy industry have exerted extraordinary influence in the United States and the world. Call them the Texas Six Pack: George W. Bush, Dick Cheney, George H. W. Bush, James A. Baker III, former Enron CEO Ken Lay, and the independent oilman and chairman of the Federal Reserve Bank of Dallas, Ray Hunt. Those six men are just the current giants in the long Texas tradition of mingling energy, business, and government for private profit.

Crony capitalism happens everywhere, you say. There's nothing new in that—businessmen and politicians have always rewarded their friends with lucrative deals. But the virulent strain of Texas cronyism now infecting America's capitalist democracy is more brazen than any of the strains of cronyism seen thus far. It's more pernicious and more corrupting and the rewards being reaped by the crony class are bigger than ever before. And it's those rascally Texans who are corralling the cash.

This book will explain how this select group of Texas Cronies came to rule America. It will expose the long history of cronyism that has bound the Texas energy business to the Texas political system and the way that tradition has now been transferred to Washington, D.C. This book will show how the Bushes, the Bakers, and the Cheneys came to power and how they enriched themselves along the way. And it will explain why, at the outset of the twenty-first century, the rest of the United States needs to care, lest Texas take over the rest of the world.

If the twentieth century was the American century, then there's little doubt that the last half of the American century belonged to Texas. Two of the last three presidents—and three of the last eight—have been Texans. Two of those three were oilmen. And all three fought major ground wars.

Like it or not, Texas rules.

No other province has a tighter hold on America's psyche, politics, and wallet.

Whether you are buying gasoline for your car, listening to the radio, or casting your vote for president, the Lone Star State is probably affecting your experience. There are 49 other provinces—as well as 14 territories and the District of Columbia—in these United States. And a few of them—like California and New York and Florida, and maybe a few of those dinky eastern states—are fairly important. But there's simply no denying that Texas has bulldozed its way to the forefront of America's domestic and foreign policy. Whether the issue is energy, presidential politics, foreign policy, or business, Texas has an outsized influence on what happens, an influence far greater than that of any other state.

California is important. It's bigger than Texas in terms of population. Its gross state product, $1.3 trillion, exceeds that of Texas by half a trillion dollars. It has cleaner beaches, nicer parks, a better climate, mountains, redwoods, surfing, the La Brea tar pits and 4,342 other wonders. But California can't keep its lights on—or its governors in office—for very long. Regardless of whether the state is run by a bunch of granola-eating vegans from San Francisco or an oversexed Austrian bodybuilder, California's economy is vulnerable.

California must import enormous amounts of crude oil, natural gas, and electricity to keep its economy afloat. Nothing proved California's vulnerability better than the electricity and natural gas price calamities of 2000 and 2001. Power that had been costing $30 per megawatt-hour was suddenly costing as much as $1,500.[2] For all of the strengths of California's massive economy, it still depends on other states and other countries to supply the energy that keeps the lights burning inside its microchip foundries, manufacturing plants, and surfboard shops.

The energy disaster proved that California had done a terrible job of managing its energy supplies, and it also showed that the real center of power in America wasn't Los Angeles or San Francisco but Houston. Young hot shots, gangs of pillage-and-plunder-minded energy traders from Houston's Energy Alley, had manipulated electricity and natural gas prices in California at their whim. Their profit was California's loss. Unfortunately for Californians, that exercise in Darwinian economics may cost them as much as $45 billion.

New York is an important state, too. And like California, it can't keep its lights on. In the summer of 2003, the blackout that hit the northeastern U.S. and parts of Canada proved that New York has a fragile electric infrastructure prone to failure. New York City is the most important arbiter and producer of American arts and media, from opera and ballet to magazines, TV, and newspapers. It's the epicenter of world banking and finance. The Empire State has given America six presidents and 11 vice presidents. But New York's economy and population are stagnant. Between 1970 and 2000, New York's population growth was nearly flat, going from 18.2 million to 18.9 million residents. During those same three decades, Texas' population nearly doubled, to 21 million people. That population shift means New York is losing clout in Congress and the electoral college. Between 1981 and 2001, New York lost five seats in the U.S. House of Representatives (and five electoral college votes). During that same period, Texas added five seats in the House and a corresponding number of electoral college votes.

California may be cool, and New York may be the Big Apple, but Texas is the Big Enchilada. And it can keep its lights on. That's because Texas has its very own power grid with few interconnections to other states, surplus electrical generating capacity, and a surfeit of natural gas to power its generators. However, electric power is just one of a panoply of factors that have made Texas into America's *über*-state.

Here are a few more:

Texas dominates the United States because the country's population is shifting away from the old, cold, Industrial Belt states of the Northeast and Midwest to the warm states of the South and West. Three of America's 10 largest cities—Houston, Dallas, and San Antonio—are in Texas. And current trends indicate that Texas will continue growing while the northern states shrink or tread water.

Texas dominates the United States because of its enormous size and location. Texas covers nearly 262,000 square miles—that's bigger than California and Oregon combined and nearly five times the size of Illinois. That vast expanse of acreage attracts industry, provides cheap housing, and allows a rock-bottom cost of living. Transportation companies have flocked to Texas. Trucking firms and railroads like Texas because it's midway between the coasts and it adjoins Mexico, one of America's biggest trading partners. Thanks to the passage of the North American Free Trade Agreement, Texas has become the primary beneficiary of the transportation systems that have been established on the trade routes into Mexico and Canada. Nearly half of all NAFTA-related trade either originates in or is destined for Texas. A massive network of rail lines in and around Houston and Fort Worth interconnect a rail system unparalleled in the United States. Texas has 14,192 miles of railroad track—far more than any other state. Those rail lines connect the rest of the country with the Port of Houston, the world's sixth-largest port. The port takes in more foreign cargo than any other American port. And most of that cargo is oil from (in order) Mexico, Venezuela, Saudi Arabia, and Iraq. The Port of Houston is now vying to become a major player in the global containerized shipping business.

Texas has an inexhaustible supply of cheap, nonunion labor. Since its statehood, Texas has been able to tap armies of immigrants from all over the world, but particularly from Mexico, who are eager to work. The state's worst jobs—janitorial work, pouring concrete, cutting meat in a slaughterhouse, hanging sheetrock—are filled by recent arrivals from Mexico, Cambodia, Honduras, and dozens of other countries.

Three of the seven largest airlines in America, including the only profitable large one—Southwest Airlines—are based in Texas. Two of the 15 biggest airports in the world (Dallas–Ft. Worth International and George Bush Intercontinental in Houston) are located in Texas.

Texas dominates the United States politically because its representatives have commandeered the U.S. Capitol. Over the past few decades, Texas politicians have made the Capitol in Washington into an outpost of the Capitol building at Eleventh and Congress streets in Austin. And that building in Austin, by the way, is *23 feet taller* than the one located in Washington, D.C.

Texans have been dominating both houses of Congress since before the New Deal. Of the last 16 terms for Speaker of the U.S. House of Representatives, five have been held by Texans.[3] Between 1931 and 1989, a Texan was serving as Speaker of the House nearly a third of the time. In 1933, when Franklin Roosevelt moved into the White House, Texans were flush in Washington. John Nance "Cactus Jack" Garner, a rancher from Uvalde, in southwestern Texas, who'd served three decades in Congress, including two years as Speaker of the House—was Roosevelt's vice president. Texans led six committees in the House, including Agriculture, Interstate Commerce, Judiciary, and Public Buildings and Grounds, as well as the powerful Appropriations Committee.[4] In the Senate, Texan Morris Sheppard chaired the Committee on Military Affairs (now the Senate Armed Services Committee) throughout the 1930s. His tenure ended only when he died, eight months before Pearl Harbor in 1941.

Texas dominates America because its representatives in Washington have steered trainloads of federal cash to the Lone Star State.

Whether the issue is building dams and highways or exotic new flying machines for the Pentagon like the fatally flawed V–22 Osprey, or incredibly expensive aircraft like the F–22 and the F–35—the Texas delegation has always pushed to the front of the line. Phil Gramm, the former U.S. senator from Texas, used to say, "I'm carrying so much pork, I'm beginning to get trichinosis."[5]

From the 1930s to the 1960s, Texas got far more than its share of federal bacon. One study found that during those three decades, Texas' share of the federal pie exceeded the national average by 27 percent! In the 1960s, the clout of Texas' politicians was made obvious during the debate over where to locate a new training center for American astronauts. The Russians had just put Yuri Gagarin into orbit, in 1961, and the Americans were determined to surpass that achievement, and do it quickly. At that time, Albert Thomas, a powerful Democrat from Houston, was the head of the committee that would choose the site. So in 1961, when it came time for Congress to choose from among sites in California, Florida, and Texas, the new space center ended up being located a few miles southeast of downtown Houston. The multi-million-dollar construction contract for the new facility was awarded to Thomas's benefactor, Brown & Root.

In the four decades since the Johnson Space Center was built in Houston, the National Aeronautical and Space Administration has pumped at least $100 billion into the Houston economy. And all of that money went to Houston because powerful Texas politicians like Lyndon Johnson, Sam Rayburn, and Albert Thomas demanded that it be done.

Throughout the 1970s Texas continued to feed at the federal trough. For example, in 1972 Texans paid about $10.3 billion in federal taxes. That same year, the state received federal outlays totaling $12.6 billion, including $5.1 billion from the Department of Defense, an amount exceeded only by California, even though California had 70 percent more people. Much of that money came courtesy of big weapons contracts that were pushed through by Texas' congressional representatives.

In the late 1980s, when Congress was picking a spot to build the superconducting supercollider, a gigantic atom-smashing machine, the Speaker of the House was Jim Wright, a Democrat from Fort Worth. When it came down to choosing the site for the supercollider, Illinois and Texas were the final contenders. It's not surprising that the final site for the collider ended up being in Waxahachie, just south of Dallas. The collider project didn't survive for long. It had a fatal collision with congressional budget cutters shortly after Wright left office. For Wright, the issue wasn't about science or technology. "To this day, I still don't know what things we intended to derive from the supercollider," he told me in early 2003. "But if they were going to build it, I wanted them to build it in Texas."

Wright left Congress in 1989 largely because of his involvement in the savings and loan debacle. And while that debacle cost the Lone Star State a powerful voice inside the U.S. Capitol, it also allowed the state to become the main beneficiary of one of the biggest transfers of wealth in modern American history. The savings and loan (S&L) disaster cost American taxpayers about $300 billion. Fully half of those losses occurred in Texas, which ended up with acres upon acres of empty federally subsidized offices, condos, and apartments that should never have been built in the first place. And it's the suckers in the lesser states who are paying the bill for that real estate subsidy.

Wright's downfall allowed other Texans to rise to prominence in Congress—but by now they were Republicans, not Democrats. In 1995, Dick Armey, a conservative Republican from Irving, near Dallas, became the House majority leader. He was backed up by the majority whip, Tom DeLay, the archconservative Shiite Republican from Sugar Land, a suburb of Houston.

DeLay once called himself a "free-market nut." It's certainly an apt description, though most Americans would probably agree that DeLay could simply leave out the "free-market" part of that phrase and be done with it. Nevertheless, DeLay, who's now House majority leader, is the most powerful man in the U.S. House of Representatives. Just as Lyndon Johnson controlled the Senate in the 1950s, Tom DeLay dominates the U.S. House in the 2000s. Like Johnson, he is ruthless, cunning, and able to raise enormous amounts of money that he can use to bolster the campaigns and causes of his allies.

Texas also dominates the American presidency. Although Texas may not own the White House outright, it definitely has a working set of keys.

In the period between 1960 and 2004, a Texan has been either president or vice president for 24 of those 44 years. And Texas may extend that streak through 2008. Cactus Jack Garner started it. Garner was the first Texan to serve as vice president, a job he said wasn't worth "a pitcher of warm spit." Since Garner served his sentence as second-in-command, Texas has gone from being an afterthought in the presidential sweepstakes to being the state that a candidate absolutely must win if he wants to live at 1600 Pennsylvania Avenue.

Since 1924, when Texas voted for the Democrat John Davis instead of the winner, Calvin Coolidge, only two men have won the White House without winning Texas. Richard Nixon did it once, in 1968, and Bill Clinton did it twice, in 1992 and 1996. But Clinton was only able to win because of another Texan, H. Ross Perot, the bantam-rooster billionaire from Dallas. In both of those races, Perot ran as a third-party candidate and his place on the ballot pulled millions of votes away from the Republicans. Of course, the only reason Perot was able to get on the ballot and run credible races was his enormous wealth. In 1992, he spent nearly $70 million of his own money. In 1996, he spent another $8 million. His enormous personal fortune allowed the bullheaded Perot to make himself into the most successful third-party candidate since Teddy Roosevelt ran as a Bull Moose in 1912.

Two other Texans, both Democrats-turned-Republicans, have

launched enormously expensive but unsuccessful campaigns for the White House in recent years. Former Texas Governor John Connally's 1980 bid, on which he spent $11 million, and Phil Gramm's in 1996, on which he spent $26 million, were both crushed by landslides of voter antipathy.

Texas has become the cornerstone of the GOP South. With Texans playing a big role in determining who lives in the White House, Texans have continued their colonization of Washington, D.C. Four of the last 15 vice presidents—Garner, Lyndon Johnson, George H. W. Bush, and Dick Cheney—have been Texans. Three of the last 15 secretaries of the treasury—Lloyd Bentsen, James A. Baker III, and John Connally—were from Texas. Two of the last seven secretaries of commerce—Donald Evans and Robert Mosbacher, both oilmen—have been Texans. The Lone Star State's importance was captured a few years ago when Karl Rove named it "America's superstate."

Texas dominates America because Big Business loves doing big business in Texas. Eighteen Fortune 500 companies are based in Houston, more than in any other city except New York. In 2003, *Forbes* magazine included two Texas cities, Austin and Dallas, on its list of the 10 best places in America to do business. Texas has long been a magnet for corporations because of its low taxes.

Texas is one of just seven states that does not charge any form of personal income tax. In fact, Texas has a constitutional amendment that prohibits the implementation of an income tax without the consent of voters. And while the paucity of tax revenue means that Texas lags behind the other states in virtually every health and human service category, the state's politicians continue to focus almost exclusively on how they can make the state even more hospitable to business. Through its politicians and think tanks, the state is now exporting that low-tax, low-service, laissez-faire, "Trust us we're Big Business and we're here to help" model to the rest of the United States.

Texas has long had a more freewheeling business culture than other parts of the country. In 2002, the *Economist* magazine said that Texas was "America on steroids.... Think of the characteristics that make America distinctive—its size and diversity, its optimism and self-confidence, its crass materialism and bravado, its incredible ability to make something out of nothing—and they exist in their purest form in Texas."

Many of the world's great fortunes have been made in the Texas energy business. And the state's Big Rich are legendary. Jerry Jones, the Snidely Whiplash of the National Football League and owner of the Dallas Cowboys, made his money in the oil business after drilling 12 successful gas wells in a row. Houston's Howard Hughes Sr. invented the rotary drill bit, which revolutionized oil drilling. He passed on his Houston-based company, Hughes Tool Company, to his son, Howard Hughes Jr., who became notorious for his manias: movies, Las Vegas, fast airplanes, and even faster women. H. L. Hunt, the eccentric billionaire oilman and die-hard supporter of Senator Joe McCarthy and other right-wing extremists, made his fortune in the East Texas oilfields. But the Lone Star State has also minted plenty of millionaires who had nothing to do with the oil business. Huge fortunes have been made in high-tech, banking, insurance, and real estate. Take the boy billionaire Michael Dell, the founder and boss of Dell Computer. He lives in a dainty 30,000-square-foot home on the outskirts of Austin. But with his fortune of $13 billion or so, Dell can afford it. And his company, which specializes in made-to-order computers, continues to crush its competitors with a brand of ruthless efficiency that John D. Rockefeller would have admired. Then there's Ross Perot, who's worth $3.7 billion or so. He made his billions by growing the Dallas-based computer services provider Electronic Data Systems into a global powerhouse. The two-time presidential candidate ran on a platform of cutting government and government waste, but in fact made his fortune thanks to EDS's ability to capture lucrative federal contracts.

Of the 400 richest people in America in 2003, 36, or 9 percent, were from Texas. According to *Forbes*, their combined wealth is nearly $80 billion. In addition to the sheer magnitude of the wealth, nearly every one of those Texas zillionaires is politically active, making big contributions to the politicians who work to allow them to keep as much of their money as possible.

The U.S. military has also been stamped with a Texas brand. Only two states—California and Virginia—get more Pentagon dollars than Texas. The commander of U.S. forces during the Second Iraq War, the U.S. Army's General Tommy Franks, hails from George W. Bush's stomping grounds, Midland. The commandant of the Marine Corps, General Michael Hagee, is from the Central Texas town of Fredericksburg. As the Second Iraq War was launched, two of the six members of the Joint Chiefs of Staff, the president's top military advisers, were Texans. In the Air Force, 41 of 282 generals—almost 15 percent—are Texans, as are 43, or about 12 percent, of 366 Army generals.[6] There is a higher concentration of Texans in the armed forces than soldiers from any other state: fully 10 percent of the personnel in the U.S. military are Texans, even though Texas accounts for just 7 percent of the nation's population. More enlisted personnel are stationed in Texas than any other state. Policy decisions about the Persian Gulf may be set in Washington, but they are enforced by soldiers stationed at Fort Hood, America's biggest military base, which is located less than 20 miles south of George W. Bush's ranch in Crawford.

Texas corporations are the ones who get contracts to take care of those soldiers. Brown & Root, a subsidiary of Dick Cheney's old company, Halliburton, does the Army's laundry and serves meals to GIs. When sailors aboard a warship in the Persian Gulf retrieve their e-mail, the system they use was probably put together by Perot's old company, EDS. When pilots take off from that same ship, they may be flying in an aircraft built by Fort Worth–based Bell Helicopter.

Texas flat knows how to vacuum up federal money. In fact, given the amount of federal money that flows into Texas, the state symbol should probably be the vampire bat, not the longhorn or the oil derrick.

Not only has Texas always managed to keep its fingers in Uncle Sam's pocket, but it has also commandeered the front porch of the American psyche. Texas myths have become America's myths. Perhaps the most enduring of these myths is the Alamo. In 1836, 182 fighters fended off several thousand Mexican soldiers, until they were finally overrun and slaughtered. That battle was part of Texas' struggle for independence, which made Texas into a nation before it was a state. Ever since those hapless souls died at the Alamo, Texas has worn a halo of self-congratulatory pomposity that permeates everything the state does. And that attitude isn't going away. One historian, H. W. Brands, put it, "Texans have long prided themselves on their individuality, including their right to be wrong in their own way. For them, the Alamo is the perfect shrine."[7]

A shrine it is. In fact, the Daughters of the Republic of Texas, the group that runs the Alamo, insist that the old Catholic church in downtown San Antonio be called The Shrine. Men are asked to remove their hats before entering the building and talking is to be kept to a minimum. The church is the most-visited tourist site in Texas. Three million people make the pilgrimage to the Mecca of Texas every year. For Texans, it is Gettysburg, the Boston Tea Party, and the Sistine Chapel all rolled up into one event, one memory, one place.

The Alamo, the cowboy, the Indian fighter, the wildcatter, the larger-than-life oilman—all of them Texas archetypes—have become so closely intertwined with America's self-image that it's impossible to tell the two sets of myths apart.

Texas' heritage, its size, its music, its movies, and a myriad of other elements combine to give it a swagger, a belief, that its destiny is more manifest than any other state's. In 2003, the Texas legislature—apparently because it didn't have anything better to do—passed a law requiring the state's schoolchildren to recite the pledge of allegiance every morning . . . *to the Texas flag*. It goes, "Honor the Texas flag; I pledge allegiance to thee, Texas, one and indivisible."

Texans have internalized this maniacal obsession with their state. It's a concept best summarized by the singer-songwriter Ray Wylie Hubbard, who in 2003 released the instantaneously classic "Screw You, We're from Texas."[8]

Flags, cowboys, and the Alamo are all part of the Texas mystique. But when it comes to explaining Texas' rise to power, it can be boiled down to one word: energy. And that leads to the thesis of this book: Texas dominates America because energy —Texas energy—dominates America. And the men who have dominated Texas energy have been extraordinarily successful at putting their politicians into power.

Texas has turned its vast energy resources into political power. This book will profile the state's crony network—the group of loosely affiliated, rich, powerful men who exert enormous influence in American business and politics. Those men include the three Texas presidents— Lyndon Johnson, George H. W. Bush, and George W. Bush—each of whom tapped into the state's veins of Big Rich oilmen to seize the reins of power.

George W. Bush is the living embodiment of a powerful crony network that includes his father, George H. W. Bush; the Bakers; the Carlyle Group; the Texas oil business; and the Saudi royal family. Vice President Dick Cheney provides a direct link to Halliburton, with its ongoing business dealings in the Persian Gulf and its long, lucrative ties to Saddam Hussein. In 2002, Halliburton dismissed its longtime legal counsel, Vinson & Elkins. (Vinson & Elkins used to represent Enron Corp. It also used to employ a lawyer named Alberto Gonzales—who is now the White House general counsel.) Halliburton replaced Vinson & Elkins with another Houston firm, one with even more influence in the nation's capital, Baker Botts. That's the outfit headed by the most powerful former secretary of state in the land, James A. Baker III.

Baker Botts is no ordinary law firm. The Baker Botts franchise has been a Republican redoubt for decades. Every time over the past 50 years when the Bush family has run into a political or legal snarl, it has called on Baker Botts. And Baker Botts loves the Bushes right back. During the 2000 campaign, Baker Botts was George W. Bush's ninth-largest contributor, giving him a total of $116,121.

Bush has rewarded the law firm and Baker with a series of very high profile appointments. One Baker Botts lawyer was named ambassador to Saudi Arabia. Another got a top spot in the Department of Transportation. In late 2003, Bush appointed Baker as his "personal envoy on the issue of Iraqi debt." Baker was given the task of convincing countries like Japan, Germany, and France to forgive much of Iraq's foreign debt. (Left unsaid in Bush's appointment was that in 1989, Baker, who was secretary of state at the time, lent crucial support to federal agriculture loans to Iraq—those loans later cost the U.S. some $500 million.)[9] Baker was successful in getting those debts reduced. He was also successful in raising his own profile and that of Baker Botts, a firm that also happens to represent the world's biggest energy company, Texas-based Exxon Mobil Corporation.

The power of the Texas energy business is not a new topic. Texas politicos have long relied on the state's Big Rich for all kinds of details. Whether it was Lyndon Johnson using a DC–3 owned by Brown & Root, or George W. Bush flying on jets owned by Enron Corp., Texas politicos and Texas interests have been stampeding to the top for decades. Texas politicians have gained clout in Washington over the past seven or eight decades because they have a huge (and growing) block of votes, they are from a big state located in a strategic spot, and they have access to huge amounts of money.

Although much has been written about the Texas energy business, the volume of the coverage has by no means exhausted the topic or blunted its importance. In fact, the energy business is more critical today, and the stakes are higher for the American economy, than at any other time in American history. Naohiro Amaya, a Japanese politician, once called oil "the blood of the twentieth century." If oil is the blood of our epoch, then Houston is the heart. And that heart is controlled by the need to feed America's insatiable energy addiction. The United States is burning more fuel now than it ever has and the trend line continues ever upward. Between 1990 and 2000, America's total energy consumption increased by 16 percent, to the equivalent of nearly 48 million barrels of oil per day. America's share of world energy consumption is rising, too. Between 1990 and 2000, U.S. energy use increased from 25.3 percent to 27.3 percent of total world consumption. In 2000, Americans burned more fuel than all of the countries of Europe combined.[10] Motorists in Europe routinely pay four dollars or more for a gallon of fuel. Yet Americans complain bitterly and call for congressional investigations when gasoline prices hit two dollars per gallon.

This is not to say that the United States shouldn't use energy or that there's anything inherently bad about this country's extravagant energy usage. These statistics simply underscore an obvious truth: *America's economy has been built on cheap energy, and America must continue to have cheap energy—in copious quantities—to continue having a high standard of living.* From the 1930s through the early 1970s, Texas provided much of the oil and gas that America needed. Texas' oil and natural gas fields yielded prodigious quantities of cheap energy that helped the country flourish. The pricing of that energy was handled by the Texas Railroad Commission, an agency that was very friendly to the state's energy interests.

But by the early 1970s, Texas' once-prolific oilfields were becoming depleted, and the same era saw the rise of OPEC. The balance of power shifted away from the God-fearing Baptists in Austin and Houston and toward the Allah-worshiping Wahhabis in Riyadh and Jeddah.

Of the six countries with 75 billion barrels (or more) of oil reserves, five—Iran, Iraq, Saudi Arabia, Kuwait, and the United Arab Emirates—are in Saddam Hussein's old neighborhood. Some 35 percent of all international oil production sails through the Strait of Hormuz. Michael Economides, an author and professor of petroleum engineering at the University of Houston, calls the strait, which connects the Persian Gulf with the Arabian Sea, a "geopolitical chokepoint." He might be more correct to call it the world's petropolitical jugular.

And if that jugular gets pinched—even a little bit—the American economy will have a coronary.

To assure that the oil keeps flowing, the United States has colonized the Persian Gulf. And the lead colonizers are Texas companies. American oilmen, particularly Texas oilmen, have long viewed the oil from the Persian Gulf as both a threat and an opportunity. In the 1950s, '60s, and '70s, that oil was a threat because it was so cheap. Persian Gulf countries could produce oil, sell it for a fraction of what the Texans could, and still make a profit. Texas producers couldn't compete with the Saudis, the Kuwaitis, the Iraqis, or the Iranians. So influential Texas politicians like George H. W. Bush and others got import quotas slapped on foreign oil.

Today, that same oil is an opportunity, and a political necessity. Texas companies like Halliburton, Exxon Mobil, ConocoPhillips Company, and dozens of others are eager to expand their presence throughout the region. But their overriding concern in the Persian Gulf and elsewhere is that energy not become too cheap, nor too expensive. If the oil gets too cheap, domestically produced energy gets hurt. If it gets too expensive, the overall American economy gets hurt. Thus, the United States has to have a way of controlling the supply. And controlling the supply requires military muscle. If America wants to continue having access to cheap Arab energy, then American warships and American troops will be stationed in the Persian Gulf for a long while to come—perhaps decades.

As the Strait of Hormuz becomes more important to America's

energy future, so, too, does Texas' energy and energy infrastructure. Texas companies produce, refine, and distribute more oil, natural gas, gasoline, jet fuel, refined products, and petrochemicals than any other state. All of the major domestic integrated and independent oil companies—Exxon Mobil, ConocoPhillips, ChevronTexaco Corp., Marathon Oil Corporation, Apache Corporation, and Anadarko Petroleum Corporation—either are headquartered in Dallas or Houston or have major operations there. Of the 48 Texas companies that made the 2002 Fortune 500 list, 18 of them were energy related. All of the 10 biggest oilfield services companies in America are based in Houston. In 2002, those 10 firms had revenues of $35.2 billion and they had operations in over 100 countries around the globe.

The enormous wealth of the Texas energy industry gives the state tremendous political power and that political power is now concentrated in the Republican Party. Nearly all of the key Texas politicians of the past quarter century have been Republicans, and all have been funded by and have championed the Texas energy business. Both George H. W. Bush and George W. Bush exemplify this. Being from the Texas energy fraternity gave both Bushes a vast reservoir of cash and political capital that they could depend upon for steady support. Being part of the world's biggest and most important industry gave them credibility and standing in the political world that could not have come from any other business.

The three Texas presidencies are the result of the state's century-long ascendance, a trek that began with the discovery of oil at Spindletop, near Beaumont, in southeastern Texas, in 1901. That rise continued with the discovery of the East Texas field in 1930 and the subsequent empowerment of the Texas Railroad Commission to regulate oil supplies. With the Railroad Commission came the rise of Texas politicians like Sam Rayburn and Lyndon Johnson, who did everything in their power to serve the oil industry by pushing tax privileges like the oil depletion allowance. As Johnson rose to power, he helped his biggest patron, Brown & Root. As Brown & Root and Halliburton prospered, so did Texas. With Halliburton leading the way, oil, business, government, and the military became ever more intertwined in outposts such as Vietnam, Iran, and Iraq. Texas Democrats began giving way to Texas Republicans, led by energy-connected politicos like Governor John Connally and Bill Clements, an energy man who in 1979 became the state's first Republican governor since Reconstruction. By the 1980s, the United States' energy interests in the Persian Gulf had attained strategic importance, and it was a Texan, George H. W. Bush, who dealt with many of the leaders of the region during the Reagan administration. Domestic oil production became a driver for investment in American real estate, a fact that helped fuel the savings and loan crisis of the 1980s.

The presidency of George H. W. Bush was another assertion of Texas influence. It allowed another Texan, James A. Baker III, to become secretary of state and, later, a major player in the lucrative world of corporate lawyer-lobbyists. It allowed Bush senior's son, George W. Bush, to tap a vast network of cronies who helped him ride out a failed career in the oil business and go on to make about $15 million from the Texas Rangers baseball team. It helped set the stage for an event that provides the quintessential example of Texas power and influence: the Florida Recount of 2000, which resulted in George W. Bush's presidency. The first Bush presidency, which gave us the First Iraq War, also provided the basis for the Second Iraq War. Both of those conflicts were the result of Texans' desire to control the supply of oil from the Persian Gulf in the same way they had dominated the supply of oil coming out of the East Texas field.

Texas now dominates America and much of the world, but it didn't rise to superstate status overnight. Understanding its rise to prominence requires looking backward at an unlikely place: Rusk County, an East Texas location that none of the experts believed would ever yield a drop of oil. None, that is, except Dad Joiner.

Chapter 2 | **From Kilgore to Baghdad**

By the spring of 1930, Columbus Marion "Dad" Joiner had been drilling for oil in East Texas for three years and all he had to show for it were some good stories and a whole lot of heartache.

But the rotund, loquacious, sixty-something, Bible-quoting promoter from Alabama just kept drilling. He *knew* that there was oil in Rusk County. Ever the optimist, he kept buying up mineral rights throughout the county, accumulating about 5,000 acres of leases at prices of $10 or $5 or even less per acre. Not that he had any money, mind you. To finance his drilling, Joiner mortgaged himself and his properties multiple times. In exchange for breakfast or lunch, the waitress at the diner might get a tiny fraction in the test well and an additional interest in a syndicate that owned acreage near the test site. To raise cash for tools and equipment, Joiner sold $25 certificates to anyone who could afford them. Joiner even created his own scrip in order to buy groceries in the nearby hardscrabble towns of Henderson and Overton.

Both towns were dirt poor. Neither had so much as a block of paved road. Joiner's promissory notes and scrip became so ubiquitous that they began to be traded almost like greenbacks. He appealed to local farm boys, offering them a fractional interest in the well if they agreed to work the rig for a few days.

Joiner had a hunch that if he could just get his drill bit below 3,500 feet—more than three times the depth of the state's first great oil well, drilled at Spindletop three decades earlier—he'd have success. He believed that a geological formation known as the Woodbine was where he'd find treasure. And the locals believed him. They lent him money. They worked on the rig. A local banker from Overton would help Joiner out after work on weekdays and on weekends. None of them knew it, but they were participating in an event that would change the course of world history and help propel Texas into the forefront of American politics.

There was really no reason for them to have confidence in Joiner. His first well, the Daisy Bradford No. 1, failed when his drill bit jammed at 1,098 feet. The Daisy Bradford No. 2 was halted at 2,000 feet when the drill pipe got hung up in the hole. By that time Joiner was broke again. The Daisy Bradford No. 3 finally got started in May of 1929. It would be, writes the historian Lawrence Goodwyn, "one of the slowest holes ever drilled in the state of Texas."[1]

Joiner often was restricted to drilling on Sundays, as that was usually the only day of the week when he could scrounge together a volunteer crew. One scout for a major oil company reportedly visited the drill site 20 different times and never once found it operating. Through the rest of 1929 and most of 1930, Joiner's progress was painfully slow. He had no money for pipe, or anything else, for that matter. But the locals kept the faith. His was the only oil well for miles around. Goodwyn explains, "As the Depression summer of 1930 passed and winter loomed, Dad's well was about the only thing people had to look forward to. It was a favorite place for people to gather after church on Sundays."

In September of 1930 there were hints of success. Sixteen months after the Daisy Bradford No. 3 got under way, Joiner's ragged drill rig finally passed the 3,500-foot mark and the core sample showed oil. Just then Joiner's bad luck returned: the drilling rig failed. On October 1, 1930, Joiner got the rig working again. This time he had plenty of company to see the work recommence, as some 8,000 people crowded around Joiner's well to watch the work. For the next two days, Joiner's men worked night and day, bailing mud out of the well. And late on the afternoon of October 3, 1930, Joiner was proved right and everyone in Rusk County, from the waitress who'd served Joiner's coffee to the local barber, was rich or about to be rich.

The Daisy Bradford No. 3 gusher blew a fine stream of sweet Texas crude out over the top of the towering wooden derrick and onto the nearby pine trees and red clay soil. The scent of prosperity—with just a hint of sulfur—was suddenly alive in the dirt-poor woods of East Texas. Two months later, a well drilled 600 feet north of Joiner's blew in. Lease prices in Rusk County skyrocketed to over $500 per acre. Then another well, this one producing 10,000 barrels per day, came in. And that well, the No. 1 Della Crim, was located *12 miles away* from Joiner's well. With that, the craze—and the trouble—began. East Texas, a land assumed to be bereft of oil, was suddenly the hottest oilfield in the world. The major oil companies—all of whom had been convinced that there was no oil in East Texas—swooped in, seeking to buy leases on every available acre. The state's biggest major oil company, Humble Oil & Refining Company, bought the Della Crim lease for $2.1 million.

Dad Joiner was a celebrity. He was also in financial trouble. Joiner was a world-class promoter and a worse-than-lousy accountant. He'd oversold the interests in the Daisy Bradford well several times over, and was in desperate need of cash to sort things out. Joiner might have gotten rich with the Daisy Bradford, if he could just borrow some money to develop the well and drill additional wells on some of his many leases. But Joiner didn't have any cash. And he couldn't borrow any. He'd tapped every line of credit known to man. And that lack of credit left Joiner vulnerable to a recently arrived baby-faced promoter from Arkansas, a man he called Boy. Other people knew him as H. L. Hunt.

Looking back, one of the few good things that can be said about the late H. L. Hunt was that he was rich. Other than that, he was a son of a bitch.

Haroldson Lafayette Hunt already had two wives when he arrived in the oilfields around Kilgore in East Texas. And he would take a third years later. Hunt was a part-time oilman and full-time bigamist, racist, anti-Catholic, and anti-Semite. He was also a skilled gambler. And he had a hunch that Joiner's well was just an indicator of a much larger oilfield. After a marathon negotiating session at the Baker Hotel in Dallas, Hunt agreed to pay Joiner a total of $1.33 million for his interests in East Texas. It was the biggest theft since the invention of slot machines.

Somehow, Hunt got Joiner to agree to take $30,000 in cash upfront. The rest of the payments would be paid out of future production payments. Armed with Joiner's leases, which covered 5,000 acres, Hunt had what he would later call a "flying start." The acreage that Hunt got from Joiner sat atop the most productive part of the East Texas field. Joiner's acreage immediately made Hunt the biggest independent producer in East Texas.[2] Within a few years, he would be one of the richest men on earth. He'd sire 14 children. Two of his sons, Nelson Bunker Hunt and Herbert Hunt, would become infamous for their attempts to corner the silver market in the late 1970s. Another son, the smartest of the bunch, Ray Lee Hunt, would become a pal of two U.S. presidents named Bush.

Other great Texas fortunes got their start in East Texas. Clint Murchison, the son of an East Texas banker, began buying up oil leases in the region shortly after Joiner's discovery. He went on to build refineries and pipelines all over North America. Like Hunt, he, too, would become an ardent anti-Communist. Dozens of other men would make fortunes in the East Texas field. The oil discovered there would accelerate the growth and prosperity of Dallas, the nearest big city. Hundreds of dentists, doctors, lawyers, and other white-collar professionals from the city invested in the field.

Joiner's strike transformed every hillbilly, cotton picker, and lumberjack in East Texas into an independent oilman, eager to get rich and determined not to let opportunity pass him by. But with so many eager capitalists sharing a common resource, conflict was inevitable. And the conflict led to calamity.

The East Texas field was an anomaly. The most experienced oilmen in the world hadn't ever seen anything like it. The field was different from all the others that came before it in two critical respects: size and ownership.

The East Texas field was gargantuan. It measured 45 miles north to south and was five to 12 miles wide, running east to west. Covering 140,000 acres, the field dwarfed anything that had come before. It contained over 5.5 billion barrels of some of the lightest, sweetest crude oil ever discovered, and there were vast, vast quantities of it. The massive pool contained a third as much as all the crude that had been produced in the United States up to that time.[3] And in some wells the oil flowed to the surface under its own pressure. It was a gusher of money.

Second, the ownership of the field was so diverse that it almost guaranteed conflict. The geology of East Texas didn't conform with the known petroleum geology theories of the time. Traditional seismic techniques hadn't detected the formation containing the ocean of oil. That meant that the major oil companies such as Humble Oil, Gulf Oil, and Texaco hadn't bought up mineral rights in the region. Not even the remnants of the huge oil empire of John D. Rockefeller, the man who founded Standard Oil (the monopoly oil company that in 1911 was forced to split up into three dozen separate companies, the biggest of which were Exxon, Chevron, Mobil, Conoco, and Amoco) would be able to dominate the East Texas field.[4] And that meant that the locals—like the grocer and banker and others who'd backed Joiner—controlled East Texas. Twelve months after Joiner's well came in, the majors still owned less than 20 percent of the giant field. And as outsiders moved in to buy oil leases and share royalties, the people of East Texas gained the capital and the knowledge needed to put their own oil deals together. And they did. Hell, if Dad Joiner—an old man armed with nothing more than a hunch, a prayer, and an oversized helping of grit—could find oil, so could they.

Promoters, scalawags, and hookers from all over the country descended on the boomtown of Kilgore. Within a few months of the field's discovery, the wells in East Texas were producing more than one million barrels of light-as-kerosene crude oil per day—fully one half of America's total consumption.[5] During one week in late October of 1931—12 months after Joiner's Daisy Bradford No. 3 blew in —a new well was being completed in the East Texas field every hour. In the first half of 1931 alone, 1,100 wells were drilled. In 1932 in Kilgore, one city block contained 44 different oil wells. By the end of 1933, nearly 12,000 wells were sucking oil out of the East Texas field.[6]

The flood of oil had a predictable result: prices plummeted.

In early 1930, before Joiner's well came roaring in, a barrel of crude oil was selling for about $1.30. By August 1931, the price was 13 cents. In parts of East Texas, a barrel of oil was selling for as little as 3 cents.[7] Dramatic price swings were nothing new to the oil industry. They'd been occurring since the first oil well was drilled when Colonel Edwin Drake hit oil in Titusville, Pennsylvania, in 1859. At that time, the price of a barrel of oil was about $15, thanks largely to the enormous value of the kerosene that could be refined from the crude. But plenty of people followed Drake's example, and a wave of Pennsylvania crude began hitting the market. By the fall of 1861, an oversupply of oil sent the price down to just 10 cents per barrel.[8]

Seven decades later history was repeating itself in East Texas, but on a much bigger scale. American oil was now part of the world market and a price crash caused by the fountain of oil coming from the field in Texas was affecting world prices. Despite the dismal prices, none of the Texas producers had any motivation to reduce their production, for they all were drawing from the same source. All of them were relying on a law that was a part of English common law known as the "right of capture." They knew that their wells were pulling oil out of the same pool and that if they stopped drilling and producing, their neighbors could simply pump the oil out from beneath their land. It was a classic example of the tragedy of the commons. On the surface, the wells were owned by different people. Below the surface, all of them were sucking oil out of the same reservoir. And as they did so, they were reducing the oilfield's long-term productivity. In its earliest days, the massive field pushed oil out of the ground under its own pressure. But as more wells tapped the field, the pressure ran out, uncontrolled, like the air from a balloon, as the new oilmen piped the precious liquid into any and all available vessels. Once the rail cars, tank trucks, wooden tanks, and pipelines were full, the producers dug huge earthen pits and filled them with oil. With each passing day, the field's pressure and production was declining. Still, prices continued to fall.

Yet the oil producers would not, could not, cooperate with one another to prolong the productivity of the resource.

The Texas Railroad Commission was an agency originally created by Governor Big Jim Hogg in 1891 to protect farmers from the avaricious railroads. In theory it had the authority to prevent the waste of oil and limit the amount of oil each producer took from his well. The best solution for all producers was to have the commission limit production so that it just met demand—a system known as prorationing. But the commission was widely ignored by the oil producers. It set production limits several times, but these were not merely exceeded, they were laughed at by the oilmen. There was simply too much money to be made.

In addition to selling the crude, many entrepreneurs set up "teapot refineries" to make even greater profits. At a time when crude oil was selling for 15 cents a barrel (or less), gasoline sold for between four and 11 cents per gallon. An oilman could spend $10,000 to $25,000 to build his own refinery and produce a dozen or more gallons of gasoline from each 42-gallon barrel of crude. The refiner's profits were only limited by the amount of oil he could process. If a plant could process 30,000 barrels of oil per month, the new businessman could make profits of $5,000 or more per month. In as little as two months, the refinery could practically be paid for and after that the take would be pure profit. Not surprisingly, lots of people saw that refining was where the real money could be made. Within a year or so of Joiner's discovery, nearly 100 refineries small and large in the woods of East Texas were turning crude oil into motor fuel, kerosene, asphalt, and other materials.

The major oil companies, led by William Stamps Farish of Standard Oil, one of the founders of Humble Oil & Refining, had long supported prorationing as the best way to assure stable prices over the long term. But the independent producers were suspicious. They viewed prorationing as a plot through which the majors could squeeze them on prices, and they distrusted Farish.

On July 31, 1931, a federal court in Houston sided with a group of independent oil producers and ruled that the Texas Railroad Commission had no right to impose prorationing. A few days later, the Texas Senate—its gallery packed with producers from East Texas—agreed with the court and rejected a bill that would have given the Texas Railroad Commission the authority to limit production in East Texas.

The pressure on Texas Governor Ross Sterling had been growing for months. As a long-time member of the Texas good old boys club, Sterling was being urged by the state's biggest oil companies to take action. He had served as the first president of Humble Oil & Refining after the company was formed, in 1917. He later became chairman of the board, a position he resigned in 1925, when the company was worth about $75 million. Humble executives pressured him. Sterling's brother worked at Humble, and wrote him a letter, telling him he had to take action. Some of the independents were even beginning to come around to the side of prorationing.

By mid-August of 1931, Sterling had seen enough. He decided that if the courts and the legislature wouldn't back him by imposing prorationing, then he'd make up the rules as he went along. At noon on August 16, 1931, Sterling signed a three-page proclamation that declared martial law in Rusk, Upshur, Gregg, and Smith counties. The document said that the oil producers were "in a state of insurrection." Their actions, he said, "openly, flagrantly and rebelliously violate the laws." Texas had to preserve its crude oil and natural gas. And to do that, he proclaimed that the "reckless and illegal exploitation of the same [must] be stopped until such time as the said resources may be properly conserved and developed under the protection of the civil authorities."[9] But to make his proclamation stick, Sterling needed muscle. For that, he turned to the commander of the Texas National Guard, Brigadier General Jacob F. Wolters, and ordered him to have his troops "without delay shut down each and every producing crude oil well and/or producing well of natural gas." At the time, Wolters was the chief lobbyist and general counsel for one of Baker Botts's biggest clients, Texaco. One of Wolters's colonels was a production executive at Gulf Oil.

Wolters commanded more than a thousand troops. Dozens of Texas Rangers were also deployed. The troops patrolled the fields on horseback. One Ranger was assigned to each patrol of 20 guardsmen, to make arrests if needed. At the outset of the occupation, Wolters ordered two military bands from the state's 50th Cavalry Brigade to serenade the troops—"Just to keep them in good humor."[10]

For the next three weeks, not a drop of oil flowed out of East Texas. The soldiers were in total control of every well and pipeline in the region. Order was restored. The Texas Railroad Commission was finally in firm control of the world's most prolific oil fields. It controlled the supply—and therefore, the price—of the earth's most important commodity. After it put the clamps on production, oil prices rallied.

Although Sterling's bold move temporarily imposed order on production, the oil producers continued to buck the Railroad Commission's authority. They began smuggling oil across state lines to avoid the state's production limits. Within months, the smuggled and illegally produced crude—known as "hot oil"—was flooding the market, causing another price crash. In 1933, the administration of the newly elected Franklin D. Roosevelt attempted to push a bill through Congress that would have given the secretary of the interior, Harold Ickes, the authority to regulate domestic oil production. It didn't work. A powerful Texas congressman, Sam Rayburn, who was chairman of the House Committee on Interstate and Foreign Commerce, killed the bill. Texas politicians wanted state, not federal, regulation.

Finally, in 1935, after months of wrangling over the prorationing problem, another powerful Texan, Senator Tom Connally, succeeded in breaking the logjam. The Connally Hot Oil Act gave the Texas Railroad Commission the authority to proration oil. It also prohibited the interstate movement of illegally produced oil. The federal law finally gave the Texas Railroad Commission the authority that Sterling had wanted it to have. Although Sterling was defeated when he stood for reelection in 1932, his role had been critical, and Humble Oil executives were quick to acknowledge that fact. W. J. Crawford, the tax administrator of Humble Oil, later told Ronnie Dugger, the editor of the *Texas Observer*, "We had to let a president of Humble quit to become governor to establish proration."[11]

With prorationing in place, the Texas Railroad Commission

quickly became the ruler of the world's oil markets. Every month it set "allowables," which determined the amount of oil each operator could produce from his wells. The allowables were set to meet current demand, and not a barrel more. Because the Railroad Commission controlled the flow of oil from the world's most prolific oilfields, the ones in Texas, the system worked. No other entity was able to control the supply of oil, and thus prices, the way the commission did. Furthermore, by controlling the prices in the burgeoning American market, it effectively determined world prices, too. Thus, in a matter of months, the Texas Railroad Commission began deciding the price of oil from Baku to Buenos Aires.

By the late 1940s and 1950s, increasing reserves of oil were being discovered in Texas, Venezuela, the Persian Gulf, and elsewhere. There was an enormous oversupply. So the Railroad Commission simply cut the allowable for Texas producers. Even in a glutted market, prices didn't fall. In fact, they rose, giving every producer even bigger profits. As a Cornell economist, Alfred Kahn, told the U.S. Senate during hearings about oil prices in 1949, prorationing allowed the oil companies to "fix their own prices and make them stick." In 1949 the Senate Small Business Committee concluded that the Railroad Commission's prorationing system forms "a perfect pattern of monopolistic control over oil production and the distribution thereof . . . and ultimately the price paid by the public."[12]

In other words, the Railroad Commission was a cartel. And cartels always have to deal with copycats.

In late 1945, a young, idealistic Arab arrived at the train station in Austin, on the banks of the Colorado River, about two miles from the Texas Capitol. He didn't know anyone in Austin. He'd never been to America. He was not royalty. He was the son of a camel owner who organized caravans that ran between Kuwait and Saudi Arabia. Yet

Abdullah Tariki had the kind of self-confidence and intelligence that breeds success. That combination had attracted the attention of the leaders of the newly established state of Saudi Arabia, and they'd sent him to Egypt, where he attended Fouad University in Cairo. There, he studied chemistry and geology. The schools in Egypt were good, but his mentors in his home country of Saudi Arabia wanted Tariki to excel in all facets of the oil business. For that, there was only one place to go. "I heard many stories about the Texans," Tariki later recalled. "They were the masters of oil. I thought 'If I go there, it's the largest state and it has the most oil. Then my word will carry weight.' That's why I went to Texas."

Upon his arrival in Austin, Tariki made his way to the University of Texas, where he became the very first Saudi Arabian ever to enroll. Tariki quickly made himself at home. He swam in Austin's famous swimming pools, including Deep Eddy and Barton Springs, and became a nut for Texas football, crying when the school's team lost. He immersed himself in classes and, after 18 months, graduated from the University of Texas with a master's degree in geology.[13] But his experience in Texas wasn't altogether happy. He was sometimes mistaken for a Mexican and was denied entry into bars, restaurants, and other public places. Those slights undoubtedly played a part in shaping Tariki's worldview. An ardent Arab nationalist who'd been steeped in the pro-Arab beliefs of President Gamel Abdul Nasser of Egypt, Tariki had long believed that the Arab states needed to exert more power over the oil being produced in their countries. His time in Texas did not change those views.

Upon graduation, he did an internship at the Texas Railroad Commission. He then moved to Midland, the West Texas boomtown that was growing rich thanks to the vast oil reservoirs of the Permian Basin. There, he worked for a major oil company, Texaco. After that, he went back to Saudi Arabia. Upon returning to his home country, he wasted little time before he began agitating for the Western oil companies to pay the Saudis higher royalties on the oil they produced. His campaign led some of the oil companies to try to discredit him, by calling him the "Red Sheikh," a name that insinuated that Tariki was a Communist.

In 1955, Tariki was appointed Saudi Arabia's first oil minister. He quickly began creating a program that would allow other young Saudis to follow in his footsteps and acquire the knowledge they would need to deal with the modern oil business. Over a four-year period, his program sent nearly 300 young Saudis to the University of Texas, where they were educated in finance and other oil-related matters. He also began looking for ways in which the Saudis and the other big Middle Eastern oil producers could gain more leverage over the Western oil companies. The best way, he decided, was by controlling production. So in 1959, Tariki arranged a meeting at a yacht club in Cairo with oil ministers from Venezuela, Kuwait, Iran, and Iraq. The result was a fledgling entity that became known as OPEC, the Organization of the Petroleum Exporting Countries. OPEC's model was simple: each oil producer—in this case, an entire country—was given an allowable. The country could produce the allowable and no more. By controlling the supply of the world's oil, OPEC would control the price.[14]

It was obvious where Tariki got OPEC's business model. Tariki was often interviewed by Jim Tanner, a long-time energy reporter for the *Wall Street Journal*. One day, Tanner began talking to Tariki about both men's alma mater, the University of Texas. At one point in their conversation, Tanner asked Tariki what he had studied while he was in Austin. Tariki smiled and replied, "I studied the Texas Railroad Commission."[15]

Chapter 3　The Supercapitalists

For modern readers, the size and scope of the oil boom that dominated Texas from the 1930s to the 1970s is difficult to imagine. Perhaps at no other time in American history have more millionaires been created than during the heyday of the oil boom in Texas, Oklahoma, and Louisiana. The men who were finding that oil—particularly the independent oilmen—were America's supercapitalists.

Unlike the dot-com boom of the 1990s, in which a bunch of pocket protector–wearing nerds from Silicon Valley were made into instant zillionaires by virtue of the estimated value of their stock holdings in newly public dot-com supernovas, the oilmen owned a real commodity that could be seen and smelled. More important, their wealth was being paid to them every month and it was being paid *in cash*. Their fortunes didn't depend on the vagaries of the stock market, or the whims of the World Wide Web. They were producing a product that was always in demand; in fact, despite occasional price fluctuations, the consumption of petroleum products was growing by leaps and bounds every year.

The old slogan "Every man a prince" was the reality of the oil business. Sid Richardson, the man who became one of Lyndon Johnson's biggest financial backers, was simply lucky. His fortune was made after he got access to land owned by the Keystone Cattle Company in the deserts of Winkler County near the New Mexico border. Before drilling his first well in Winkler County in 1935, Richardson had run through some $15 million of his own money and that of his investors, and, as one writer put it, "could drink every drop of oil he had to show for it." The Keystone Field changed that. Richardson's first well produced 250 barrels of oil per day. Over the next few years, nearly 400 wells would be drilled in the Keystone field and only 17 of them would be dry holes. By 1940, Richardson owned more than 120 producing wells, including 33 in the Keystone field alone. Richardson later would acknowledge his good fortune, saying, "People get luck and brains mixed up, and that's when they get in trouble."[1]

Before the oil boom, America's great fortunes were based on mining, shipping, or manufacturing, all of which required substantial infusions of capital, technology, and labor. In the gold rush days of the oil business, people could get rich with little or no capital and a bare minimum of technology and labor.

No other industry in American history has ever been quite so democratic. A dirt-poor cotton farmer in East Texas whose only asset might be his 40-acre farm could be made wealthy by a single oil well. The farmer had only to give permission to the company drilling the well. He didn't have to put up any capital or participate in the labor. His only requirement for entry into the leagues of the middle and upper class was the ownership of his land. The well might be drilled by people he'd never met. And the royalty checks might come from a company whose headquarters was hundreds of miles away.

In the annals of world capitalism, those royalty payments were wholly anomalous. And they still are. "The notion of landowners owning the mineral rights is *uniquely American*," explains Michael Economides, an energy expert from the University of Houston who has worked in numerous countries around the world. "In none of the developed world or the oil producing countries, do land owners own the mineral rights."[2]

Landowners whose understanding of the oil business went no further than the nearest gas station could, like the fictional Jed Clampett of the *Beverly Hillbillies,* be made rich overnight. In fact, many Jed Clampetts made fortunes. "A few oil wells makes ranching a fine business," was one the Texas sayings that became commonplace during the boom years. By the mid-1950s, Texas was providing about 40 percent of all the oil consumed in America, and the royalties from that production were making Texans rich. In 1955, some $500 million (equal to $3.3 billion in 2002 dollars) in royalties, rents, and bonuses was paid to Texas landowners. Land owned by the state—vestiges of Texas' brief period of nationhood after the Alamo—contained small oceans of oil and the royalties from that oil provided tens of millions of dollars for the endowments of the University of Texas and Texas A&M University. By 1990, the endowment topped $3.5 billion. Those endowments paid for engineering and geology programs, which began pumping out hundreds more engineers and geologists, who then jumped into the Oil Patch, further accelerating the development of the state's vast resources.

The oil royalties contributed to a higher standard of living for Texans than for average Americans. Between 1930 and 1960, per capita incomes in Texas increased nearly 500 percent, as compared to 350 percent for incomes in the United States as a whole.

Even though many landowners got royalties from the oil business, that of course did not mean that the means of production were democratic. The vast majority of the state's oil drilling and the enormous profit potential that came with it was controlled by a small group of executives from major oil companies and a select group of independent oilmen. Those men met at exclusive watering holes like the Fort Worth Club, the Petroleum Club in Houston, or the Dallas Petroleum Club. Those were the places where deals were made over a sandwich and a glass of bourbon. Those were the places where the capital needed to make deals happen could be obtained—assuming, of course, that the prospect and the reputation of the promoter were good enough.

The potential of the average Jed Clampett to strike it rich in the oil business, either by drilling a well himself or letting someone else drill on his land, gave the oil business allure. And nowhere was the romance of the oil business stronger than in Texas. Texas oil had sex appeal to burn. But the world of Texas oil was not only about glamour and glitz and nouveaux riches. With World War II, Texas oil became a weapon.

Many factors contributed to the Allies' victory in World War II. But one of the main reasons—maybe *the* reason—was that the Germans and the Japanese simply ran out of gas. Joseph Stalin happily acknowledged this fact during a banquet in Moscow right after the war ended. In raising his glass to Britain's Prime Minister Winston Churchill, the Russian dictator offered a toast, saying the conflict had been a "war of engines and octanes. I drink to the American auto industry and the American oil industry."[3]

The engines came from Detroit. The octanes came from Texas.

During World War II, Texas oilfields and Texas-based pipelines provided critically important fuel for the war effort. At the outset of the war, German submarines were wreaking havoc on American tankers in the Atlantic carrying fuel from Texas to the East Coast and Europe. Secretary of the Interior Harold Ickes sought an alternative way to move the oil, warning, "I do not believe we can win the war without at least this one pipeline"—a pipeline from the prolific East Texas field to the East Coast. After months of wrangling, and a hard push from the Texas oilman J. R. Parten, the massive project was approved and in a matter of months, two big pipelines, the Big Inch and Little Big Inch, were built by an army of workmen. By the end of the war, the two pipelines had carried more than 350 million barrels of crude oil and petroleum products (equal to 14.7 billion gallons) from Texas to the East Coast. The pipes ensured that the Allies had the octanes needed to feed the armada of engines needed to win the war.

Meanwhile, as the oil flowed through the new pipelines, German and Japanese forces were repeatedly stymied in their efforts to find new oil supplies. That lack of fuel doomed their plans. The Germans desperately needed to capture the oilfields in the Caucasus in order to continue their march across Russia. Hitler himself recognized this when he refused to provide more soldiers and materiel to one of his field marshals, who was begging for reinforcements to assist in the battle of Stalingrad. "Unless we get the Baku oil," Hitler told him, "the war is lost." The same problems confronted the Germans in North Africa, where the renowned German general Erwin Rommel was hamstrung by a lack of fuel.

"The bravest men can do nothing without guns, the guns nothing without plenty of ammunition, and neither guns nor ammunition are of much use in mobile warfare unless there are vehicles with sufficient petrol to haul them around," wrote the man known as the Desert Fox. After his Afrika Korps was defeated at El Alamein, a dejected Rommel wrote to his wife, "Shortage of petrol! It's enough to make one weep."[4]

The Japanese military wept for lack of fuel, too. In the late 1930s Japan produced just 7 percent of the oil it consumed. The rest was imported—80 percent from the United States, and about 10 percent from the Dutch East Indies. As Daniel Yergin points out in his seminal book on the history of the oil industry, *The Prize*, oil was "central to Japan's decision" to invade Asia and thus begin World War II. Other historians go further, asserting that "the entire Japanese foray into Indonesia and Southeast Asia was for oil."[5] Shortly after Pearl Harbor, the Japanese navy landed at Balikpapan, a refinery town in Borneo, but the entire complex had been destroyed by employees of Royal Dutch/Shell before the Japanese arrived. In 1943, the Japanese even drilled a wildcat well in central Sumatra in an attempt to increase their oil stocks. The oilfield they discovered was enormous, the largest one between California and the Middle East, but the Japanese still had to transport the oil over very long distances in tankers that were vulnerable to Allied submarines and surface vessels. The Japanese even converted some of their ships to burn coal because oil was in such short supply. By April 1945, the Japanese battleship *Yamato* went into battle against American forces with enough fuel for just a one-way trip. It was quickly sunk by a swarm of American warplanes.

Persian Gulf oil was critical to the war effort—so critical that in the middle of World War II, President Franklin D. Roosevelt and his interior secretary, Harold Ickes, began talking with American oil executives about the government's buying part of their interests in Saudi oilfields so that the companies could build a refinery at the Saudi Arabian port town of Ras Tanura, on the Persian Gulf. Roosevelt and Ickes discussed buying a $40 million stake in the California-Arabian Standard Oil Company (which later became the Arabian-American Oil Company, or Aramco). The deal fell through, but America's interest in Saudi Arabia continued. After the Yalta Conference in early 1945, Roosevelt had a private meeting aboard an American warship in the Suez Canal zone with the Saudi king, Abdul Aziz bin Abdul Rahman bin Faisal al Saud. Afterward, a reporter for the *New York Times* wrote of the meeting, "The immense oil deposits in Saudi Arabia alone make that country more important to American diplomacy than almost any other smaller nation." Roosevelt's alliance with King Abdul Aziz meant that American oil companies could increase their operations in Saudi Arabia. In the postwar years, four American companies, Exxon, Chevron, Mobil, and Texaco, joined forces under the Aramco banner.[6] They developed the Saudi oilfields, built refineries and pipelines—and made enormous profits. Saudi Arabia was, said one oil executive at the time, a "gold mine."[7]

Of course, the American oil companies had lots of other interests in the Persian Gulf. Chevron had been working in Bahrain ever since it discovered oil there in 1932. Exxon had been producing oil in Iraq since the 1920s. Gulf Oil had an enormously valuable concession in Kuwait.

All of the companies' investments signaled a dramatic increase in American involvement in the Persian Gulf, and those investments caught the attention of the U.S. State Department. In 1945, one of the agency's reports called the Persian Gulf oilfields a "stupendous source of strategic power, and one of the greatest material prizes in world history."[8]

It wouldn't be the last State Department assessment of the Persian Gulf's strategic value.

The events of World War II dramatically reinforced the Texas oilmen's sense that they were on a mission from God. The war, America's booming economic growth, and the consequent insatiable hunger for oil—all combined to give the Texans and their companies a special sense of purpose, a belief that their oil rigs, their oilfield technology, their oil*men* could—and would—dominate the world. And that dominance would happen with or without any intervention by the federal government.

The Texas oilmen knew their job wasn't ordinary. The oil business was equal parts religion, capitalism, alchemy, and up-by-your-bootstraps entrepreneurship. Their quest for energy had an epic quality. The oil industry had always operated on the frontier of the possible. Whether the challenge was Dad Joiner's gambit to find oil in Rusk County in 1930 or the technology that allowed Brown & Root to construct and operate the first offshore oil well drilled out of sight of land, off Morgan City, Louisiana, in 1947, Texas oilmen made their livings by bucking up against the impossible. Texas oil men not only hailed from a frontier state, they were living on the frontier of the doable. They were looking for, drilling for, and finding oil in places that had never been drilled before. They were building the pipelines and the refineries to bring it to market. And they were making enormous fortunes.

The Texas oilmen were superindividualists who believed in the federal government only to the extent that it could protect their investments and the United States' borders. All other uses of government—particularly those that encouraged unions, provided for the needy, guaranteed civil rights or voting rights for blacks and Mexicans, or imposed environmental restrictions—were verging on the Communistic. And they didn't want to pay for any of those government programs.

During World War II, income tax rates for the wealthiest Americans soared, reaching as high as 94 percent. In the postwar years the high tax rates continued and the newly rich oilmen were outraged. The "frustration was severe at that time, particularly with the socialistic ideas that were starting to sprout in the Roosevelt years and Truman years," says George Strake Jr., a Houston oilman and longtime Republican donor and politico. With the income taxes at such high levels, "You had to invest as much money trying to hang on to your money as you actually saved."[9]

To the oilmen the tax burden was onerous, but they had a savior: a tax loophole known as the depletion allowance. And that tax dodge had to be protected by Texas politicians at all costs.

Chapter 4   Depleting the Federal Treasury

The Shamrock Hotel had refrigerated trash bins.

Its swimming pool, which measured 165 feet long and 142 feet wide, was the largest hotel pool in America. The pool was so big, the hotel occasionally staged water-skiing exhibitions on it.

The Shamrock, built a few miles south of downtown Houston, was the ultimate example of Texas excess, the perfect expression of a completely over-the-top "I don't give a shit what you think about it" kind of attitude that flourished in the state after the war. The hotel was built in the late 1940s by the "King of the Wildcatters," Glenn McCarthy. He didn't care that his new 18-story hotel cost $21 million. McCarthy had more cash than he could spend.

The pugnacious son of an itinerant oilfield worker, McCarthy was an Irishman who'd gone from roughneck to millionaire by the age of 26. And he intended to outdo all of his fellow oilmen when it came to living large. By 1949, when he was 42, McCarthy was worth $200 million. But his never-ending eagerness for a stiff drink and a fist fight made him too coarse for Houston's country club set. So he built himself a hotel, a place where Frank Sinatra, Bob Hope, and Bing Crosby would entertain. And just to make sure the country club swells noticed, McCarthy made sure that no one would ever forget the open-ing of the Shamrock, on Saint Patrick's Day, 1949.

For the festivities, McCarthy rented an entire train, the Santa Fe Super Chief, to carry a few dozen movie stars from Los Angeles to Houston. Another 3,000 guests were invited to the $1 million shindig. The movie actress Dorothy Lamour was to do a live radio broadcast. The liquor and food flowed. It turned into a near riot. The crowds out-side the hotel were so large that it took the mayor of Houston two hours to get to the party inside. The public address system quit work-ing. Fans crashed into the dining rooms in order to get a glimpse of the visiting movie stars.

"It was," recalled one guest, "one hell of a party."[1]

It was also one hell of a hotel. McCarthy—who allegedly served as the inspiration for the character Jett Rink in Edna Ferber's novel *Giant*—wanted to be certain that everyone knew of his Irish heritage. So he had the hotel's Steinway grand painted green. The rest of the hotel interior was green, too—67 shades of it! When Frank Lloyd Wright, a man who had more than a passing acquaintance with per-sonal eccentricities, visited the Shamrock, he was less than impressed. "I always wondered what the inside of a juke box looked like," he sniffed.[2]

There are many stories about the predilections of Texas' nouveau riche energy barons, and the saga of the Shamrock Hotel—which McCarthy owned for just five years—is just one of them. It illustrates the incredible size of the Texas oil fortunes, which for a time dwarfed the money being made anywhere else on earth. But the story of the accountants behind those great fortunes has largely been neglected. How *did* the Texas independent oilmen like McCarthy, H. L. Hunt, Sid Richardson, Clint Murchison, and the others get so rich? And how did they do it so quickly?

The short answer: the oil depletion allowance.

The Texas Railroad Commission's power to set prices was a key factor in enriching the state's oil barons. So, too, were the fantastic amounts of oil that the independent oilmen produced. McCarthy drilled 1,000 wells. Hunt reportedly owned 500 wells in the East Texas field alone. Richardson found vast riches in the Keystone field in West Texas. Murchison owned producing properties from Canada to the Texas Gulf Coast. Those gushers of oil and gas were fountains of liquid currency that, once the initial investment in the well was made, required little further investment on the part of the owners. One estimate said that the early Texas oilmen were getting a return of $60 for each $1 that they invested.

But the gushers of oil were also an income tax headache. In 1949, the year that McCarthy opened the Shamrock, the highest marginal income tax rate was 82 percent. Fortunately, though, the depletion allowance enabled the oilmen to dodge those high tax rates on significant amounts of their income. First enacted in 1913, it allowed investors who owned mineral deposits (including oil and gas) to make significant deductions on their taxable income for the depletion of the deposits.

With the depletion allowance, oil producers could deduct 27.5 percent of the income they received from their wells. And better still, there was no limit on the amount the oil producers could deduct. By using the depletion allowance and another oil industry giveaway known as the intangible drilling cost allowance, oilmen were legally able to avoid much, and in some instances, *all*, of their personal income tax liabilities.

A very modest depletion allowance was included in the tax code when the original income tax law was passed in 1913. The first law allowed producers to use the depletion allowed to deduct just 5 percent of their income and the deduction was limited to the original cost of their property. But in 1926, the depletion allowance was dramatically expanded to allow the 27.5 percent exemption.

For Texas oilmen, the depletion allowance was akin to motherhood, football, and the Alamo in the pantheon of the sacred. For decades it was seen as a birthright. And thanks to a group of Texas congressmen—from populist Democrats like Sam Rayburn to country club Republicans like George H. W. Bush—it almost became one. Thanks to them, the oil depletion allowance was one of the longest ongoing bank robberies in the history of the republic.

Numerous studies showed that the oilmen were getting a tax break that was unprecedented in American business. While other businessmen had to pay taxes on their income regardless of what they sold, the oilmen got special treatment. They argued they were selling a wasting asset, one that would soon be used up. They claimed the depletion allowance was a matter of national security and that without it, domestic oil companies would have less incentive to search for oil.

A quick example of how the depletion allowance worked will illustrate why the oilmen loved it so. Let's assume there are two businessmen. One is a grocer who buys a $500 refrigerator for his store. The other is an oilman. The grocer buys the refrigerator. When he files his income taxes, he is allowed to depreciate the cost of the refrigerator over 10 years, taking a depreciation of $50 per year.

The oilman drills a well that costs $100,000. He finds a reservoir containing $10,000,000 worth of oil. The well produces $1 million worth of oil per year for ten years. In the very first year, thanks to the depletion allowance, the oilman could deduct 27.5 percent, or $275,000, of that $1 million in income from his taxable income. Thus, in just one year, he's deducted nearly three times his initial investment. But the depletion allowance continues to pay off. For each of the next nine years, he gets to continue taking the $275,000 depletion deduction. By the end of the tenth year, the oilman has deducted $2.75 million from his taxable income, even though his initial investment was only $100,000. Meanwhile, the grocery store owner was only allowed to deduct the cost of the $500 refrigerator.

This example—although it sounds outlandish—was, in fact, fairly close to reality. A study done by the U.S. Treasury Department found that in 1949, the depletion allowance was allowing oil and gas producers to deduct more than 19 times the cost of their original investment.

While the depletion allowance was a boon to Texas and Texas oil producers, the non-oil-producing states were none too happy with the loophole. And they began trying to overturn it. They thought it could be done quickly. It took them five decades.[3]

In 1933, the newly elected Democratic administration of Franklin Roosevelt began trying to repeal the tax break. Roosevelt's treasury secretary, Henry Morgenthau, said the depletion allowance was a "pure subsidy to a special class of taxpayers" and he tried to get Congress to eliminate the loophole. He failed. Patriotism didn't work, either. Six weeks after the Japanese attacked Pearl Harbor, Morgenthau went back to Congress asking them to repeal the "special privilege" enjoyed by the oil industry. Nothing happened. In 1950, President Harry Truman attacked the depletion allowance, saying, "I know of no loophole...so inequitable." Years later, in 1969, Senator Edward Kennedy of Massachusetts would ask, "Is there any justification at all for the present tax treatment of depletion [and] intangible drilling costs?" Another senator, Paul Douglas of Illinois, demanded to know why the oilmen could deduct 27.5 percent of their income, "world without end, amen?"[4]

The short answer to Douglas's question was simple: Texas oilmen wanted it. And in order to keep the depletion allowance they contributed enormous amounts of money to politicians from Texas and other states. Over the decades that Texas politicos were strengthening their positions in Washington, Texas oilmen pumped millions of dollars into the pockets of their favorite politicos. And always, the first item on the oilmen's to-do list was—no surprise—the perpetuation of the oil depletion allowance.

Sam Rayburn, the powerful Texan who served three nonconsecutive terms as Speaker of the U.S. House of Representatives, was one of the most ardent supporters of the depletion allowance. Rayburn held his seat in Congress for nearly 49 years. He was so forceful in the backing of the provision that he interviewed prospective members of the House Ways and Means Committee (which writes tax policy) for their views on the tax dodge. If the congressmen didn't agree with Rayburn on depletion, they didn't get on Ways and Means. There was simply no way that Rayburn would allow any measure reducing the depletion allowance out of committee. For if that happened, Rayburn knew that "they'd cut it to fifteen, ten, five percent—maybe even take it away altogether. Do you think you could convince a Detroit factory worker that the depletion allowance is a good thing? Once it got on the floor, it would be cut to ribbons."[5]

There was another Texan who was backing the depletion allowance in the 1950s. Born poor in 1908 to a hard-luck cotton farmer who tried to eke an existence out of the rocky, hardscrabble hills near Hye, in Central Texas, he'd also been born with a voracious appetite for power and influence. Standing six feet four inches tall in his bare feet, he was a lion of a man, a sometimes crude, sometimes charming personality who *knew* that he was destined to change the world, who *knew* that he would live in the White House. His name was Lyndon Baines Johnson.

Johnson had been one of Rayburn's key allies throughout Rayburn's years in the U.S. House of Representatives. And in 1948, Johnson decided that a man of his own stature belonged in the Senate. His opponent for the Democratic nomination was the state's governor, Coke Stevenson. During his campaign, Johnson preached the gospel of the depletion allowance. Not only should the depletion allowance be kept in place, Johnson argued, it should be increased to 30 percent. Increasing the depletion allowance—now *that* was a campaign pledge that the Texas oilmen could really support.[6]

Chapter 5

1948: Lawyers, Airplanes, and Money—Part I

I t came down to lawyers, airplanes, and money.

Johnson's backers knew that Coke Stevenson was running ahead in the polls in their race for the Democratic nomination for a seat in the U.S. Senate. Stevenson, the Texas governor, was a popular, even beloved, figure, a pipe-smoking politician who was unpretentious and hard-working. But Stevenson wasn't fighting only Johnson, he was also fighting a powerful crony network of wealthy people who had hitched their wagons to Johnson's star—and they were *not* going to lose. Losing would have meant catastrophe for this crowd—one whose magnitude grew after Johnson launched a bitter, negative campaign against Stevenson.

To assure Johnson's victory, his backers gave him everything he needed. Johnson's lawyers—who would come to play a pivotal role in the election—were also working for George and Herman Brown, the owners of a rapidly growing construction company called Brown & Root. Johnson had a fleet of aircraft at his disposal. He used converted heavy bombers, sturdy DC–3s, and a brand-new technology, the helicopter. Those aircraft helped ferry the rivers of money Johnson needed. His aides used the planes to transport grocery sacks filled with hundred-dollar bills to the campaign's headquarters, to be used for whatever expenses were most pressing.

The primary race pitted Stevenson, a West Texas rancher and staunch opponent of the New Deal, against Johnson, who'd been a key ally of the late Franklin Roosevelt and his New Deal policies. Both were Democrats, but Stevenson was the more conservative candidate. He was suspicious of anything that had to do with big government and—as a friend of his once wrote—he had "an ingrained hatred of debt of all kinds." Johnson, on the other hand, had an ingrained love of practical politics. If a federal project meant money for his district, then he was for it, regardless of whether the money was borrowed or not. It was a showdown about government philosophy and Johnson and his supporters couldn't afford to lose.

The Browns knew that if Stevenson won, their federal defense contracts might evaporate. Their other businesses were "regulated in a thousand ways," one of their lawyers said later. Stevenson would make things very difficult for Brown & Root if he won. "The Browns had to win this. They *had* to win this. Stevenson was a man of vengeance, and he would have run them out of Washington. Johnson—if he lost, he was going back to being nobody. *They* were going back to being nobody.... That was the acid test. That was *it*. All or nothing."

Johnson's lead lawyers, Charles Francis and Alvin Wirtz, were among the state's most influential cronies. Both had used the revolving door between business and government to their advantage; both had close ties to the oil and gas business and both worked for Brown & Root.

Charles Francis had gotten into the oil game early. While still in high school, he invested in a gas pipeline. In 1914 he went to the University of Texas, where he got his law degree. He became one of the most prominent oil and gas attorneys in the state.[1] By the 1948 election, Francis had served in the Roosevelt administration as a special assistant to the U.S. attorney general, and during World War II he'd been a special consultant to the Department of the Interior.[2] He was also a partner at Vinson & Elkins, one of the state's most powerful law firms, which represented Brown & Root as well as dozens of other industrial interests in Texas. In addition to his law firm's ties to Brown & Root, Francis was also a business partner with the Browns. Francis, along with George and Herman Brown and several others, owned stock in Texas Eastern Transmission Corporation. The company had purchased one of the most valuable assets built during the war, the Big Inch and Little Big Inch pipelines. Although they'd been built to carry crude oil and refined products to the East Coast, Texas Eastern converted them to carry natural gas, which was rapidly replacing fuel oil as the fuel of choice for space heating and industrial use.

Alvin Wirtz, a former Texas state senator and an expert in oil and water law, was Johnson's lead strategist. Wirtz and Lyndon had been pals since the early 1930s; they'd worked together when Johnson was the state director of the National Youth Administration, the youth employment agency created during the New Deal. Wirtz had known Johnson's father. Although Johnson was 20 years younger than Wirtz, the two became allies. Wirtz supported Johnson when he ran for Congress in 1937, to fill the position left open after the death of U.S. Representative James P. Buchanan. Buchanan had been the chairman of the House Appropriations Committee and played a pivotal role in providing federal funding for one of Wirtz's pet projects, the Lower Colorado River Authority, the agency that was trying to build a series of dams and provide electrification in Central Texas. During his eight years in the Texas Senate, 1922 to 1930, Wirtz authored the bill creating the river authority. Shortly after the new authority was created, Wirtz became its general counsel. During that same time period, Wirtz held another job, as an attorney for Brown & Root. Thus, Wirtz was representing the river authority on legal matters while also working for Brown & Root, which was in the midst of building the

Marshall Ford Dam on the Colorado River, near Austin, the biggest and most complex construction job the little road-paving company had ever undertaken. It wasn't a conflict of interest. It was just business.

Wirtz's ability to mix business, politics, and law was a hallmark of his life. He'd been a delegate to the 1928, 1932, and 1940 Democratic National Conventions and he was an active booster of Franklin Roosevelt's renomination bids in 1940 and 1944. In 1940, Johnson, through his friendship with President Roosevelt, got Wirtz appointed undersecretary of the interior, a position that was second in power only to that of the interior secretary himself, Harold Ickes. The White House press release announcing Wirtz's appointment made it clear that Johnson had been responsible for Wirtz's appointment.[3] In turn, Wirtz took care of Johnson. He played a key role in helping Lyndon and Lady Bird Johnson buy the radio station in Austin, KTBC, which would later make the Johnson family enormous amounts of money.[4] In 1941, Wirtz quit his job at Interior, returned to Texas, and helped run Johnson's unsuccessful campaign for the U.S. Senate against W. Lee O'Daniel in a special election in that year.

Wirtz was also one of the first Texas politicos to talk with the Saudis about controlling the flow of oil out of the Persian Gulf. During World War II, Wirtz was one of Roosevelt's key negotiators with the Saudis to procure the oil the Allies needed for the war effort.

By 1948, Wirtz was Johnson's go-to guy. And by helping Johnson, Wirtz was helping himself. Wirtz organized one of Austin's biggest law firms, Buell, Wirtz, Rauhaut and Gideon. By getting Johnson into the Senate, Wirtz would further the interests of all of his clients, particularly the Browns. Lady Bird Johnson once said that Wirtz, the Browns, and Johnson all "shared a vision of a new Texas and they were going to be part of it. By gosh, they were going to make things happen—bring Texas whatever industry and whatever had made the eastern part of the United States the so-called elite and rich part. . . . They were all builders, strong, young, aggressive, determined."[5]

Johnson had other cronies. His key aide, a lawyer who handled the mail and the phone calls, was a man whose name was destined to become as synonymous with Texas as Johnson's. He was tall, smart, gorgeous, and could charm the skin off a rattlesnake. And like Johnson, he believed that he was destined for the White House. His name was John Bowden Connally.

Like Johnson, Connally, born dirt poor, was a self-made, independent man with big aspirations. He grew up on his parents' farm near Floresville, South Texas, and was able to attend the University of Texas thanks to a stipend provided by the National Youth Administration. He became a champion debater, president of the school's main theater association, the Curtain Club, and later, the president of the student body. He went to law school and in 1939 began working for Johnson in Washington. He quickly became Johnson's protégé. By 1948, he was Johnson's campaign manager and key confidant.

Coke Stevenson's lead lawyer was Clint Small, who had his own power base. Small was a former state senator and district court judge. In 1930, he'd run against Ross Sterling for the governor's job and come in third. He ran again, unsuccessfully, in 1934. Small went on to work as an attorney for Humble Oil.

Small was diametrically opposed to everything that Wirtz and Johnson stood for. Where Wirtz and Johnson were closely tied to Roosevelt and were ardent proponents of the New Deal, Small was a member of the Texas Regulars, a group of ultraconservative politicos and businessmen who were anti-union and opposed to Roosevelt and everything having to do with the New Deal. The Texas Regulars' funding came largely from independent oilmen like Hugh Roy Cullen, the publishing mogul Oveta Culp Hobby (whose family owned the *Houston Post*), and others who were convinced that America was under siege from Communists. In 1944, Small and the Texas Regulars produced an eight-point political platform that included a provision that called for the "restoration of the supremacy of the white race, which has been destroyed by the Communist-controlled New Deal."[6]

The airplanes his oilmen friends provided Johnson gave him a key advantage. While Stevenson traveled the state in an old Plymouth that didn't even have a loudspeaker, Johnson was in the air. Throughout the summer of 1948, he flew every chance he got. Johnson's most ostentatious air travel occurred aboard a plane provided by Sid Richardson. It was a B–24 Liberator, a gigantic bomber with a 110-foot wingspan, 4,800 horsepower, and huge fuel tanks that allowed it to fly 2,100 miles without refueling. These planes had played a key role in the Allied victory in World War II, and thousands of them had been built in the Dallas area. After the war, Richardson bought a B–24 and converted it into a passenger plane for his personal use. In the summer of 1948, Richardson's plane became a regular part of Johnson's campaign apparatus, used for ferrying Johnson to Houston or carrying Lady Bird Johnson from South Texas to Austin.

The DC–3s came from Brown & Root. The company had been using them since World War II to keep track of their ever-expanding business interests, and also to further their political goals. On many occasions the DC–3s would carry Johnson and other Texas politicians back and forth from Austin or Houston to Washington. On other occasions they were used to ferry Johnson to the political "powwows" that the Browns held at their hunting and vacation retreat at Fort Clark, in West Texas, near the Rio Grande.

The airplanes provided an incalculable advantage to Johnson during the race. At that time, commercial airplane service was still spotty and expensive. Private planes meant Johnson and his aides could visit multiple cities in a single day. Meanwhile, Stevenson, the traditional candidate, was driving from place to place. During the final, critical, week of the campaign, Johnson used the private planes to work the state's biggest cities, going to rallies in Dallas, Houston, Fort Worth, and San Antonio.

The airplanes were great for covering long distances between major population centers, but Johnson didn't stop with planes. He also used a then brand-new technology, the helicopter.

The Johnson-Stevenson race was very competitive. Polls consistently showed Johnson trailing Stevenson, and the wisdom of the day assumed that Johnson couldn't defeat him. Johnson knew he needed something new, something that would distinguish him from the pipe-smoking conservative. Johnson found it shortly before the campaign began, during a special demonstration held in Washington by Larry Bell's aerospace company.

Bell staged an event for congressmen to demonstrate the capabilities of a new aircraft that could rise straight up in the air. During Bell's demonstration, LBJ realized that a helicopter was just what he needed. With a helicopter he could effectively shrink Texas. Yes, the state would still be 800 miles long and nearly 800 miles wide. But if Johnson could travel by helicopter from town to town, he could travel much more quickly. With a helicopter, Johnson could land right in the center of town and give a speech right on the landing spot, eliminating the need for time-wasting car trips to and from the airstrip. He could speak to more people, shake more hands, and solicit more campaign contributions than if he stayed on the ground throughout the campaign.

Johnson's first-choice helicopter was a Sikorsky S–51, an ungainly-looking four-seat aircraft made by the Connecticut-based aerospace company Sikorsky. When it arrived, the campaign outfitted it with amplifiers and loudspeakers so that Johnson could blast his message out to potential voters as he flew by, entreating them to meet him in the nearest town, where they could hear his speech.

Helicopters were still a novelty everywhere, and they were particularly novel for the rural people of Texas, so whenever Johnson went to a small town—or a large town, for that matter—his arrival was a major news event. Joe Phipps, a radio broadcaster who traveled with Johnson and acted as his emcee on the stump, recalled that Johnson wanted to "guarantee that nothing would lessen the impact of this strange, insect-like craft settling itself down on dusty roads, playgrounds, parking lots, on courthouse squares—the harbinger of a bright, new world to come."[7]

One reporter said the aircraft, which the campaign dubbed the *Johnson City Windmill,* achieved exactly what Johnson had envisioned. With "Lyndon Johnson for U.S. Senate" emblazoned on the fuselage, the craft caused a sensation. "Coming down on those rural people in those little towns who had never seen anything like it, with that tremendous roar and the dust swirling up, it was an awesome thing," recalled the reporter. "As it was approaching, there was a lot of hurry-up: latecomers rushing to get there. But as it actually started to come down, there was silence—the silence of awe." The awe inspired by the helicopter brought big crowds. On one Saturday, Johnson made seven "hoverings" and 13 landings, speaking to some 15,000 people.[8]

Reporters loved it. *Time* magazine wrote, "Long Lyndon Johnson, one of Texas' most ebullient congressmen, has introduced the first new gimmick in Texas politics since the hillbilly band and the free barbecue.... Out in the bottoms and the back country, the Johnson City Windmill wowed the citizenry."

Johnson was fully aware of how much the helicopter was helping his campaign. On one occasion he flew in the helicopter to Austin, where he was met by another congressman, John Lyle, a Democrat from Corpus Christi. "That thing sure makes a lot of noise," Lyle said. To which Johnson replied, "That thing sure gets a lot of votes."

The helicopter could fly at 80 to 90 miles per hour, allowing Johnson to speed around the state and make multiple appearances every day, reaching voters who might otherwise have never seen a candidate for the U.S. Senate. There were no traffic lights, railroad crossings, or pothole-infested roads to slow him down. Johnson could carry all of his campaign literature with him and drop leaflets from the air or land and have campaign workers pass them out to voters.

The Sikorsky worked well, but the campaign only used it for about two weeks. After that it was replaced by the smaller Bell 47-B. The pilot of the Bell, Joe Mashman, says his boss, Larry Bell, the founder and owner of the company, which was based in New York State at the time, offered the chopper to the campaign because he could see the strategic value of making friends with someone like Johnson. Mashman recalls Bell's telling him, "I want you to take a helicopter down to Texas and fly this young congressman around who wants to become a senator. He started his election campaign late, but thinks he still has a chance. We're interested in helping him out because helicopters are new and if we get an important person such as a congressman showing enough confidence to fly in our aircraft, it would help us and the overall industry."

For Bell, the deal made perfect sense.

By 1948, Larry Bell had already turned the aerospace business on its ear. The daring designer from Indiana created several important airplanes, including the rocket-propelled X–1, in which the fabled test pilot Chuck Yeager broke the sound barrier in 1947. Bell built the P–59 Airacomet, the American military's very first jet-powered airplane, which was tested with great secrecy during the early days of World War II.[9] During the war, he also envisioned and began building the machines that would assure his place in aviation history: helicopters.

In 1946, the Bell 47-B became the first commercially licensed helicopter in the world, when the Civil Aeronautics Board (forerunner of the Federal Aviation Administration) gave it clearance to operate. By 1948, Bell had built only a handful of the aircraft and the company was anxious to increase the visibility of its machines. Supplying one to the Johnson campaign gave the company the opportunity to do a favor for an influential member of Congress who just might land a seat in the U.S. Senate. And from there, the senator would have opportunities to do great things for Bell.

Mashman recalls that Johnson "was considered a young, forward-thinking congressman. He was close to the technical people in our government." Plus, he'd been serving on the House Naval Affairs Committee, an entity that could provide the push needed for the military to begin buying aircraft from Bell. According to Mashman, the Johnson campaign never paid Bell anything for the use of the aircraft, even though at that time Bell had only a few of the model 47-Bs on hand. Nor did it pay the salaries of Mashman or the mechanic who came with him to work for the Johnson campaign. Those costs were borne by Bell.

Larry Bell's helicopters helped get Lyndon Johnson elected. In return, Bell got the exposure he was hoping for. Shortly after the 1948 election, Bell moved his company from New York State to the east side of Fort Worth. It made sense for many reasons: The wide-open spaces of Texas were a better location for the flying that Bell needed to do to test his designs. Texas was a nonunion state. Plus, by being in Texas, Bell's company, now called Bell Helicopter, would have the political backing that Bell would need to sell his helicopters to the U.S. military. Indeed, over the next few decades Bell sold many, many aircraft to the Pentagon.

Johnson's 1948 race was reportedly the most expensive political campaign ever waged in Texas.

The money flowed to Johnson like an inexhaustible river. By befriending Richardson, Murchison, Hunt, and other oilmen like Amon Carter of Fort Worth, Wesley West of Austin, and J. R. Parten of Houston, Johnson assured himself of nearly unlimited funding. When his campaign accounts were running low, Johnson dispatched

John Connally, now his smooth-talking bagman, to get more cash. As Robert Caro reports in the second volume of his biography of Johnson, *Means of Ascent,* Connally would get on a private plane in Austin, fly to Houston, or Dallas, or West Texas, and return with grocery sacks filled with cash. On one occasion, it was $50,000 in $100 bills. On another, Connally brought back $40,000.

Brown & Root was one source of Johnson's sacks filled with cash. On several occasions, one of Johnson's campaign workers visited Herman Brown, who would give him $25,000 in cash, which the worker would then give to Johnson's lawyer, Alvin Wirtz. Throughout the 1948 race, Brown & Root was providing virtually everything that Johnson needed. For the Browns it made good business sense. The company had been Johnson's biggest patron throughout his career, starting in the late thirties. In return, Johnson had done everything the company had asked. That had been the arrangement ever since Johnson's very first day in Washington, D.C.

When LBJ arrived in the capital as a newly elected congressman on May 13, 1937, his very first assignment was to make sure that federal money kept flowing for Brown & Root's dam construction project on the Lower Colorado River near Austin. George and Herman Brown had bet their entire company on the Marshall Ford Dam project. They were deeply in debt, having spent about $1.5 million on equipment and a giant cableway. They'd started construction on the dam before the Bureau of Reclamation, the agency responsible for federal dam projects, had obtained the necessary authorization from Congress. When the bureau investigated further, it found that it was paying to build a dam on land that it didn't own. The site was owned by the state of Texas. The funding question left the Browns fully exposed on their capital investments on the Marshall Ford project.

Just 11 days after Johnson got to Washington he had the matter straightened out. He convinced the Rivers and Harbors Committee to authorize money for the dam and to ratify all federal contracts with

Brown & Root. Thereafter, the Browns bankrolled Johnson every step of the way. In 1941, when Johnson made his first bid for the U.S. Senate, the Browns were his key patrons. In fact, Johnson would later say the entire 1941 campaign was "Brown & Root funded."[10]

In 1948, the Browns made another big bet on Johnson. Their cash and the cash from the other Texas Big Shots was used to pay campaign operatives who traveled the state to promote Johnson and spread rumors about Stevenson. It was used to pay off labor bosses, precinct chairmen, and political bosses, who in turn assured the votes—real or manufactured—of dozens of others. The cash paid for Johnson's personal needs, for hotels, telephones, salaries, and all the other necessities of a campaign.

Even though the aircraft and the cash played critical roles in pushing Johnson first to the finish line, in the end the election was decided by the lawyers and the courts.

The polls closed on August 28, 1948. After weeks of campaigning, and days of ballot counting, it was 494,191 to 494,104 in Johnson's favor—just 87 votes separated the two Democrats in the critically important primary. Johnson's margin was less than one tenth of one percent of the votes. Johnson was ahead, but the winner wouldn't be determined by the voters. The winner would be the candidate who was able to muster more supporters, more money, more legal muscle, more influence.

And the contest wasn't just about Lyndon Johnson. If Stevenson's crowd was allowed to rule the state's Democratic delegation, Harry Truman, the incumbent president, would be in trouble, too. Truman, who was trailing the Republican candidate, Thomas Dewey, in the polls, desperately needed to win Texas if he was going to return to the White House. Stevenson's supporters and the right-wingers in the Texas Regulars were threatening to abandon Truman and the Democrats and back Strom Thurmond, the virulently racist governor from South Carolina, who was gathering support in the Deep South for his States' Rights Democratic Party, popularly known as the Dixiecrats.

Truman's future, Johnson's future, Brown & Root's future, all hinged on the legal scrap that began immediately after the ballot counting stopped. The questions were simple: Who had really won the election and, more important, had votes been stolen and if so, where had the stealing been the most blatant? The focus quickly began centering on Precinct 13 in Jim Wells County, a region controlled by a South Texas political boss and Johnson ally named George Parr. Stevenson zeroed in on the precinct, demanding to see the list of voters from the election. An investigation showed that 202 names had been added to the voter list—in alphabetical order and in the same handwriting—after the polls had closed.

The matter quickly went to the courts. Each side hired a platoon of lawyers whom they dispatched all over the state to investigate suspicious votes and argue in the courts and in the newspapers as to which ballots should be counted and which candidate had perpetrated the most egregious acts.

The two sides fought before the canvassing committee of the Texas Democratic Party. Stevenson's lawyer, Clint Small, told the committee members that "the issue before this committee is whether or not Precinct 13 in Jim Wells County is to elect a United States Senator" with votes that were clearly illegal. Johnson was trying to win a seat in the Senate "with votes of people who never appeared at the polls," he went on, saying that the tally from Jim Wells County "reeks with corruption and fraud."[11]

Stevenson got a friendly federal judge, T. Whitfield Davidson, who opposed the New Deal, to issue a temporary restraining order, which prevented Johnson's name from being put on the November ballot. Davidson also appointed a group of commissioners to investigate the electoral shenanigans that had occurred in Jim Wells County and elsewhere. Davidson's order set off a vicious battle in the courts and created a huge problem for Johnson. There were suggestions of a statewide recount, a solution that Johnson's camp hated because it would take days and might reveal further vote fraud. Another suggested solution was to put both candidates' names on the ballot in the November general election, opposite those of the Republican candidate. Numerous scenarios were discussed about how that might affect Johnson and his chance to win. One state newspaper called the hot-running legal battle the "greatest political controversy of all time in Texas."[12]

Meanwhile, time was running out for Johnson. The deadline for finalizing the statewide ballots was October 3. If his name wasn't on the ballot, he might be forced to campaign again, this time to convince voters to write in his name—always a hard route to victory.

Johnson's lawyers, led by Wirtz, decided that their candidate's best chances lay with the U.S. Supreme Court. On September 28, 1948, one month after the election, Wirtz led a group of Johnson's lawyers into the chambers of Supreme Court Justice Hugo Black, who was a strong supporter of the New Deal. For several hours that day, they argued their case with Black, asking him to side with Johnson. The next day, Black agreed, signing an order that set aside Judge Davidson's injunction. Black criticized Davidson's intervention in the state election and he put a stop to the investigation into the vote fraud in Jim Wells County.

On September 29, a month and a day after the polls closed, Lyndon Johnson was declared the winner of the Democratic nomination for the U.S. Senate. His name would be on the ballot in the November general election. It had been a bruising battle, a battle that pitted two different political views, two markedly different candidates. Johnson won the war. His lawyers, airplanes, and money had prevailed in a race that was incredibly close. That same template would be used by another Texas candidate almost precisely 52 years later—only the stakes in that race would be much higher.

The 1948 Senate race is a key demarcation line in the history of Texas politics. Johnson's controversial victory helped start the movement that transformed the state from one dominated by Democrats to one dominated by Republicans. The change started with Stevenson himself. His defeat at the hands of Johnson turned Stevenson into a Republican. In 1952, he vocally supported Dwight Eisenhower. In 1960, he came out for Richard Nixon. In 1964, he touted Barry Goldwater. In 1968, he supported Nixon again.

Stevenson's supporters, bitter at the defeat of their candidate, began drifting into the Republican Party. Years later, Clint Small told the writer Ronnie Dugger that Johnson's win "was just a straight-out steal of the damned election."[13] In 2003, 55 years after Johnson beat Stevenson, Peter O'Donnell, the Big Rich Republican activist who helped convince George H. W. Bush to make his first run for office in the 1964 race for the U.S. Senate, told me that Johnson's tainted victory played a key role in the formation of the Texas Republican Party. "People here identified with Coke Stevenson. They were conservative Democrats. They thought he [Johnson] stole the election." That election, combined with several other events, fueled resentment and "sowed the seeds" of the GOP's rise in Texas politics, O'Donnell told me.

Thief or not, Lyndon Johnson went on to face Jack Porter, a Republican oilman, in the general election in November of 1948. Johnson crushed him, beating him by a margin of more than two to one, and began seizing the reins of power.

By early 1949, Johnson and the rest of the congressional delegation were part of the rapidly growing Texas power base in the nation's capital. Sam Rayburn, Johnson's longtime ally, was once again the Speaker of the House. Another Texan, Tom Clark, was U.S. attorney general. The state had a surfeit of oil and gas and more was being discovered. The Texas Railroad Commission governed oil prices. A growing maze of pipelines carried oil and natural gas from Texas to energy-starved cities to the north and east. Houston and Dallas were growing like kudzu. The state's rapidly expanding industrial base as well as its huge military presence assured lots of clout when it came to federal appropriations. Locally owned banks and insurance companies were giving the state the capital it needed to grow without relying on outsiders from New York, Boston, and Chicago.

And few of the people in the state stood to benefit from Texas' surging influence more than George and Herman Brown and their company, Brown & Root.

TIMELINE: BROWN & ROOT, HALLIBURTON, AND THE INFLUENCE GAME

1919: Brown & Root founded by Herman Brown and Dan Root. Erle Halliburton begins his oil-well-cementing company the same year.

1929: Dan Root dies. Herman Brown brings his brother, George, into the business.

1937: The Browns back Lyndon Johnson in his run for the U.S. House of Representatives.

1937: Eleven days after Representative Johnson's arrival in Washington, he secures federal funding for the Marshall Ford Dam (now known as Mansfield Dam) on the Lower Colorado River outside of Austin, which was being built by Brown & Root. The dam project becomes the basis of their empire.

1940: Johnson helps the Browns again, directing the U.S. Navy to award a military base construction contract to Brown & Root.

1941: Brown & Root begins building warships for the U.S. Navy.

1947: The Browns and a group of investors buy the Big Inch and Little Big Inch pipelines from the U.S. government and form Texas Eastern Transmission Corporation. The deal immediately makes them one of the biggest pipeline companies in America.

1948: The Browns again back Johnson, this time for the U.S. Senate, providing him with lawyers, airplanes, and money. Johnson also gets key backing from the independent oilmen and wins his seat after a bruising legal battle.

1949: Johnson, doing the Browns' bidding, brands Leland Olds, the head of the Federal Power Commission, a Communist. Olds's career is destroyed. Johnson's attacks open the door for another anti-Communist, Joe McCarthy.

1962: Shortly after the death of Herman Brown, George Brown agrees to merge Brown & Root with Halliburton for a pittance, $36.7 million. Brown continues to run the company as a nearly autonomous unit of Halliburton.

1965: Brown & Root joins the RMJ-BRK consortium, which provides a myriad of construction services for the U.S. military in South Vietnam. It's the first time the U.S. military uses private construction companies in a theater of war.

1967: The General Accounting Office finds that Brown & Root and its fellow contractors "could not account for the whereabouts of approximately $120 million worth of materials which had been shipped to Viet Nam from the United States."

1969: Former Texas Governor John Connally joins the Halliburton board. Richard Nixon later appoints him to serve on the President's Foreign Intelligence Advisory Board (PFIAB), the super-secret entity that monitors all of America's intelligence operations.

1982: Halliburton board member Anne Armstrong is appointed by President Ronald Reagan to serve as chair of the PFIAB. For the next eight years, she serves on both the Halliburton board of directors and the PFIAB.

1983: George Brown dies.

1991: In the wake of the First Iraq War, Halliburton gets enormous contracts in Kuwait and Saudi Arabia.

1992: Halliburton does study for Pentagon on privatizing logistics functions for the military. Shortly afterward, it is awarded a huge cost-plus logistics contract by the Pentagon.

1995: Halliburton hires Dick Cheney, defense secretary in the first Bush administration, as president and CEO.

1997: The General Accounting Office finds that while working for the Army in the Balkans, Brown & Root was charging the Army $86 for sheets of plywood that cost $14.

1998: Cheney engineers the merger between Halliburton and Dallas-based Dresser, an oilfield equipment and services company. In doing so, Halliburton takes on enormous asbestos liabilities associated with a Dresser subsidiary. To complete the transaction, Dresser's construction subsidiary, Kellogg, is merged with Brown & Root to become Kellogg Brown & Root, or KBR.

2000: General Accounting Office finds that Halliburton's work for Pentagon in Kosovo was fraught with excessive charges.

2000: George W. Bush picks Halliburton CEO Dick Cheney to head his vice-presidential search team. A few weeks later, Bush picks Cheney as his running mate. Cheney leaves Halliburton with a retirement package worth $33.7 million.

2000: Halliburton provides airplane to Bush campaign during the Florida recount.

2001: George W. Bush appoints Halliburton board member Ray Hunt to the PFIAB. He becomes the third person to serve on the Halliburton board and the PFIAB at the same time.

2001: Halliburton pays Vice President Cheney $205,298 in deferred compensation.

2002: Halliburton pays Vice President Cheney $162,392 in deferred compensation.

March 2003: Pentagon quietly awards a no-bid contract to Halliburton to do rebuilding in Iraq. Contract is worth up to $7 billion.

December 2003: A preliminary audit by the Defense Department finds Halliburton has overcharged the government by as much as $61 million to import gasoline into Iraq.

January 2004: Bloomberg reports that from March 2003 to December 2003, the Pentagon earmarked $2.3 billion to pay Halliburton for work done to restore Iraq's oil production.

January 2004: Halliburton wins another contract from the Army Corps of Engineers, worth up to $1.2 billion over two years, to rebuild oil facilities in southern Iraq.

February 2004: Halliburton becomes focus of an international investigation into $180 million in bribes allegedly paid to secure a gas project in Nigeria. The company also agrees to repay the Pentagon for more than $30 million for overcharges involving work it did for U.S. troops in the Persian Gulf.

February 2004: Corporate Crime Reporter reports that a Baker Botts lawyer, James Doty, who represented George W. Bush when he bought the Texas Rangers baseball team, is heading the investigation into Halliburton's alleged bribes in Nigeria. Doty was general counsel at the Securities and Exchange Commission when the agency investigated Bush's sale of stock at Harken Energy.

Chapter 6   Brown & Root Cleans Up

By 1949, George and Herman Brown were millionaires several times over. The paving company they'd started three decades earlier had made them richer than they'd ever imagined. No longer would they have to rely on small paving contracts like the one they got in the 1920s to pave the streets of Houston's ritzy new River Oaks neighborhood. Now, the two men were rich enough to live in River Oaks. And much of that wealth had been made possible by Lyndon Johnson. After assuring federal funding for the Marshall Ford Dam, Johnson began helping Brown & Root secure other federal contracts. And those contracts—made before, during, and after World War II—transformed George and Herman Brown's company into a construction superpower.

Brown & Root's contract to build the 2,000-acre Corpus Christi Naval Air Station was, like the dam, a key to their success. Johnson's influence assured that Brown & Root's lack of experience in building military bases was not a problem, nor did the company have to bother with competitive bidding. On June 13, 1940, President Roosevelt signed a contract for the construction of the base on a cost-plus basis: the base was to cost $23.4 million, and Brown & Root would be paid a $1.2 million profit. But $23.4 wasn't the final price. In a development that would become a Brown & Root trademark, the budget for the project grew. And grew. And grew some more. By 1941, the cost for the base was $45 million. Before it was finished, the air base had cost the federal government $125 million.[1] The project also gave Brown & Root credibility within the Defense Department, which would lead to many more contracts building bases and doing other work.

After the air base contract, the Browns got into the shipbuilding business for the U.S. Navy, thanks to another friend in Congress, Representative Albert Thomas of Houston. Brown Shipbuilding, a newly created subsidiary, won a contract to build ships even though the firm had never built so much as a canoe. By 1943, Brown Shipbuilding, located on a sprawling yard on the banks of the Houston Ship Channel, had 23,000 employees and was churning out destroyer escorts and submarine chasers.[2] By the end of the war, the Browns' new venture had produced $500 million worth of ships, 355 vessels, and had repaired or converted 90 others.

Brown & Root was the best shipbuilder the U.S. Navy had. When Great Lakes shipbuilders complained that the Gulf Coast was getting too many contracts, the Navy conducted studies that found that Brown & Root was building the best ships and doing it faster and at better cost than any other shipyard under contract to the Navy. The company won the Navy E for excellence award every year it built ships.[3]

The Browns made a fortune during World War II, but their wartime profits wouldn't come close to the mountain of money they were to make in the fecund decades after the war. In 1946, Brown & Root won a contract to build a military base on the island of Guam. The original contract was for a $21 million project. But like the Corpus Christi base, the project grew. By 1955 the costs had reached $250 million. The company also built military facilities in Spain and elsewhere. By 1954, Brown & Root had done $1 billion worth of work for the Pentagon and more work was coming their way.[4]

The Browns minted money by purchasing surplus war equipment and transforming it into saleable material. Within months of the bombing of Hiroshima, the two brothers, foreseeing the massive demobilization of America's arsenals, formed a company that bought, chopped up, and melted down almost 21,000 airplanes purchased from the War Assets Administration. The Browns set up smelting furnaces that could produce 100,000 pounds of aluminum from the recycled planes per day. Shortly thereafter, they had a corner on the aluminum market. They also sold spare parts they'd salvaged from the airplanes back to the U.S. military. In the end, the Browns made tens of millions of dollars on the surplus-aircraft business.

The war had been very, very profitable. But the Browns' biggest potential profits lay in Texas Eastern Transmission Corporation, the entity they had founded to buy the Big Inch and Little Big Inch pipelines from the federal government. In 1947, Texas Eastern paid $143 million for the pipelines (slightly less than the amount the government had spent to build them).[5] With that purchase, they instantly became dominant players in the American energy business. Their pipelines were the key conduit through which natural gas from Texas was flowing to states in the north and east. The venture was incredibly profitable from the outset. In November of 1947, when Texas Eastern sold stock to the public, the Browns had a major windfall: on the very first day of trading, their stock holdings in Texas Eastern were worth more than 66 times their initial investment.

But they were still just getting started. By the time Lyndon Johnson moved into the White House in 1963, Texas Eastern was one of the most valuable companies in America. Its assets were worth nearly $1.5 billion and its profits were about $40 million per year. It owned interests in 1,000 oil wells and was buying and selling crude oil, refined products, and natural gas in 19 states.[6] In addition to huge profits, the Browns' businesses had synergy. Between 1947 and 1977, Brown & Root did $1.3 billion worth of upgrades and repair work on the Big Inch and Little

Big Inch pipelines and other Texas Eastern assets.[7] Texas Eastern and Brown & Root became the two pillars of the Browns' empire.

But in the early days of Texas Eastern's existence, the Browns were worried that federal regulators would limit their ability to make big profits. They needed friends who could help them at the Federal Power Commission, the agency that regulated the rates that could be charged for the use of interstate pipelines. Unfortunately for the pipelines' owners, the head of the Federal Power Commission at that time, Leland Olds, was a friend of American consumers, not of the Texas crony network. And that meant the Browns and the other oilmen had to get rid of him.

To do that, they needed help—and by 1949, with Lyndon Baines Johnson comfortably ensconced in the U.S. Senate, the Browns had an able assassin, ready and willing to do their bidding. All Johnson would need for his killing was a stout dose of red baiting.

Originally appointed to the Federal Power Commission by Franklin Roosevelt, Leland Olds was renominated for the same position by Harry Truman. But Johnson and his allies were not going to allow Olds to serve another term. Olds had sided with the consumers in reining in the power of the big utilities. He'd also led the government's efforts to control natural gas prices—a fact that was anathema to independent oilmen and major oil companies alike. For years the oilmen had been lobbying for deregulation of the gas industry. In 1949, Senator Robert S. Kerr of Oklahoma, an oilman, introduced a bill to do that. Olds testified against the bill. He believed that the Federal Power Commission's policy, which allowed the gas producers a 9.5 percent return on their investment, provided good protection for consumers; otherwise they might be abused by the pipeline owners, who held a monopoly on the natural gas delivery business. President Truman agreed with Olds's position and vetoed Kerr's bill.

The veto got the oilmen's attention. Billions of dollars in profits were at stake over the natural gas issue. The energy producers wanted to get rid of Olds and replace him with someone more amenable to their positions, someone who would allow them to charge higher prices and make bigger profits. But getting rid of Olds meant destroying his reputation, so that his nomination would not be confirmed. And Johnson and the oilmen were happy to do just that. Hugh Roy Cullen, an archconservative Houston independent oilman, claimed that Olds "did not believe in our form of government." Charles Francis, who was a partner in Texas Eastern Transmission Corporation as well as a lawyer for the Browns, said that Olds should be tossed out because of "his political views, and unjudicial temperament."

John Connally, Johnson's longtime lawyer and adviser, said the defeat of Olds was a "real bread-and-butter issue to these oilmen. So this would prove whether Lyndon was reliable, that he was no New Dealer. This was his chance to get in with dozens of oilmen—to bring very powerful rich men into his fold who had never been for him, and were still suspicious of him."[8]

Johnson saw that the best way to take care of Olds was to brand him a Communist. In the 1920s, Olds had worked for a wire service, and during that time he'd praised some aspects of the system of government in Russia. He'd also shared a speaking platform with a Communist leader, Earl Browder. In 1928, Olds had supported Herbert Hoover, a Republican, in his bid for the presidency, saying that Hoover was "the leader of progressive capitalism." Those phrases and several others snipped from Olds's writing were enough ammunition for Johnson and a Texas Congressman from Corpus Christi, John Lyle, to use to lead the charge in branding Olds a Communist. Johnson was appointed to the subcommittee in charge of considering Olds's nomination and he immediately began attacking him, charging that he was planning to "plot a course toward confiscation and public ownership." Olds, Johnson said, chose "to travel with those who proposed the

Marxian answer." All the while Johnson was slapping around Olds, he was getting his scripts from his lawyer back in Austin, Alvin Wirtz.

Wirtz, who was still working for Brown & Root—and Texas Eastern—had plenty of other clients who wanted to see Olds destroyed, including Texas' biggest energy companies: Houston Natural Gas Company (which later became Enron), Humble Oil & Refining Company, Sun Oil Company, Amerada Petroleum Corporation, Hunt Production Company, and several others. The oil companies simply could not allow Olds to have control over the movement of their products. Wirtz fed Johnson a string of questions "of the type a lawyer might ask in court," to help Johnson in his grilling of Olds.[9]

Under questioning, Olds repeatedly denied that he was a Communist. It didn't matter. Lyndon Johnson, the man who just ten years earlier had led the fight to create publicly owned power generation plants at the Lower Colorado River Authority, was now leading an attack on Olds, a man who was committed to protecting consumers from greedy corporate interests. Analyzing Johnson's actions, Ronnie Dugger, one of his biographers, wrote that by "joining in the political crucifixion of Leland Olds—driving in the nails himself—Johnson had used most of the tricks of what would come to be known as McCarthyism, and he nauseated some of his colleagues, but he had achieved his purpose—he had convinced the oilmen back in Texas that he was their man."[10]

Leland Olds lost his bid to stay at the Federal Power Commission: the Senate nixed his confirmation 53 to 15. And the Texas oil and gas producers reveled in their victory. Johnson had killed their enemy. He'd done it by raising the specter of Communism. And the Texas oilmen loved anyone who carried the flag of anti-Communism. By the late 1940s, Texas politicos had been on an anti-Communist jihad for several years. Indeed, Johnson's attack on Olds was modeled on the methods of another Texan, Martin Dies, Jr.

In 1938, Dies, a congressman from East Texas, who had originally been elected in 1930 as a supporter of the New Deal, became the first chairman of the House Un-American Activities Committee (HUAC). In fact, creating it was his idea. Dies had been railing against the dangers of the red menace for years. An anti-Semite, Dies never minded expressing his antagonism toward Jews. He once said that a person shouldn't be labeled a Fascist or a Nazi "simply because he expressed anti-Jewish views."[11]

In 1943, Dies nearly got a measure passed in the U.S. House of Representatives that would have barred workers from public employment if they were "communistic." The type of conduct that could be considered "communistic" was not well defined. Dies's bill was defeated by the thinnest of margins: 153 to 146.

Dies also led a crusade against alleged Communists at the University of Texas, which he charged was overflowing with the vermin. He was backed up by an archconservative oilman, Orville Bullington, who claimed that "more than a thousand communists had infiltrated the university" and that the school contained a "nest of homosexuals.[12] None of Bullington's or Dies's charges against officials of the university—or anybody else, for that matter—ever proved to be true. But Dies's methods were very effective, and Lyndon Johnson imitated them in crafting his attack on Leland Olds. Dies got tremendous publicity for his witch hunts. He also got political backing from Texas oilmen, who saw the anti-Communist attacks as a way to further their political interests in the United States and abroad.

The oilmen were the first true globalists. They were actively seeking oil in all parts of the world, and they were not eager to risk their capital in banana republics where the next dictator might expropriate their wells, drilling rigs, and profits. Supporting the anti-Communists was simply a way to provide some insurance. If Texas independent oilmen like Cullen, H. L. Hunt, and Clint Murchison were going to make multi-million-dollar bets on oil wells in South America, Asia, and the

Persian Gulf, they wanted to make sure their investments would be safe. As one of the newly rich Texans told *Fortune* magazine in 1954, "We all made money fast. We were interested in nothing else. Then this Communist business suddenly burst upon us. Were we going to lose what we had gained?"[13] But they had other motives. By funding anti-Communists like Dies, they also could attack the labor unions and the supporters of the New Deal. Murchison admitted as much when he told one writer that the anti-Communist crusade was useful in keeping "the albatross [of Communism] hung about the neck of" the New Deal.[14]

When Dies's attacks began to run out of gas, he was replaced by another charlatan who would be even more strident in his attacks on alleged Communists. And like Dies, he would depend heavily on Texas oilmen for money. His name was Joe McCarthy.

Within a few months of Johnson's destruction of Leland Olds, Joe McCarthy, the Republican senator from Wisconsin, began proclaiming that America had been overrun by Communists. His declarations immediately gained him a huge base of support in Texas.

McCarthy tapped into the funding base of the Texas Regulars, the ultraconservative anti–New Deal group that had supported Coke Stevenson. One of the leading funders of that group was Hugh Roy Cullen, the Big Rich Houston oilman who had opposed the nomination of Leland Olds at the Federal Power Commission. In 1952, Cullen was the single biggest contributor to McCarthy's reelection campaign. The Houston oilman once announced at a press conference: "McCarthy is the greatest man in America."[15] McCarthy was also backed by Jesse Jones, the real estate and banking magnate from Houston who had served as Franklin Roosevelt's right-hand man. Shortly after leaving Washington, Jones became an avid critic of the New Deal and McCarthy's strident anti-Communism appealed to Jones' conservative nature. McCarthy got enormous amounts of additional funding from Murchison, Hunt, and other Texas oilmen. The Wisconsin Republican got so much money from the Lone Star State he became known as "the third senator from Texas."

In 1954, McCarthy held a $100-per-plate Republican fundraiser in Dallas. It was only the second time such a high-dollar Republican fundraiser had ever been held in Texas. One thousand people showed up to hear McCarthy expound on his topic, "Twenty Years of Treason."[16]

The commoners in Texas also supported McCarthy. In the fall of 1953, when McCarthy married his former research aide, Jean Kerr, a group of Houstonians, led by a printer named E. M. Biggers, decided they'd give the newlyweds a present and called on the public to donate. "I guess we had an Oldsmobile in mind until somebody said 'Hell, why not a Cadillac?'" recalled Biggers. The group set a $100 top limit on donations and within a few weeks had raised $6,000—enough money to buy the car. "I had to call the newspapers and tell them we had enough," he said. The group raised so much money that Biggers added all kinds of options to the Cadillac. "We put more gadgets on that car than any Cadillac ever had in Houston. . . . We gave the car everything except a left turn indicator . . . and we figured Joe didn't need that."[17]

Biggers's daughter-in-law, Virginia Biggers, was perhaps even more staunch in her support of McCarthy. She was a leader of a group of crazed Houston housewives known as the Minute Women who were convinced that the city's schools were being afflicted with "creeping socialism." The Minute Women kept up their paranoid, anti-Communist rants for several years—firmly convinced that they were saving the city from what Mrs. Biggers called "every Red, Pink. . .and misguided 'liberal' in the United States."[18]

For Texas oilmen, extremism in the defense of McCarthy was no vice. By 1954, the Houston oilman Jack Porter, who'd been the Republican nominee for Senate in the 1948 race, was a member of the Republican National Committee. Porter defended McCarthy's zealotry, saying, "Somebody had to raise unshirted hell to get those people out of the government, and Joe's raised it.... He's a great patriot doing his best to protect America."

Hunt, an oilman who'd gotten rich in the East Texas field, held identical views. By 1954, Hunt was the financial backer of a radio and TV program called *Facts Forum,* a show that fervently espoused McCarthy's claim that America was being overrun by Communists. Hunt spent about $1 million per year on *Facts Forum* and two related programs, which were featured on 80 TV and 384 radio stations across the country. Hunt's ultra-right-wing beliefs were so extreme that one of his friends said that Hunt believed Communism came to America "when the government took over the distribution of mail." Even the president of the *Dallas Morning News,* E. M. Dealey, who was also a staunch supporter of McCarthy, referred to Hunt as a "latent Fascist."

Hunt's Fascism was no match for that of McCarthy, whose downfall occurred shortly after the American public began witnessing his destructive inquisition on television. In the summer of 1954, McCarthy's career was mortally wounded by a Boston attorney named Joseph Welch, who after witnessing McCarthy's grilling of Fred Fisher, uttered the famous lines: "Until this moment, Senator, I think I never really gauged your cruelty or your recklessness.... Let us not assassinate this lad further, Senator. You've done enough. Have you no sense of decency, sir? At long last, have you left no sense of decency?" His challenge effectively ended McCarthy's career.

But Welch did not put an end to the strident anti-Communism that existed in Texas. In fact, despite McCarthy's downfall, conservative, anti-union, anti-Communist, pro-military sentiments continued to gain steam in Texas. This environment provided the ideological breeding ground—and the money—for the next major politician to emerge from Texas: George H. W. Bush.

Chapter 7

Bush and Baker Join Forces

George Herbert Walker Bush's first political defeat was exactly one week old when he sat down to write a letter to his pal, former vice president Richard Nixon. "We got whipped, and whipped soundly," Bush wrote, "but out of the gloom of November 3rd there are some bright spots." Those bright spots, Bush said, included the fact that he'd received more votes than any other Republican candidate in Texas history. Plus, he had "a good campaign with the best people in Texas involved; a wonderfully dedicated spirit; a sense of humor.... I think we have a base for a future race should the opportunity present itself." Bush also thanked Nixon for coming to Houston during the campaign. "Your visit was great and all of us here appreciate it. It was a terrific help in fund raising."

Two days later, on November 12, 1964, Nixon, writing from his law office in New York, responded to Bush's letter, saying that he hoped "this defeat, far from discouraging you, will only whet your appetite for making another race the next time the proper opportunity is presented." Nixon added that he'd seen a lot of candidates in the previous years and "in terms of political aptitude and that very hard to define mystique which makes a successful political leader, you rate among the very top of the list."[1]

Bush's attempt to capture a seat in the U.S. Senate had failed. The liberal incumbent Democrat, Ralph Yarborough, beat him by 300,000 votes. Yarborough had succeeded in branding Bush a carpetbagger, a Yankee. But the signs were encouraging. Bush had won more votes in Texas than the presidential nominee, Barry Goldwater. He'd expanded the reach of the Republican Party in Texas by showing that a virtually unknown candidate could run hard and get lots of media attention. Several of the state's big newspapers, including the *Fort Worth Star-Telegram,* the *Dallas Morning News,* and the *El Paso Times,* had endorsed Bush over Yarborough. He'd run on a conservative platform that had found wide support. Bush opposed President Lyndon Johnson's civil rights bill, saying that Texas "has a responsible record in this field" and that it "is capable of solving its own problems." His platform was pro-military, anti-union, and against federal control of public education— the bedrock positions for Texas conservatives.[2]

Bush's candidacy proved that he and other Texas Republicans could raise the kind of money they would need in order to succeed at capturing some of the key statewide offices. Bush's campaign was awash in money. The day after the election, the *Houston Chronicle* estimated that Bush had outspent his opponent by "at least 7–1."[3] The majority of that money came from the energy business. Bush had tapped into his family's East Coast network in investment banking and politics, but the big support came from his network of friends in the energy industry.

At the time of Bush's run for the Senate, he was the chairman of Zapata Off-Shore Company, an oil drilling contractor based in Houston with operations all over the world. In the previous decade Bush had developed close ties to oilmen in both Midland and Houston. He'd spent about a decade drilling for oil in the Permian Basin. Bush landed in Odessa in 1948 and later moved to Midland. There, he met a Tulsa native, Hugh Liedtke, who had followed the footsteps of his father, a Gulf Oil Corporation lawyer, into the oil business. In 1953, Bush and

Liedtke, along with John Overbey and Bill Liedtke, formed Zapata Petroleum Corporation. Their luck was remarkable. Shortly after they started Zapata they drilled 127 wells in the West Jamieson field, in West Texas, without a single dry hole.[4]

They weren't alone in seeking—and making—their fortunes in the oil business. Midland had an astounding concentration of energy interests: by 1950, 215 different oil companies had operations in the city—there was an oil company for every 100 residents. The city was breeding millionaires by the limousine load. And every one of those oilmen wanted to keep the federal government out of their business and away from their wallets. It was an attitude expressed perfectly by the writer Larry L. King, who once described Midland as "bedrock conservative territory with the nut wing among Rightists well-represented."[5] In addition to looking out for good energy deals, Bush worked to strengthen the Republican Party in Midland.

By the late fifties, the two men decided to split Zapata into two companies. Liedtke would head Zapata Petroleum, which would focus on oil exploration and production. Bush would take over the drilling business, known as Zapata Off-Shore Company. However, Bush knew that if he wanted to be in the offshore drilling business, he couldn't stay in Midland. So in 1959 he moved his company to Houston, and Bush immediately resumed the activities that he'd started in Midland, namely, looking for energy deals and drumming up support for the Republican Party. Within a short time, he became chairman of the Harris County Republican Party. He also became business partners with one of the most successful drillers in the oil business, William P. "Bill" Clements Jr., the founder and boss of Dallas-based Southeastern Drilling Company, or Sedco. The two men had a joint venture in the offshore drilling business, known as Seacat-Zapata Off-Shore. And that deal led to Bush's first exposure to the Persian Gulf. About the same time Bush was running for the Senate, one of their oil-drilling vessels was drilling a well off the Kuwaiti coast for Royal Dutch/Shell.[6] Seacat-Zapata also owned another drilling vessel that was working off the coast of Iran.[7]

When Bush decided to run for the Senate, Clements, who lived in Dallas, agreed to be his finance chairman. And Clements raised a ton of money—most of it from Bush's brethren in the energy fraternity. "To get things done down here, you had to have the backing of wealthy individuals back then, and that was the energy business," explains George Strake Jr., an oilman who went on to serve as chairman of the Texas Republican Party. It wasn't the major oil companies who supported Bush, he said, it was the independent energy guys. Bush's campaign chairman was a Midland lawyer, Martin Allday, whose firm specialized in oil and gas work. Allday himself donated $1,000 to Bush's campaign. (When Bush became president, he appointed Allday to the Federal Energy Regulatory Commission. Allday immediately became chairman and served at the FERC for four years.)

Bush's pal Robert Mosbacher headed a committee, Oil Men for Bush, that was charged with shaking money out of the oil patch. Bush got $2,000 from Houston's most ardent anti-Communist oilman, Hugh Roy Cullen. Another $500 came from Perry Bass, the nephew of the Fort Worth oilman Sid Richardson. Bass, along with the then Texas governor, John Connally, was one of the executors of Richardson's vast estate. (Perry Bass and his four sons—Sid, Ed, Robert, and Lee—have since parlayed Sid Richardson's fortune into a megafortune. In 2003, *Forbes* estimated that the five men were worth a total of $6.6 billion. The Basses continue to be huge donors to the Republican Party.) Bush also got big donations, totaling $23,000, from a group of Corpus Christi men who were doing offshore drilling in Asia with Clements's company.

Bill Clements himself wrote a gigantic check. "I recall giving him about five hundred thousand," Clements told me in mid-2003. Told that was the equivalent of nearly $3 million in 2003 dollars, Clements shrugged and said risk came with the territory. "That's what politics is all about isn't it? I thought he'd be good for the country. And I was proved right."

Bush burned through the money building up his name identification. He had billboards put up across the state blazed with his name and picture. During the Republican primary against a former state representative from West Texas, Jack Cox, Bush's campaign spent nearly $2.60 per vote, to Cox's $1.20.[8]

Although Bush lost his bid for the U.S. Senate, he was well positioned for the future. He had the staunch backing of the Dallas wing of the Republican Party, led by Peter O'Donnell. The offshore drilling business was booming. And he had allies. His newest and best friend was a young, ambitious attorney who, like Bush, had been a Republican since he was in diapers. He'd helped Bush on the campaign, sizing up the crowds, offering advice. His name was Jimmy Baker.

Looking back, it seems inevitable that James Addison Baker III and George Herbert Walker Bush would become buddies on a tennis court—at a country club, no less. The Houston Country Club was a natural habitat for both men. It was an exclusive, members-only, ultra-WASP playground located in the Memorial section, one of Houston's best neighborhoods. Baker and Bush were both from high-profile families. Both had gone to exclusive East Coast schools. They were about the same age, and both had been in the military. Bush, six years older, was a decorated World War II Navy flyer who had been shot down by the Japanese; Baker had been a Marine. Both were young, wealthy, good-looking, and ambitious. Both had strong ties to the oil business. Both had pure GOP DNA.

They quickly became best friends and their alliance would shape the American political scene for decades to come.

Although Bush had lots of contacts and friends, Baker was the man who could really provide him with entrée to the right people in Houston. Baker belonged to all of Houston's best clubs, including the Bayou Club, the crème de la crème of the oil Mecca's high society. He ate lunch at the Houston Petroleum Club. All well and good for George Bush to come from a good Eastern family, and for his father, Prescott Bush, to be a U.S. senator. But he wasn't Houston royalty. Jimmy Baker was. By the time Bush moved to Houston in 1959, Baker's family had been in Texas for more than a century.

Baker's great-grandfather, James Addison Baker, moved to Texas from Alabama in the 1850s. He first settled in Huntsville and in 1861 was elected to the Texas legislature. A year later, while serving in the Confederate Army, he was elected to serve as a judge.[9] In 1872, he moved to Houston and added his name to the law firm that became Baker Botts.[10]

Within a short time, Baker began working for the most infamous robber baron of the age, the railway magnate Jay Gould—a man so hated that he dared not travel the streets of New York without his bodyguard. In 1873 the *New York World* editorialized, "There is one man in Wall Street today whom men watch, and whose name, built upon ruins, carries with it a certain whisper of ruin.... They that curse him do not do it blindly, but as cursing one who massacres after victory." A few weeks after that article appeared, Gould bought the newspaper.[11]

Judge Baker quickly became one of Gould's chief lawyers. His job was to help Gould expand his influence in Texas, and expand he did, in Texas and beyond. By 1882, Gould controlled the biggest rail network in America, and probably the world. It extended from Boston to New York, to Chicago, St. Louis, Kansas City, Omaha, and Denver. He also had a stranglehold on Texas, owning rail lines into Fort Worth, Dallas, El Paso, Laredo, Galveston, and on to New Orleans. At the zenith of his rail empire, Gould owned nearly 16,000 miles of railroads, or about 15 percent of all the tracks in America.[12] And Baker Botts played a key role in that expansion by helping Gould integrate his Texas railroads with the ones he owned in other states. Judge Baker became one of Gould's main advisers and the firm became the general counsel for Gould's Missouri Pacific Line. Thanks to its lucrative association with Gould, Judge Baker's firm quickly became one of the foremost law firms in the state.[13]

It also began a tradition: for the next century and more, Baker Botts would specialize in representing looters, polluters, and plutocrats.

The law firm's influence continued into the early 1900s under the leadership of Judge Baker's son, Captain James A. Baker. By the 1920s Captain Baker was perhaps the single most powerful man in Houston. He was involved in millions of dollars' worth of real estate deals and investments. Baker Botts had multiple interconnected dealings with railroads, banks, oil companies, mortgage companies, and utilities. The firm was on retainer to several big corporations, including Texaco, which kept the law firm's partners on its payroll from 1914 through 1954.[14] It was in these decades that Baker Botts began gaining experience with the legal issues surrounding foreign oil exploration and production. In the mid-1930s, Texaco became one of the original partners of the Arabian-American Oil Company, now known as Aramco, the venture created to exploit the immense oil wealth of Saudi Arabia. Baker Botts lawyers became corporate chieftains and players in Washington, D.C. One of them, Robert Scott Lovett, became head of the Union Pacific Railroad. Another partner, Edwin Parker, simultaneously acted as general counsel for Texaco.[15] The firm was very active in Washington. Parker served on the War Industries Board in World War I. During World War II, one of the firm's partners, Brady Cole, was the assistant general counsel for the War Emergency Pipelines, the federal agency that built the Big Inch and Little Big Inch pipelines.[16]

In Houston, Captain Baker served as the chair of Rice University's board of trustees—a position in which he could exert control over monies in the school's endowment and see that it was lent to favored friends and businesses. In addition, he sat on the board of one of Houston's biggest banks, Texas Commerce Bank. Captain Baker and another Big Rich Houstonian, Jesse H. Jones, played pivotal roles in obtaining the federal money needed to drain and dredge swampland to widen the Houston Ship Channel, the port that would connect the city to the Gulf of Mexico and the rest of the world. All of Captain Baker's business ties meant yet more legal work for Baker Botts. His deals helped bind the firm's "expanding circle of influence with one of the strongest of all glues, money."[17]

James A. Baker Jr., Jimmy Baker's father, inherited Captain Baker's influence. Less visible than Captain Baker, he was a capable corporate lawyer. He married Bonner Means, a daughter of the family that had been one of the original landowners in the great Humble oilfield, in a town a couple dozen miles north of downtown Houston. The discovery of that field, in 1904, had helped spur the development of Houston's oil business. It had also provided the discoveries that became the nucleus of Humble Oil & Refining. Bonner Means's great-great-uncle had been the governor of South Carolina when the Civil War began, and so the traditions of the Old South became the heritage of the next generation of Bakers when, in 1930, James Addison Baker III was born. From the outset, it was clear that he, like his father, grandfather, and great-grandfather, would be a corporate lawyer.[18]

Jimmy Baker grew up in the lap of luxury. His boyhood home, at 1216 Bissonnet, was a sprawling, English manor–style house that had been built in 1926 in Shadyside, the most exclusive neighborhood in the city. The men who built houses there included Joseph Cullinan, who founded Texaco; William Hobby, the publisher of the *Houston Post;* and William Stamps Farish, one of the founders of Humble Oil.

The young Baker attended the best schools, starting in elementary school with the Kinkaid School, Houston's oldest independent coeducational school. While attending Kinkaid, Baker, then ten years old, was the target of an extortion attempt. In October of 1940, his father, James A. Baker Jr., received a hand-written letter—the text in big, block letters—at the Bakers' home on Bissonnet demanding that he "donate" $10,000 to the extortionists. If he didn't do so, the four-page letter warned that it was "much easier to kill eight and ten year old children than to kidnap them and hold for ransom and have to kill them later . . . We are not going to try to harm you or kidnap any of your close relatives and get caught with the evidence. We will start killing a close friend of yours. . . ." Baker's father turned the letter over to the Federal Bureau of Investigation, which followed up on the letter, but no arrests were ever made. According to FBI files, no further threats were made against the young Baker's life.[19]

It's hard to assess the effect the extortion attempt may have had on Baker or his family. By nature, the lawyers at Baker Botts sought to avoid any publicity. The Bakers' ethos had always been to keep a low profile in all matters, and the extortion attempt probably only strengthened that preference.

As a teenager, Baker attended the Hill School in Philadelphia, where he was captain of the tennis team, and from there he went on to Princeton, at that time (and until 1969) still a males-only university. There he met a number of the cronies who would become part of America's political elite. One of his classmates was Frank Carlucci, who after holding a series of jobs in the federal government became Ronald Reagan's defense secretary. After leaving the Pentagon, Carlucci went on to form the Carlyle Group, an outfit that—thanks to help from Baker, George H. W. Bush, and other power players—became one of the biggest private equity firms in the United States. Two years behind Carlucci and Baker was a macho Princeton man who also was destined for the big time: Donald Rumsfeld.

After Princeton, Baker joined the Marines, got married, got discharged, and went to law school at the University of Texas. After graduation he quickly became a corporate lawyer—not at Baker Botts, which had an antinepotism rule, but at Andrews & Kurth, another old-line Houston firm. Andrews & Kurth was so stuffy that it was considered "suffocatingly conservative, even by conservatives," according to one account written during Baker's stint at the firm. Andrews & Kurth worked for railroads, oil companies, and other industrial interests. Its most famous client during Baker's tenure was the Hughes Tool Company, the oilfield equipment firm owned by Howard Hughes Jr., the billionaire playboy and aviator whose business interests sprawled all over the planet.[20] Andrews & Kurth didn't handle the legal affairs of Baker's buddy, George H. W. Bush. Those tasks were handled by the Baker family's law firm, Baker Botts.

By the early 1960s, Baker Botts was one of Houston's leading law firms serving the needs of oil and gas companies. Its work in railroads had helped it move into legal work on natural gas pipelines. One of the firm's biggest clients was Tenneco, a Houston-based pipeline giant that had interests in a myriad of businesses across the country. Right after World War II, Baker Botts had tried in vain to help Tenneco acquire the Big Inch and Little Big Inch pipelines but had lost out to George Brown and the other investors in Texas Eastern Transmission Corporation.

The firm also worked for a number of independent oil companies. One of them was Zapata Petroleum Corporation, the company created by Hugh Liedtke and George H. W. Bush. That legal work would provide huge benefits to Baker Botts and its client Liedtke over the coming years.

In the late 1950s, when Bush and Liedtke split up Zapata, with Liedtke taking control of the exploration and production company and Bush taking control of the drilling company, the lawyers at Baker Botts continued working for both companies. Baker Botts attorneys worked closely with Bush on Zapata Off-Shore's initial public offering.

Baker Botts did more than provide legal services to Bush. It also became part of his political network in Houston. When Bush needed money for his campaign or that of another Republican, his mailing list often included the white-shoe lawyers at Baker Botts. A pattern was developing: when the Bush family needed help, they called Baker Botts.

After the unsuccessful 1964 campaign, Baker helped Bush put his life back together. When the campaign office was shut down, all of the papers from the campaign were delivered to James A. Baker III. They haven't been seen since. Thus did the lives and destinies of George H. W. Bush, James A. Baker III, and Baker Botts became ever more intertwined.[21]

Bush and Baker became inseparable allies, more like brothers than friends. The lawyers at Baker Botts looked after the legal matters. Bush and Baker talked about everything. They plotted strategy for future political races, played tennis together, and networked with other Republicans. They did favors for each other. One such favor involved finding a paying position for a gangly teenager, a boy who would grow up to be president of the United States. On June 6, 1962, George W. Bush got his very first summer job . . . working in the mail room at Baker Botts.[22]

Chapter 8

Bleeding Oil

I bled and died for the oil industry.

—George H. W. Bush (quoted in Daniel Yergin,
The Prize: The Epic Quest for Oil, Money and Power)

Instability in the Middle East severely threatens sources
of our petroleum imports from that region of the world.

—George H. W. Bush, 1970

The sting of George Bush's loss in the 1964 Senate
race didn't last long. In 1966 he won a seat in the
U.S. House of Representatives, representing northwest Houston's
newly created Seventh District, an area that included about one third
of Houston. The district contained several working-class neighborhoods as well as what may be the most oil-rich enclave on earth, River
Oaks. Every energy man of any consequence lived within a few
blocks of the River Oaks Country Club. Hugh Roy Cullen lived there.
George Brown of Brown & Root lived there. They and the rest of the
city's oil moguls were represented in Washington by George H. W.
Bush.

Bush knew that one of his main jobs—maybe his only job—at the
U.S. Capitol was the preservation of the depletion allowance. He
understood this as a Texan, as an energy man, and as a Republican.

Support for the depletion allowance had long been a litmus test for
candidates seeking votes in Texas, and that had been particularly true

during the 1960 presidential election. As a U.S. senator, John F. Kennedy had voted to reduce the depletion allowance, a move that made many Texas voters suspicious of him and his motives. Despite having Lyndon Johnson, a favorite son, on the presidential ballot, a strong Texans for Nixon campaign had sprouted in the state and it was growing. It wasn't surprising. Texas had voted Republican in both the 1952 and 1956 presidential elections. And the oil industry had been favoring the Republican Party for years. In 1956, officials at the nation's biggest oil companies gave nearly $350,000 to Republicans while giving less than $15,000 to Democrats. In 1960, the officers and directors of the American Petroleum Institute, the industry's primary lobby organization, gave over $113,000 to the GOP's candidates and just $6,000 to the Democrats. In 1964, the officials from that same group gave twice as much to Republicans as Democrats.

During the 1960 campaign, Johnson loyalists were worried that Kennedy might waffle on the depletion issue. Having a strong statement from Kennedy in favor of depletion was critical to Johnson, too. Johnson was running for two offices at the same time. Thanks to a law passed just for his benefit by the Texas legislature, Johnson was running for reelection to the Senate and for the vice presidency. Johnson's political adviser, John Connally—who was also working as a lawyer-lobbyist for the oilman Sid Richardson at the time—understood the gravity of the depletion allowance issue. Connally warned Johnson that Kennedy had to be forceful in his support of the depletion allowance. If the oilmen believed that Kennedy was going to cut depletion, Connally said at the time, "I'm not kidding when I say we are lost. . . . If Kennedy comes out for repeal—or anything that can be interpreted that way—there is no power on earth that can save us." In Connally's view, if the oilmen saw the depletion allowance as endangered by Kennedy, Johnson could not only lose his bid for the vice presidency but he could also lose his seat in the Senate. Johnson, the powerful Senate majority leader, would be out of a job.[1]

Fortunately for Johnson and Kennedy alike, the Kennedy campaign realized that it absolutely had to win Texas if it was to defeat Richard Nixon. In October of 1960, Kennedy wrote a letter to his Texas campaign manager, saying he wanted to make "clear my recognition of the value and importance of the oil-depletion allowance. I realize its purpose and value.... The oil-depletion allowance has served us well." The Kennedy campaign went on to win Texas by just 46,000 votes—votes that helped Kennedy win one of the closest presidential elections in U.S. history.

Despite Kennedy's support of the depletion allowance, the attacks on the tax dodge continued. In 1962, Philip M. Stern published *The Great Treasury Raid,* in which he found that the depletion allowance was the single biggest special-interest tax preference in existence. Stern showed that the depletion allowance and other tax breaks for the oil and gas industry were costing the U.S. Treasury $2 billion per year ($11.9 billion in 2002 dollars). He also found that in 1957, while U.S. corporations paid an average of 48.7 percent of their profits in federal and state taxes, oil companies were paying less than half that amount.[2] The depletion allowance was so broadly written that American oil companies operating overseas were even allowed to take the exemption on their foreign wells, which reduced their tax liabilities in the United States.

When he got to Washington in early 1967, Congressman George Bush immediately found himself in a position where he could protect the depletion allowance: he was appointed to a spot on the House Ways and Means Committee. It was the first time a freshman had been put on the powerful tax-writing committee in 63 years, and it wasn't an accident. His father, Prescott Bush, a recently retired senator from Connecticut, used his influence to prevail on his former colleagues to put his son on Ways and Means. Once on the committee, Bush became a lead defender of the depletion allowance. The key critics of the tax break were eastern Republicans and liberal Democrats, who were gaining strength in their effort to repeal the measure, and they had plenty of ammunition to attack Bush. By the late 1960s, representatives on Capitol Hill were estimating that the depletion allowance had cost American taxpayers $140 billion in revenue ($696 billion in 2002 dollars) since it had been instituted.[3] Depletion became as much of a villain among northern state senators as segregation. "In an era when civil rights became the great moral issue that galvanized liberals, the targeted oil depletion allowance was not far behind," wrote one Bush biographer.[4]

One of Bush's sharpest critics was a New York Democrat, Representative James Scheuer, who confronted Bush over the depletion issue, demanding to know: "Why should we take the risk out of your oil business? You don't want us to limit your profit, George, why do you want us to limit your risk?"

For Bush, protecting the depletion dodge wasn't just about protecting the fat cats in the oil business; it was about protecting the Texas economy. In 1969, Texas was producing 35 percent of all the oil used in the United States. In addition, the Lone Star State itself was heavily dependent on energy taxes. In 1968, about 40 percent of the state government's revenue came from taxes on oil and gas. Any change in America's oil policies would cost jobs, Bush argued: "Not only would unemployment problems be severe; fewer job holders would face the responsibility of paying larger tax payments to offset revenue losses resulting from declining production."[5]

But depletion was only part of Bush's battle. He was also fighting for his buddies in Texas against another foe, one that threatened their profits as much as the rollback of the depletion allowance: imported oil. And the greatest threat was coming from the countries of the Persian Gulf.

Production costs in places like Saudi Arabia and Kuwait were far lower than in Texas. That cost advantage meant foreign oil was substantially cheaper than oil produced in Texas and other states. The solution—at least for the oil industry—was an oil import quota. Established in March of 1959 by President Dwight Eisenhower, the Mandatory Oil Import Program set a limit on oil imports. Imports of foreign crude were limited to about 20 percent of domestic production. The rationale behind the import quota was the same as the one that existed for the depletion allowance: protecting domestic oil producers.

By 1969, Bush was smack in the middle of the fight over both the depletion allowance and the oil import quota. He became one of President Richard Nixon's key advisers on the matter. Nixon appointed a cabinet-level task force to examine the oil industry tax breaks. Nixon and Bush both understood that Texas oilmen had contributed hundreds of thousands of dollars to Nixon's campaign. Many of Bush's friends, including his former business partner, Bill Clements of Sedco, had been big supporters of Nixon in 1968. Their money would be needed again for Nixon's 1972 presidential race.

By the fall of 1969, after months of wrangling in Congress, Bush and other oil state representatives were ready to concede defeat on the depletion allowance and they were considering a compromise on oil quotas. Representatives from the non-oil-producing states had finally amassed enough votes to get rid of the depletion allowance. To get to the crux of the matter, Bush invited Nixon's treasury secretary, David Kennedy, to his home in Houston. On November 12, 1969, Bush and Kennedy huddled with a group of Houston oilmen, who expressed their industry's woes and explained that the industry could not stand to have either the depletion allowance reduced or the oil import quotas removed. Shortly after the meeting, Nixon's chief of staff, Bob Haldeman, wrote in his diary that the Republicans risked losing "at least a couple of seats, including George Bush in Texas," if they changed federal oil policies on depletion and imports.[6] In February of 1970, Nixon made a decision: the depletion allowance would stay at 27.5 percent and the oil import quota would stay in place.

George H. W. Bush had done his job.

Exactly one week after Nixon made his decision, Bush spoke to an oil industry group in Beaumont, Texas, telling them that he was introducing legislation that would give them even more protection from foreign oil. Bush's legislation would further reduce the amount of foreign oil that could be imported into the U.S. to 12 percent of total demand—a decrease from the 20 percent limit that was being enforced at the time. Bush told the group that imposing the quota would stimulate oil and gas drilling in Texas and make the country less dependent on foreign oil. "This is particularly true now," he told them, "when instability in the Middle East severely threatens sources of our petroleum imports from that region of the world."[7] Bush didn't need to bother to add that by restricting imports, the oilmen would get higher prices for their oil.

Bush did nothing to hide his slavish devotion to the oil industry. In fact, around the same time he wrote a letter to Treasury Secretary Kennedy thanking him for meeting with his oil friends in Houston. "I was also appreciative of your telling them how I bled and died for the oil industry," Bush wrote. "That might kill me off in the *Washington Post* but it darn sure helps in Houston."[8]

Bush "bled and died" for the oil industry because he knew that his Big Rich backers in River Oaks and Dallas's ritzy Highland Park neighborhood held the keys to the kingdom. Their money decided which politicians went to Washington and which ones stayed home. Bush knew that he would need their support for his future political races. Richard Nixon understood this, too. By keeping the depletion allowance in and foreign oil out, Nixon was protecting the oilmen. Furthermore, he was pulling all of them—and their wallets—closer to the Republican Party.

The oilmen showed their appreciation by giving Nixon money. Lots and lots of money.

Chapter 9   **Texas CREEPs for Nixon**

The Pennzoil Company's plane left Houston with a light load—just a few passengers and a briefcase stuffed with $700,000 in cash, checks, and securities. It landed in Washington on the evening of April 5, 1972. As the plane's engines shut down, a Pennzoil vice president grabbed the satchel and by 10 P.M. that night, he'd delivered it straight to President Richard Nixon's Committee to Re-Elect the President (CREEP). Every dime of the money came from Big Shots in the Texas energy business. And it was being delivered just in time. A new federal law was about to take effect that was going to require political campaigns to disclose the names and contributions of their donors. Beating the deadline meant the Nixon campaign wouldn't have to identify who gave the money or account for how it was spent.[1]

The scheme might have worked. It should have worked. But unfortunately for Nixon and his backers, just a few weeks after the Pennzoil plane delivered the money to CREEP, some of the money from that briefcase ended up in the pocket of one Bernard Barker, who was arrested at the Watergate Hotel while he and several others who were part of a group known as the "plumbers" were burglarizing the Democratic National Headquarters.

The Watergate break-in, and the subsequent cover-up and lying about the incident by Nixon and his loyalists, was perhaps the biggest political scandal in American history. It resulted in Nixon's resignation in August of 1974, and the jailing of several Nixon administration officials. But it was the discovery of the $700,000 contribution to CREEP that shows just how far the Texas Big Oil Big Shots were willing to go to elect a president whom they knew would be amenable to their issues. The $700,000 is also indicative of the corrupt relationship that existed among Nixon, George H. W. Bush, Baker Botts, James A. Baker III, and, of course, the Texas energy interests.

Nixon's close ties to the Texans played a pivotal role in the rise of the Texas crony network. Nixon's money and political appointments empowered dozens of motivated Texas Republicans, who began recruiting others to join their party. And it wasn't limited to the Bushes and the Bakers. Lots of other familiar names began their political careers with Nixon. Dick Cheney worked in the Nixon administration. So too, did a young economist named Ken Lay. The Nixon administration would be a key nexus of up-and-coming players in the Texas Republican Party, and veterans of his administration would come to rule the state's party—and its money.

By providing huge contributions to Nixon's campaign, the Texas oilmen knew that they'd get even greater influence in Washington than they already had. They knew that once Nixon was reelected, he would allow them to guide federal policy and provide the personnel needed to fill federal appointments. And once those jobs were filled with people sympathetic to the industry, they would ensure that decisions were taken that led to increased profits.

George H. W. Bush's pals, the Liedtkes, understood this perfectly. Hugh Liedtke, Pennzoil's CEO, and his brother, Bill, Pennzoil's president, had taken the company that used to be known as Zapata Petroleum Corporation and turned it into a sprawling energy conglomerate with pipelines, oil wells, and gas distribution systems—and lots of reg-

ulatory concerns in Washington. Bush convinced Bill Liedtke to be the
regional finance chairman for Nixon's presidential campaigns in both
1968 and 1972. By doing so, Liedtke clearly saw the opportunity to
ingratiate himself with Nixon. And he was very good at raising money.
In 1972, Liedtke, acting on instructions from Nixon's chief fundraiser,
Maurice Stans, began soliciting contributions for CREEP—most of it
in cash—from Texas oilmen.

Bill Liedtke made sure that the checks and cash got to Washington
before April 7, 1972. On that date, new federal laws were going into
effect that required all political campaigns to report contributions of
$100 or more, as well as the identities of the contributors. Throughout
Nixon's years in the White House, his political operatives had continually appealed to energy barons in Texas and elsewhere for cash contributions. The Nixon operatives could then apply that cash to any
purpose that they wanted, like, say, paying the Watergate burglars—or
making contributions to favored Republican candidates like George H.
W. Bush. The new law would change all that.

In fact, the $700,000 that Liedtke sent to Washington on the
Pennzoil plane was only a part of Nixon's cash horde. Nixon loyalists
had been operating a secret $3 million political slush fund out of a
townhouse in northwest Washington for several years before the
Watergate burglary. In 1970, that slush fund gave $112,000 to George H.
W. Bush's Senate campaign. At least $6,000 of that money was in cash
and was never declared by the Bush campaign.[2]

Watergate investigators later found that Nixon was giving political
contributions to candidates like Bush in an effort to assure their loyalty
if they were elected. In addition to the cash he gave to Bush, Nixon
met with two Texas oilmen in September of 1970 to talk about energy
policy. During that meeting, according to a memo written by Charles
Colson, a Nixon White House aide, Nixon got a pledge from the oilmen that they would pump even more cash into Bush's campaign.
After the meeting, Colson wrote that the oilmen "put $25,000 cash

into Bush's campaign in Texas and I suspect they will do considerably more."

While the Liedtkes were raising money, James A. Baker III was working as the 13-county chairman of Nixon's Houston-area CREEP. Given Baker's importance to the Nixon campaign, it's difficult to believe that he knew nothing about the Liedtkes' extraordinary efforts to provide cash to CREEP. But Baker, the wily corporate lawyer, escaped any taint of blame.

Meanwhile, the Baker family law firm, Baker Botts, which represented Pennzoil, was doing all it could to ingratiate itself with the Nixon administration. But that was to be expected: Baker Botts's ties to the national GOP went back two decades. Back in 1952, Dillon Anderson, a Baker Botts partner, was a leading supporter of the Dwight Eisenhower–Richard Nixon Republican ticket. Anderson's allegiance was rewarded. In 1953, Anderson joined the Eisenhower administration as a consultant to the National Security Council. It was during Anderson's tenure on that body that Eisenhower approved the Central Intelligence Agency's plan to overthrow the democratically elected leader of Iran, Mohammad Mossadegh, a move that gave U.S. and British oil companies control over Iran's oilfields (which Mossadegh had planned to nationalize). Coincidentally, that overthrow was good for one of Baker Botts's clients. Right after the CIA ousted Mossadegh and installed the Shah of Iran, five U.S. oil companies were given major shares of the Western consortium that controlled the country's oil. One of those companies, Texaco, had been a Baker Botts client for decades. In 1955, Anderson became Eisenhower's national security adviser, a position he held for two years.

Baker Botts's influence over federal energy policy continued when Richard Nixon won the White House in 1968. Nixon appointed a Baker Botts lawyer, Rush Moody Jr., to the three-member Federal Power Commission, the agency that regulates natural gas pipelines. That appointment was good for Pennzoil.

With Moody on the three-member panel, the commission approved a series of deals that allowed Pennzoil to divert natural gas from Louisiana to other markets where the prices were substantially higher. The result, during the winter of 1972, was huge profits for Pennzoil and devastating gas shortages in Louisiana. Louisiana's Governor Edwin Edwards said the "health and safety of millions of Louisiana's citizens are gravely threatened." He added that Pennzoil was showing an "absolute disregard of the public interest in this state." Industrial plants had to lay off workers because they couldn't keep running for lack of fuel. One big utility that depended on gas from Pennzoil had to buy other fuel to keep its generators operating, which cost its customers some $200 million.[3]

By working together, the Liedtkes, Pennzoil, and Baker Botts were gaining power in Washington and big profits for themselves. By any measure, Baker Botts's influence at the Federal Power Commission was remarkable. While Rush Moody Jr. was a commissioner, another Baker Botts lawyer, Gordon Gooch, was working as the agency's general counsel. And Gooch's chief assistant was yet another Baker Botts attorney. Gooch served as general counsel for the Federal Power Commission from 1969 to 1972. That year, he left the agency to work as a fundraiser for Nixon's CREEP and to work in Baker Botts's Washington office.[4] Gooch and his fellow fundraisers were very successful. In 1972, Nixon's campaign raised $6.1 million in secret contributions from the oil industry.[5]

While Nixon was rewarding Baker Botts, he also made sure to solidify the Republicans' base in Texas. He did that by giving a job to one of Texas' most influential Republican women, Anne Armstrong. A longtime pal of George H. W. Bush, Armstrong had married Tobin Armstrong, a member of one of the richest ranching families in South Texas. She'd been raising money and agitating for the Texas GOP for years. In 1971, Armstrong was elected the cochair of the Republican

National Committee. In 1972, Nixon gave her a job at the White House, where she became one of his top advisers. In 1976, she was appointed U.S. ambassador to Great Britain by President Gerald Ford. Shortly after that job ended, Armstrong joined the board of directors at Halliburton.

Nixon also helped Bush. In 1970, Bush ran for the Senate but lost to the Democrat, Lloyd Bentsen. Shortly afterward, Nixon appointed him the U.S. ambassador to the United Nations. In 1972, right after Nixon won reelection, he appointed Bush to become the chairman of the Republican National Committee. "We have a chance to build a new coalition in the next four years," Nixon told Bush, "and you're the one who can do it." Nixon gave another key appointment to a Texas energy titan when, in late 1972, he appointed Dallas drilling contractor Bill Clements to work at the Pentagon as deputy secretary of defense.

However, Nixon's favorite Texan was a man who was, in almost every way, his polar opposite: John Connally.

In December of 1970, Nixon appointed Connally, the pompous, polished protégé of Lyndon Johnson, to be his secretary of the treasury. Connally, who had presidential aspirations of his own, would become one of the most powerful members of the Nixon administration. Although he was nominally a Democrat, Connally had seen the shift in Texas politics and he saw that his future, and the state's future, lay in the Republican Party, not the Democratic Party. By aligning himself with Nixon, Connally saw a chance to get ahead, and he took it.[6]

"Nixon was in love with Connally," says Robert Strauss, the politically active lawyer who co-founded the huge Texas-based law firm Akin Gump Strauss Hauer & Feld. Strauss, a former chairman of the Democratic National Committee, told me "When Connally came into the room, Nixon ignored everyone else. Nixon loved everything about Connally."[7]

In Connally, Nixon saw everything that he was not. Where Nixon was secretive and ill-at-ease in public, Connally was exuberant and had the never-met-a-stranger type of personality that made him a natural politician. On the stump, Nixon was stilted and preferred written speeches. Connally was at ease giving impromptu speeches that could last half an hour or more. Whatever their differences in outward style, Connally insisted that the two politicians "had much in common. . . . We both put a high value on discipline, of the mind and manner, and are wary of those who lose control. . . . We excelled at debating and began our political careers in college in the 1930s. We each met our wives in an amateur theater group, married in the same year, and served as naval officers during the war."[8]

Whether the two came together because of political expediency or true mutual admiration is difficult to say. But it was obvious that both men saw the utility of the relationship. Connally thought that Nixon could help him achieve his life's goal, which was to become president of the United States. With Connally, Nixon got a key ally in Texas. Connally could raise lots of money and help assure Texas' electoral college votes in the 1972 presidential race. Nixon also got a man who could help further his standing among the nation's corporate bosses. Perhaps no other businessman-politician of the era had better connections than Connally, who knew every important CEO in the country. He'd made his connections over the preceding three decades, first as Lyndon Johnson's assistant, then as Navy secretary under President John Kennedy, then as governor of Texas. Before Kennedy named him Navy secretary in the early 1960s, Connally had been a director or officer of 27 different corporations.[9]

As treasury secretary, Connally could tap all of those connections. And he did. Connally became the driving force behind the creation of the Business Roundtable, the fraternity–cum–lobbying group whose members include the CEOs of America's biggest corporations. Connally saw the Roundtable as an essential pipeline between corporate America and top government officials. That same pipeline provided huge financial contributions to the GOP.

The creation of the Business Roundtable was an extension of Connally's worldview: he always viewed the world of government and business as two sides of the same coin. And Connally was hip-deep in both worlds. During his six years as Texas governor, from 1963 to 1969, Connally met dozens more corporate leaders, in addition to the ones he had gotten to know alongside Johnson, many of whom were eager to hire him when he left office in early 1969. Shortly before his term as governor ended, Connally announced that he was joining one of Texas' most powerful law firms, Vinson Elkins & Searls. The firm was so excited to get him that it agreed to add his name to the outfit, making it Vinson Elkins Searls & Connally. His salary at the firm was to be $100,000—a huge amount at the time. He also joined a raft of corporate boards, including those of Texas Instruments, Gibraltar Savings, and the United States Trust Company.

Connally also joined forces with his old pal George Brown. With Connally out of politics (at least temporarily), Brown quickly put him to work on the board of Brown & Root's parent company, Halliburton.

Shortly thereafter, Nixon appointed him to serve on the President's Foreign Intelligence Advisory Board, one of the most secretive positions in the American government. Created in 1956 by President Dwight Eisenhower, the board is charged with monitoring all of America's intelligence operations for the president. It can ask for any classified information. All of the board's findings are classified as top secret and only a scant handful of its reports have ever been declassified.[10] With his appointment to the PFIAB, Connally became the first of three Halliburton directors (Anne Armstrong and Ray Hunt are the others) who would have simultaneous positions on the spook board and the Halliburton board. (When Nixon appointed Connally to head the Treasury Department in late 1970, Connally had to relinquish his positions on the PFIAB and the Halliburton board of directors.)

By this time, Brown & Root had become a money-making machine for Halliburton. It was pioneering offshore oil exploration in the frigid waters of the North Sea. It was working all over the Persian Gulf. And it was making a fortune in Vietnam.

Chapter 10   Brown & Root Goes to Vietnam

The Vietnam War changed the United States. And while it was changing the United States, it was also changing Brown & Root. Before Vietnam, Brown & Root was an arm's-length civilian contractor to the U.S. military. During the war in Vietnam, Brown & Root became *part of* the military. The war also established Brown & Root as one of the biggest and most important construction companies in America.

During World War II, Brown & Root built ships and air bases, turned them over to the military, and then moved out of the way. During the Korean War, Brown & Root's factory in Houston refurbished tanks for the U.S. Army. After Korea, Brown & Root built military bases in France and Spain and on Guam. All of those projects were "turn-key," meaning that Brown & Root was given specifications and budgets for a project and told to deliver it at a certain time. On that date, the keys to the facility would be handed over to the Pentagon and Brown & Root employees went home.

All that changed in Vietnam. "For the first time in history," wrote one Vietnam historian, civilian contractors "assumed a major construction role in an active theater of operations. Without their valuable contribution, many more troops would have been required to do the job."[1] Brown & Root and its partners became part of America's war-making apparatus. It was a historic shift.

Brown & Root was breaking down the old barriers between the military world and the civilian world. Civilian engineers and workers from Brown & Root were doing construction and engineering jobs normally done by soldiers from the Army Corps of Engineers and the Navy's Seabees, and they were doing them in a territory halfway around the world, in a land that was in the midst of a vicious, protracted war. Vietnam—the most divisive and unpopular war in America's history—began the mass privatization of military duties. That privatization was very profitable for Brown & Root and its parent company, Halliburton. But they were not the only Texans whose fortunes were changed by the war.

In fact, the entire Vietnam War was fought with a Texas twang. America's involvement in the war was accelerated by a Texas president, Lyndon Johnson. The troops he sent into battle rode into combat behind pilots who got their training at Fort Wolters, Texas, a base in Mineral Wells, Texas, named for Jacob F. Wolters, the man who'd commanded the National Guard troops during the 1931 takeover of the East Texas field. Most of the helicopters flown in Vietnam were built in Fort Worth. And the pilots were often landing those aircraft at bases built by Brown & Root.

Bell Helicopter, the company that provided a helicopter to Johnson during his 1948 campaign, secured its future during the Vietnam War by building the UH–1, better known as the Huey. The first turbine-powered helicopter to be mass-produced, the Huey revolutionized the aviation industry. Its 1,300-horsepower turbine allowed the 5,000-pound 'copter to take off carrying a load nearly equal to that weight. It could climb 2,000 feet per minute—as fast as a World War II fighter.[2] Plus, it could fly at 125 miles per hour for about three hours, and do so in all kinds of weather while carrying nine fully equipped soldiers and a crew of four. Most important, the helicopter was cheap to build, cheap to maintain, and relatively easy to fly.

The Huey was the perfect vehicle for Vietnam. In a country with few roads, thousands of square miles of impenetrable jungle, and an elusive enemy, American commanders could put squads of soldiers in areas that were completely inaccessible to wheeled or tracked vehicles. In addition, the helicopter could carry huge payloads and was flexible enough to handle a panoply of different missions, from helicopter gunship to medical evacuation to reconnaissance.

In 1967, during the height of the war, Bell's plant on the eastern edge of Fort Worth employed 11,000 workers who were cranking out 200 helicopters per month, 160 of which were destined for the American military. "We went from shipping fifty helicopters to shipping two hundred helicopters per contract order. That was a huge jump," said one employee who worked at Bell in the early 1960s.

Texas was also providing the pilots for Vietnam. In 1967, the training base at Fort Wolters—a desolate, windblown place about 40 miles west of Fort Worth—was churning out 600 new helicopter pilots every month. By 1969, Bell Helicopter was selling nearly $600 million worth of Hueys and other helicopters to the U.S. military every year. As the former Bell employee told me, "Vietnam made Bell."

Vietnam also helped make Brown & Root.

George Brown's company went to war alongside his longtime ally, Lyndon Johnson. Johnson began sending huge numbers of American combat troops to Vietnam—200,000 in 1965 alone. That year, Brown & Root joined Raymond International of New York, Morrison-Knudsen of Idaho, and J. A. Jones Corporation of North Carolina to form a consortium of American companies that could undertake large, complex construction projects in Vietnam. Called RMK-BRJ, the consortium was awarded government contracts worth nearly $2 billion over the next few years. Brown & Root's 20 percent interest in the deal meant revenues of more than $380 million ($2.1 billion in 2002 dollars).[3] Brown & Root was assured of a profit on its work in Vietnam. The company—in a move that would later become its standard operating procedure—enjoyed a cost-plus contract. Whatever it spent doing each project, the government guaranteed that it would pay the company a profit on top of its costs.

Within a few weeks of Brown & Root's joining the consortium, the company's signs became a common sight for American G.I.s stationed in South Vietnam. The company expanded the harbors at Saigon, Cam Rahn Bay, and Da Nang. It built the Phan Rang Air Force Base, one of the consortium's biggest projects. The consortium was put in charge of doing everything from drilling water wells to building living quarters for the troops.

By July of 1966, about a year after Brown & Root joined the group, RMK-BRJ had 52,000 employees working at 50 locales across South Vietnam. With the war raging, speed was more important than budgets. Construction costs in South Vietnam were approximately two and a half times those in the United States, but the Pentagon didn't worry about costs in the early days of the war as it rushed to build the infrastructure needed to accommodate the flood of G.I.s coming into the country. And that caught the attention of the General Accounting Office. In 1967, the GAO slammed RMK-BRJ, saying it had been "unable to maintain control over the hundreds of millions of dollars worth of materials and equipment that have been purchased and shipped to Viet Nam for the construction program. . . . The contractor was not prepared to control the receipt, storage and issuance of this steady stream of materials and equipment and as a result, materials and equipment were 'dumped' at contractor depot sites, unidentified, unsegregated and unprotected from the elements or theft." The agency charged that RMK-BRJ "could not account for the whereabouts of approximately $120 million worth of materials which had been shipped to Viet Nam from the United States." It added that "normal management controls were virtually abandoned."[4]

The report provided ammunition for opponents of the war, including Senator Abraham Ribicoff, a Democrat from Connecticut, who said federal money was "being squandered because of inefficiency, dishonesty, corruption and foolishness."

Whether by foolishness or design or just business, Brown & Root found the Vietnam decade to be an extremely profitable one. In 1960, it had 10,000 employees. By 1969 it had more than doubled in size and become the biggest construction company in America.[5] Its skilled, strictly nonunion workers could build almost anything, from drilling rigs to undersea pipelines, refineries, dams, and bridges, and do it under impossible conditions, using little more than spit and duct tape. "Brown & Scoot" had a reputation that dared companies to come up with bolder, riskier plans. Brown & Root, the company founded in 1919 with a few mortgaged mules, was famous.

Meanwhile, though, the management of the company had changed dramatically. George Brown, who'd joined the business after Dan Root's death in 1929, was in charge of the company. In 1962, his brother, Herman, had died. Rather than run the outfit himself, George decided to sell. In December 1962, shortly after Herman's death, George Brown sold Brown & Root to Halliburton for the bargain basement price of $36.7 million. It was a steal for Halliburton. Brown & Root made Halliburton into a successful company.

In 1919, Erle Halliburton founded the New Method Oil Well Cementing Company and began working in the boomtown of Burkburnett, Texas, not far from Wichita Falls in the north-central part of the state. He quickly gained renown for its expertise in well cementing, the process that seals the space between the well bore and the pipe. Halliburton's technology held steel pipe inside the oil well, kept water out, and reduced the possibility of explosions. Within a few years, Halliburton had named his company after himself, and his cementing technology was being used in fields from South Texas to Saudi Arabia. In addition to cementing, it offered a myriad of other oilfield services and equipment. But by the early 1960s, Halliburton was in a serious slump. Between 1957 and 1962, the company's revenues had been flatter than a West Texas highway. Halliburton had good clients, but few major growth opportunities. The acquisition of Brown & Root changed all that.

In 1962, before the Brown & Root purchase, Halliburton's revenues were just $195 million. In 1970, Halliburton's revenues were $1 billion, and 70 percent of that revenue came from Brown & Root, which was making a fortune in Vietnam. In addition to its operations in Vietnam, the company was working on the North Slope in Alaska, as well as in Saudi Arabia, Iran, Turkey, Libya, Yemen, Nigeria, Kuwait, Abu Dhabi, Egypt, Argentina, Dubai, Colombia, Angola, Oman, Qatar, Morocco, Equatorial Guinea, and other countries. It was laying undersea pipelines in the frigid waters of the North Sea and in the warm Persian Gulf waters off the shore of Kuwait.

All of those contracts were profitable. But even bigger contracts for Brown & Root were looming a few thousand miles west of Saigon, in Tehran.

Chapter 11 All the Shah's Texans

The Shah of Iran had a long to-do list.

Upon arriving in Washington in July of 1973, he was to meet privately with President Richard Nixon in the Oval Office to talk about several issues, including the recent oil production cuts by OPEC. There was going to be a state dinner at the White House. The next night the Shah and Empress Farah were going to host a swank party at the Iranian embassy for a few hundred of their closest friends. They were to attend a performance at the Kennedy Center and host a champagne reception (Dom Perignon, of course) during intermission. In his spare time, the Shah also planned to shop for a few billion dollars' worth of weaponry.

That wasn't new. In the previous eight years, the Shah had become America's favorite military hardware junkie. Over that time, American arms makers had sold the Shah nearly $4 billion worth of airplanes, guns, electronics, and other gear and they were eager to continue feeding his habit.[1] To make sure the Shah got first-class treatment during his shopping spree, the Nixon administration assigned him a high-profile chaperone, a Texan who'd given lots of money to Nixon's political campaigns and was a former business partner with George H. W. Bush. Of course he was an energy man.

His name was Bill Clements. And his 1973–77 stint as deputy defense secretary under Nixon would help propel him into the top ranks of the Texas Republican Party, a move that would make him one of the most important politicians in the state's history and help elevate the Texas crony network to national prominence. Clements deserves notice for his accomplishments as a politician, but it's his business dealings with Iran—particularly those done during his tenure at the Pentagon—that deserve special attention. Those dealings, along with those of other Texas companies, show that the oilfields of Iran were just another stop on Texas' long drive to colonize the countries of the Persian Gulf.

By law, the job of deputy secretary of defense gave Clements power within the Pentagon equal to that of the secretary of defense himself. And Clements was involved in everything. The Dallas-born energy magnate–turned–Washington–insider oversaw the deployment of American troops overseas and participated in the development of billions of dollars worth of weapons systems. He played a key role in the conceptualization of the Tomahawk cruise missile. When OPEC began hiking oil prices in the early 1970s, Clements also became one of the Nixon administration's foremost advisers about defense policy as it pertained to energy. Overseeing military contracts was another one of Clements's main jobs.

When in the course of his Washington visit the Shah was ready to see America's latest aircraft, Clements squired the man he considered his "longtime personal friend" to Andrews Air Force Base outside the capital.[2] There, the Shah inspected two of America's latest, most advanced fighter jets, the F–14 and the F–15. Pilots even took the Shah—a.k.a. King of Kings, Center of the Universe, Shadow of the Almighty, Regent of God, and Light of the Aryans—for joy rides on the multi-million-dollar airplanes.[3] The Shah enjoyed himself so much he ordered 80 F–14s. Cost: $2.2 billion.[4]

Under normal circumstances, Clements's dealings with the Shah, as well as his tenure at the Pentagon, wouldn't be considered remarkable or merit an extra moment of attention. But Clements's tenure at the Pentagon was remarkable, because for three of the four years Clements was overseeing America's military, *he was also business partners with the Shah.*

Many Texas Big Shots have merged politics, oil, and business, but few have done it more boldly than Bill Clements. Beginning in 1973, the same year that Clements was sworn into office at the Pentagon, Clements and the Shah became coinvestors in a drilling company called Sediran Drilling Company, which was awarded a prime contract by the consortium of Western oil companies that controlled much of Iran's oil production. The contract was worth tens of millions of dollars and just to sweeten the Shah's interest in the deal, the loan for his share of the venture was backed by U.S. taxpayers.

Clements's financial ties with the Shah were just one part of a vast network of connections Texas companies developed in the Persian Gulf during the 1970s. Perhaps no other state had more connections to the Shah's empire than Texas. Whether the issue was oil production or defense contracts, Texas companies were invariably the lead contractors.

The close ties that developed between Texas and Iran were part of a broader trend. By 1973, the Texas Railroad Commission was no longer setting the world price of oil. Instead, prices were being determined by the Saudis, Iraqis, Iranians, Venezuelans, and other members of OPEC. In addition, in the seventies the Arabs were nationalizing the oil operations in their countries, and the major oil companies such as Texaco, Mobil, Gulf, and Exxon were being tossed out. In Saudi Arabia, the royal family took ownership of the massive Arabian American Oil Company (Aramco). Just five weeks before the Shah arrived in Washington in July 1973, the Libyan dictator Muammar al-Qaddafi nationalized the oil operations of one of Texas' most famous oilmen,

Nelson Bunker Hunt, son of the Texas zillionaire oilman H. L. Hunt and half brother of Ray Hunt.

Changes were afoot in Iraq, too. Once a reliable source of crude for America's biggest oil companies, Iraq began to change with the rise to power of General Ahmed Hasan al-Bakr in the late 1960s, the leader of the Baath Party. One of his top lieutenants was Saddam Hussein. The Baath Party quickly consolidated its power and in 1972 began nationalizing the holdings of American oil companies operating in Iraq.

A tectonic shift in the global economy and the global power structure was under way. The Arab revolution envisioned by Abdullah Tariki more than twenty years earlier was finally happening.

The Texas Railroad Commission—which had kept oil prices rocksteady for decades—had become irrelevant. OPEC was in control. Between early 1973 and late 1974 the price of oil quadrupled, going from $3 per barrel to $12. Supertanker-size loads of cash were flooding into countries like Iran, Iraq, Kuwait, and Saudi Arabia. So what were the Texans to do? Like opportunists everywhere, they simply followed the money. By the mid-1970s, half of the $7 billion in annual trade between the Mideast and the United States was being done by companies operating out of Houston. By 1977, Texas companies were working on construction, drilling, consulting, and armaments contracts worth at least $35 billion ($104 billion in 2002 dollars) in the Persian Gulf.

The Arab countries' new dominance was made clear by the founder of OPEC, Abdullah Tariki. In April of 1976, Tariki returned to his alma mater in Austin to talk about energy policy at the University of Texas. "The oil companies made billions of dollars from our country," Tariki told a group of his fellow alumni. "In the past, they were the bosses, and now they are becoming the employees."[5]

The Arabs' new-found wealth meant good things for Texas. Big Shots like Jordan's King Hussein came to Houston for their medical checkups at the Texas Medical Center as did dozens of Saudis. Hundreds of Saudi businessmen moved to Houston to work at newly established companies like Aramco Services Co., a subsidiary of the giant Saudi oil company.[6] The Arabs also teamed up with Texas Big Shots. In the mid–seventies, two rich Saudis, Ghaith Pharaon and Khaled bin Mahfouz, went into business with a former governor— none other than John Connally. Together they bought a Houston bank. While Connally was cutting deals, his law firm, Vinson & Elkins, was negotiating legal details for clients like Brown & Root, which was doing a plethora of deals throughout the Persian Gulf. Lawyers from Baker Botts did similar work, handling legal details for oil companies working in the Arab world.

Iran attracted more attention from American investors than any other country in the Persian Gulf. Awash with petrodollars, Iran in the 1970s was one of the world's fastest-growing countries and the Shah was spending money like a drunken sailor. Ever since 1953, when the Central Intelligence Agency installed him as Iran's ruler, the Shah had governed the country with an iron fist, using his dreaded secret police

OIL PATTERNS

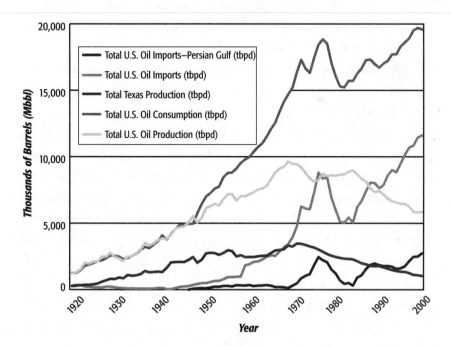

organization, SAVAK. Opposition was not allowed. The Shah determined where and how tens of billions of dollars would be spent. The Shah understood that he owed his allegiance first and foremost to the United States. And he showed that allegiance by producing more oil than any other country in the Persian Gulf except Saudi Arabia. Iranian wells were producing 6 million barrels of oil per day—much of it flowing straight into the gas tanks of cars in the United States.

Oil was the only reason the Shah was in power at all.

In 1953, the Shah was put into power by the Central Intelligence Agency because the Iranian leader at the time, Mohammad Mossadegh, Iran's democratically elected prime minister, just wouldn't cooperate with the oil companies. For months, Mossadegh had been insisting that Iranians, not the Anglo-Iranian Oil Company (which changed its name to British Petroleum in 1954 and is now called BP), should be in control of his country's oil. Anglo-Iranian was making tens of millions of dollars in profits every year from its Iranian concession. The British assured the Iranians that they were getting fair compensation for their oil, but the Iranians believed—rightly—they were being cheated and under Premier Mossadegh's leadership, legislation was passed in Iran to nationalize the oil company.[7]

The British appealed to the Americans for help. But American President Harry Truman refused to pressure Mossadegh. His successor, Dwight Eisenhower, wasn't so reluctant. Shortly after Eisenhower got to the White House in January 1953, he was convinced by a number of intelligence officers that the longer Mossadegh ruled Iran, the more likely it was that Iran would become a Communist nation. With anti-Communist fever sweeping America, Eisenhower agreed to a plan put forth by the Central Intelligence Agency to overthrow Mossadegh. The plan would be executed by a CIA agent, Kermit Roosevelt, who was the grandson of former U.S. president Teddy Roosevelt. On August 19, 1953, the coup succeeded. Mossadegh was tossed into jail and the Shah, who had been forced to leave the country by

Mossadegh's followers, was brought back and installed once again on Iran's Peacock Throne.

A short time later, the Shah signed an agreement that gave control of the country's oil to a consortium of Western oil companies: a 40 percent share of Iran's oil production went to BP; 35 percent was split among Mobil, Gulf Oil, Chevron, Exxon, and Texaco; and the remaining 25 percent was split among American, French, and Dutch oil companies.

The signing of the consortium deal was Bill Clements's big opportunity. Within months of the coup against Mossadegh, Clements began negotiating a contract with the new oil consortium to handle the country's drilling needs. By early 1958, Clements's company, Southeastern Drilling Company, better known as Sedco, was drilling wells in one of Iran's biggest natural gas fields and building pipelines to carry that gas to residents of Tehran.[8] It was the beginning of a long relationship. For the next 21 years, Sedco was one of the most active American companies in all of Iran.

Founded by Clements in 1947, Sedco was one of the biggest beneficiaries of the offshore oil boom that began after World War II and has continued right up to the present day. Clements was able to parlay a pair of used drilling rigs he'd purchased in Mississippi, into a worldwide drilling company. He got rich on his operations in Iran, the North Sea, and elsewhere: in a little more than two decades, Clements's stake in Sedco was worth $100 million. Not surprisingly, that money made him popular with politicians. In 1964 he was George Bush's biggest financial backer. In 1968 Clements headed Nixon's fundraising effort in Dallas County. Thanks to work by Clements and others, Nixon nearly won Texas in the 1968 presidential race. Hubert Humphrey won the state but lost the election. Shortly after Nixon beat Humphrey, he appointed Clements to work on a commission that analyzed the workings of the Defense Department. In 1972, Clements backed Nixon again, co-chairing the Texas chapter of Nixon's Committee to Re-Elect the President.

After Nixon crushed the Democratic presidential nominee, George McGovern, in the November 1972 election, he appointed Clements deputy secretary of defense. In 1973, as Clements began preparing for his new government job, he did not sell his Sedco stock or put it into a blind trust. Instead, he kept the stock and turned over the running of Sedco to his son, Gill Clements.

Sedco's ties to the Iranians grew closer during Clements's tenure as deputy defense secretary. In November of 1973, the Export-Import Bank, an export credit agency that is backed by the U.S. Treasury, approved a direct loan of $11.25 million to Sediran Drilling Company,[9] a new company that was half owned by Sedco. The remainder was owned by Bazargani Bank of Iran (30 percent) and the Pahlavi Foundation (20 percent), which was controlled by the Shah. The Export-Import Bank loan, part of the flood of American financing that flowed into Iran in the years before the Shah was deposed, allowed Sediran to purchase eight new drilling rigs. Between 1968 and 1979, Ex-Im provided nearly $4.5 billion in financing and insurance to Iran.[10]

Although the Pahlavi Foundation did some good works—it gave pensions to distant relatives of the royal family and operated boarding houses, nurseries, and youth centers—it also was used to enrich the Shah. He used the foundation to invest in banks, hotels, casinos, resorts, sugar mills, cement plants, and even a skyscraper in New York. Its assets were also used to maintain good political connections. In addition to its ties to Clements, the Pahlavi Foundation had a former secretary of state, William P. Rogers, on its payroll to act as a consultant.[11] By some estimates, the Shah's holdings through the Pahlavi Foundation and other entities were worth as much as $25 billion.[12]

Shortly after Sediran got the loan from the Export-Import Bank, it was given a long-term drilling contract by the Western oil consortium working in Iran. Sedco too continued getting big contracts. In 1975, a Sedco subsidiary was given a $108.3 million contract ($342 million in

2002 dollars) to build a pipeline from Esfahan to Tehran. The contract called for Sedco to do the engineering, procurement, construction, and a year of maintenance on the pipeline. The drilling contract was lucrative, too. In 1978, Sedco's Iranian operations had nearly $60 million in revenue. That year, about 15 percent of Sedco's $390 million in revenues came from its Iranian operations.[13]

There was nothing unusual or untoward about doing business with the Pahlavi Foundation, says Clements. "My attitude was we should turn it over to the local people as soon as we can and get the hell out," he told me in the summer of 2003. When asked how the Export-Import Bank became involved in the deal, Clements began explaining that the process for creating Sediran started before he went to the Pentagon. "Contracts had already been signed. The work to create Sediran had started," he said. When asked to elaborate, he stopped short, saying, "I don't remember all that. I'm sure whatever connection there was, it was totally unimportant."[14]

Clements went on to say that the work Sedco was doing in the Persian Gulf was part of the Texanification of the world oil business. "Pipelines, floating drilling rigs, we were doing all those things in the Gulf of Mexico before we ever went to the Persian Gulf. We took all that technology out of the Gulf of Mexico and took it to the Persian Gulf, as did Halliburton and Brown & Root. We all did the same thing," Clements said. "The real base of that is our engineering schools here in Texas. Whether it was Texas A&M, or Rice, or the University of Texas or SMU, all of those institutions had graduates in Kuwait, Iran, and Iraq doing the work that needed to be done."

The massive investments made by American companies like Sedco made Iran a magnet for Americans. By 1977, there were more than 20,000 Americans living in the country, including some 5,000 working in the oil industry (the biggest contingent), 2,000 businessmen and teachers, 1,300 military advisers, and about 13,000 dependents.

Of course, not all of these were Texans, but still, by the mid-1970s

Tehran was looking a lot like Dallas. El Paso Natural Gas, Electronic Data Systems, Bell Helicopter, Texas Instruments, and Brown & Root were all doing big business with the Shah's government.

El Paso Natural Gas, a Texas-based energy company that owned huge pipelines to California and elsewhere, was a key part of the invasion of Iran. By 1975 it had signed on to a deal with the state-owned National Iranian Oil Company to build a $5.6 billion plant to liquefy natural gas, which would then be exported to other countries. Electronic Data Systems, the Dallas company headed by H. Ross Perot, was working on a contract to computerize Iran's social security system. The basic contract was for $48 million. But clauses in the contract meant that EDS's total revenue from the deal could reach $90 million.[15] Texas Instruments was part of a group of companies building an air defense system that called for radar installations to be installed throughout the country. Cost: up to $15 billion.

Bell Helicopter, which had made a fortune in Vietnam, hit another gold mine in Iran. The Shah loved anything that flew, and in the early 1970s he agreed to a contract with Bell that called for the company to build 489 helicopters, train pilots, and construct a maintenance facility in Iran. Bell managed the training by hiring about 1,500 pilots who'd flown Hueys in Vietnam. After the contract was signed, a Bell executive (a former Army general) boasted that when Bell was finished, Iran would have "the largest air mobility force in the free world next to the United States."[16] The total value of the contract eventually reached $1.8 billion. By the late 1970s, Bell, with 14,000 employees, was the biggest American employer in Iran.

But such contracts to Bell, EDS, and other companies were small potatoes compared to what George Brown's company was doing.

By 1975, Brown & Root and other divisions of Halliburton were working on projects in Iran worth $9.2 billion ($30.8 billion in 2002 dollars).

The projects included a $1.2 billion highway that extended hundreds of miles across the Great Salt Desert from Tehran to Chah Bahar, on the Gulf of Oman. The highway was the first stage of an even bigger project: a giant naval port on the Gulf of Oman. The Shah planned to transform Chah Bahar, a small fishing village, into a major deepwater port that would allow the Iranian military to project military power deep into the Indian Ocean and the Persian Gulf. The port was going to cost $8 billion and Brown & Root was the lead contractor.

Better still, Brown & Root never had to worry about competitive bidding. The company's work during the Vietnam War convinced the Shah that Brown & Root was the company for him, and he gave the company the contract to build Chah Bahar without seeking bids from any other construction companies.[17] In trumpeting the deal, a Brown & Root publication said the port at Chah Bahar "encompassed the widest range of shipyard facilities ever assembled in a single project." Brown & Root was to handle the design, engineering, and construction of the facilities at Chah Bahar and at another site called Bandar Abbas.

Brown & Root's paychecks on the Chah Bahar deal were directly tied to Iran's oil exports. When the company needed more funds, it drew money from accounts in banks in both Tehran and Houston. When those accounts were depleted, they were replenished by proceeds from the sale of 100,000 barrels of Iranian oil, which was shipped to a refinery in the Bahamas.

The rewards of the Chah Bahar project for Brown & Root were not only monetary. By building Chah Bahar for the Shah, the company was helping the U.S. Navy achieve its goal of having a significant presence in or near the Persian Gulf. Just as in Vietnam, Brown & Root's work in Iran was done in very close partnership with the military. Throughout the life of the Chah Bahar project, the U.S. Navy had officers working on the project even though the contract was between the Iranians and Brown & Root. Brown & Root was no longer just a contractor, it was an integral part of America's ability to wage war and project power. And it was doing it in one of the most oil-rich areas of the world.

The U.S. Navy badly wanted Chah Bahar to be built and it was working closely with the Shah to get it done. The Shah's new port at Chah Bahar was designed to give the Navy a harbor and drydock facilities big enough to handle an American aircraft carrier and accompanying ships. The push for the drydock and other facilities came from Admiral Elmo R. Zumwalt, who was the Navy's chief of naval operations from 1970 to 1974. Zumwalt told the *Washington Post* that the Shah of Iran was "quite clear" that when it was finished the new port could be used by U.S. Navy ships. He added that the details of the port construction were part of "unique, personalized arrangements" between the Shah and the Nixon administration.[18]

Today, there is no port facility for U.S. Navy vessels at Char Bahar. Events in Iran overtook the plan, and by the time the Shah was removed from the throne, he'd spent just $350 million of the billions that had been planned for the port at Chah Bahar. The Shah's successors, led by the Ayatollah Khomeini, quickly canceled the project, leaving Halliburton in the drydock. But the company was barely fazed, for during the 1970s it had doubled again in size, becoming one of the world's biggest construction firms.

When the Shah fell from power, Halliburton and Bell Helicopter left Iran—and waltzed straight into the waiting arms of the dictator next door, Iraq's Saddam Hussein.

SNAPSHOT: HOW HALLIBURTON'S BUSINESS BECAME AMERICA'S BUSINESS

Headquarters: Houston

Annual revenues (2002): $12.5 billion

Employees: 83,000

CEO: David Lesar (2002 compensation: $7.75 million)

What it sells: Oil and gas services, construction services. Halliburton operates in more than 100 countries around the world. As of 2003 its prime contract was to clean up the damage caused by the Second Iraq War. It also has numerous lucrative contracts with the Defense Department to provide services to American troops stationed overseas.

Cash-and-carry story 1: Dick Cheney. In 2000, the year Dick Cheney was elected to serve as U.S. vice president, his retirement package from Halliburton was worth $33.7 million. In 2001 and 2002, he received deferred compensation payments from Halliburton totaling $367,690. Between 1995 and 2002, Halliburton gave $432,375 in soft money to Republican-affiliated entities at the federal level. During that same time period, it gave zero dollars to the Democrats.

Cash-and-carry story 2: George W. Bush. In recent years, the Halliburton board of directors has provided a cash pipeline to George W. Bush. The members of the Halliburton board and their recent donations to Bush are Dick Cheney ($1,000 in 1999, $1,000 in 2000; Cheney's wife, Lynne, gave identical amounts on identical dates to Bush); Robert Crandall ($1,000 in 1999); Charles DiBona ($1,000 in 2000); Ray Hunt ($1,000 in 1999, $5,000 to the Florida recount in 2000, $100,000 to Bush's inaugural in 2000, $2,000 in 2003); J. Landis Martin ($1,000 in 1999, $5,000 to the Florida recount); Jay Precourt ($1,000 in 1999, $1,000 in 2000); C. J. Silas ($1,000 donation in 1990).

Cash-and-carry story 3: The George Bush Presidential Library. The Brown Foundation (created by George and Herman Brown, founders of Brown & Root) gave $500,000. Dresser Industries (merged into Halliburton in 1998) gave $100,000. The Halliburton Foundation gave $50,000. Brown & Root gave $10,000. Halliburton's old law firm, Vinson & Elkins, gave $10,000. Halliburton's old CEO, Dick Cheney, and his wife, Lynne, gave $10,000. (These figures were made available by the George Bush Presidential Library and Museum.)

The crony factor: Halliburton's law firm is Baker Botts, the Houston-based law firm headed by former Secretary of State James A. Baker III.

Chapter 12   Brown & Root and Saddam

In 1979, with the Shah gone and American hostages being held in Tehran by allies of the Ayatollah Khomeini, Brown & Root simply moved across the Shatt al-Arab and began working for Saddam Hussein and his Baath Party. And the glue that bonded Brown & Root to Saddam—as it had been with the Shah—was crude.

Halliburton's work for the Iraqis is perhaps one of the best examples of why the United States has such tortured relationships with the nations of the Persian Gulf. When one oil-rich ally falters, the U.S. abandons the country and embraces the nearest repressive government, no matter how unsavory their policies. And Halliburton's three-decades-long relationship with the hypercorrupt Baath Party is a prime example of this practice.

Brown & Root's work for the Baath Party's oppressive regime began in earnest in 1973, before the fall of the Shah, when it was awarded a $117 million contract ($475.6 million in 2002 dollars) to build two oil terminals, Mina al-Bakr and Khor al-Amaya, on the Iraqi side of the Persian Gulf. The contract was significant for many reasons. It was one of the first major contracts awarded to an American company by Iraq's socialist rulers. In fact, when Brown & Root got the contract, the Iraqis had not had diplomatic relations with the United States for six years. Iraq severed its ties to the U.S. because of America's support for the Israelis during the Six Day War of 1967. But the Baathists wanted to increase Iraq's oil production capability from less than two million barrels per day to about five million barrels per day. And to do that they needed an outlet on the Persian Gulf, where oil could be loaded directly onto tankers. They also needed American technology to build not only the port but the pipelines that would connect their oilfields to the loading facilities. And Brown & Root was perhaps the most experienced company in the world when it came to undersea pipelines.[1]

The timing was important for another reason: just two weeks after Brown & Root won the construction contract, shortly after the beginning of the Yom Kippur War of 1973, Iraq announced on Radio Baghdad that it was nationalizing the last of the American oil companies' operations in the country. The reason given was that America's staunch support of the Israelis "necessitates directing a blow at American interests in the Arab nation so that Arab oil may be a weapon in our hands and not in the hands of the imperialists and the Zionists." The move meant that two of America's biggest companies, Mobil and Exxon, which had been operating in Iraq for decades, were pushed out of Iraq.[2]

The Baath Party, nominally led by Ahmad Hassan al-Bakr but with Saddam Hussein running the country behind the scenes, was showing the Americans that the Iraqis meant business. Companies like Brown & Root, the ones who could help Iraq increase its production, could stay. But companies like Exxon and Mobil, which were profiting from Iraq's oil production itself, could not.

Brown & Root completed the work on the two oil-loading terminals in 1975, but they didn't stay in operation very long. In 1979 Saddam Hussein took power for good. In 1981, Hussein's troops invaded Iran. Within weeks, Iranian gunboats took control of Mina al-Bakr. Saddam's forces counterattacked and regained control of Mina al-Bakr, but the terminal was badly damaged. Khor al-Amaya, the other terminal built by Brown & Root, was also damaged.[3] Neither could be used. And even if they could be used, tankers refused to dock there for fear of being attacked by Iranian forces.

In early 1981, while the Iran-Iraq War raged, the Iraqi government turned to Brown & Root again. That year Brown & Root entered into a contract with the State Company for Oil Projects of Iraq which called on the company to develop an interim solution that could allow Iraq to load oil onto tankers in the Persian Gulf while repairs were made to Mina al-Bakr. Under the terms of that contract, signed on March 5, 1981, the Iraqis paid Brown & Root $2.4 million. But that was just the beginning of Brown & Root's work for Saddam. The price of oil assured that.

By November of 1983, the worldwide price of oil was $29 per barrel and the United States was increasingly concerned about ensuring the flow of oil from the Persian Gulf. The Iran-Iraq War had helped drive up world oil prices. The U.S. was boycotting oil from Iran and Libya. In 1982, the Syrians, in a show of support for Iran, had shut off a pipeline that carried Iraqi crude from the oilfields at Kirkuk across Syria to the Mediterranean. That meant that Hussein's government could only export oil through a single pipeline that ran to the Turkish port of Ceyhan. The lack of export capacity meant that Iraq was only exporting about 850,000 barrels of oil per day—a steep drop from the 3.3 million barrels a day it was shipping before the war with Iran began.

So on November 26, 1983, President Ronald Reagan signed National Security Decision Directive 114, which said that the United States was ready to deter any attacks on "critical oil productions and transshipment facilities in the Persian Gulf." The directive went on to state that it was American policy to "undertake whatever measures may be necessary to keep the Strait of Hormuz open to international shipping.... Because of the real and psychological impact of a curtailment in the flow of oil from the Persian Gulf on the international economic system, we must assure our readiness to deal promptly with actions aimed at disrupting that traffic." At about this same time, the Reagan administration made a decision to strengthen its ties to Saddam Hussein—a move that was firmly backed by Vice President George H. W. Bush, who took part in the discussions about how the U.S. could help Saddam.[4] In late November 1983, the Reagan administration dispatched a special envoy to Baghdad to meet with Saddam Hussein. The principal topic of discussion was finding new ways for Iraq to increase its oil exports. That meant finding a new pipeline route. Reagan's envoy believed that a new pipeline would allow Iraq to increase its oil exports, strengthen Saddam against the Iranians, and ensure supply to the United States. The envoy had lots of experience in defense matters. He was Bill Clements's former boss at the Pentagon, Donald Rumsfeld.

Iraq's ability to export oil was one of Rumsfeld's main topics of discussion. According to top secret notes of the meeting, which have since been published by the National Security Archive, Rumsfeld and Hussein even discussed specific pipeline routes through Saudi Arabia and Jordan. "Both pipelines were important and Iraq wanted to develop both," say notes from the meeting. "Rumsfeld agreed that one did not want to be dependent on only one route."[5] The United States had just two concerns: "its ability to project military force in the Middle East, and to keep the oil flowing."[6] During Rumsfeld's mission and in subsequent talks with the Iraqis, the United States ignored the fact that Hussein had been using chemical weapons against his adversaries.

Within a few weeks of Rumsfeld's visit, Saddam Hussein's henchmen turned once again to their favorite American company: Brown & Root. The Iraqis hired the company to work on two major pipelines. One line, projected to cost over $2 billion, would connect Iraq's oilfields near Basra with Saudi Arabia's pipeline that ended at Yanbu on the Red Sea. The other pipeline would connect Iraqi oilfields at Kirkuk to the Jordanian port of Aqaba. Partial funding of the $1 billion Aqaba pipeline was to come from the U.S. Export-Import Bank, which was going to guarantee $485 million in loans for the project.

Brown & Root's contracts with Iraq clearly had the blessing of the U.S. government. Within a few days of Rumsfeld's talk with Hussein, Under Secretary of State for Political Affairs Lawrence Eagleburger (and later, secretary of state under George H. W. Bush) was writing the head of the Export-Import Bank to encourage him to extend financing to Iraq with the express purpose of increasing Iraq's oil exports. Doing so, wrote Eagleburger, would allow Iraq to have "an additional 50% increase in its oil exports by the end of 1984."[7] (After leaving government service, Eagleburger went into the corporate world. One of the boards he joined was...Halliburton's.)

A few months after Eagleburger wrote his letter, another Texas company with a long history in Vietnam and Iran began negotiating with Saddam Hussein's henchmen. In October of 1984, more than a month before the U.S. and Iraq restored diplomatic relations, Bell Helicopter began talking with Iraqi officials about a big helicopter deal. Although America had pledged not to sell weapons to either Iran or Iraq, the 45 large helicopters that Bell wanted to sell the Iraqis could easily be used for military purposes. Furthermore, American diplomats were aware that the Iraqis had used helicopters for some of their chemical attacks. When word of the sale first surfaced, the State Department insisted that it would not allow it to take place. But in September of 1985, about the same time the Iraqis were attacking Iranian oil installations on Kharg Island, the U.S. approved the sale of the 20-seat 214 Super Transport helicopters, all of them built at Bell's factory in Fort Worth. The deal was worth $200 million to Bell. It also put the United States clearly on the side of the Iraqis in the Iran-Iraq War.

During the Iran-Iraq War, Brown & Root once again found opportunities to increase its ties to the Pentagon. As the war raged, oil tankers in the Persian Gulf were being threatened—and in some cases, attacked—by Iranian soldiers firing Chinese-made Silkworm missiles. Some of these missiles were hitting Kuwaiti ships, and the Kuwaiti government appealed to the United States for help. In response, in early 1987, the U.S. put 11 Kuwaiti tankers under the U.S. flag and provided warships as escorts.[8] But the U.S. Navy needed more than just warships to protect the tankers as they traversed the Persian Gulf. The solution came from Brown & Root. The company owned two huge barges, the *Hercules* (400 feet long and 140 feet wide) and the *Wimbrown VII* (250 by 70). The Navy decided that the barges could be converted into small, floating fortresses that could be anchored in the middle of Persian Gulf shipping lanes. The two barges could work as bases for helicopters that could patrol the area around Iran's Farsi Island, which had been used as a base by Iranian gunboats.

The Kuwaitis paid Brown & Root to retrofit the barges and then lease them to the U.S. Navy, which used them for 21 months. Welders attached heavy steel plate armor to the barges and built living facilities for several hundred men.[9] According to Rear Admiral Harold Bernsen (ret.), who had come up with the idea of using the *Hercules* and the *Wimbrown VII* as military bases, the Kuwaitis "paid for the whole thing. They even paid for the food."[10] So it came to pass that Brown & Root's barges helped keep the Persian Gulf shipping lanes open.

The deal provides one of the clearest examples of how U.S. military, economic, and commercial interests in the Persian Gulf were beginning to blur and overlap. The ending of the Iran-Iraq war didn't change that—if anything, it spurred the phenomenon. On September 27, 1988, just five weeks after the war ended, workers from Brown & Root arrived at Mina al-Bakr to survey the damage done by the Iranian attacks. After several days of work, Brown & Root determined that "the terminal could probably be repaired so that by June 1, 1989 there would be oil flowing through at least one berth."[11] By early 1989, Brown & Root had 250 workers rehabilitating the Iraqi oil terminal, welding new pipe, installing new valves, and putting in a new computer-controlled delivery system. The Brown & Root crews stayed on Mina al-Bakr throughout 1989 and into 1990. The work went so well that the Iraqis began handing over additional tasks to Brown & Root and Halliburton. In May of 1990, Halliburton signed a contract with the Iraq Oil Exploration Company to provide equipment and training designed to help the company upgrade its seismic capability—which would enable the Iraqis to better develop their oil and gas resources.[12]

By August 1990 Brown & Root had completed most of the work on the Mina al-Bakr platform, and Saddam Hussein's government had paid the Houston construction giant more than $57 million for their efforts. There were just a few more details to finalize, and about 40 Brown & Root employees were attending to those tasks when, on August 2, 1990, Saddam Hussein's army swooped into Kuwait. Within a few hours, Kuwait City was made into a suburb of Baghdad.

"Had the Iraq-Kuwait war not begun," a Brown & Root employee later wrote, the company's work at Mina al-Bakr would have been completed by mid-August. "As a result of the war, however," Brown & Root's personnel "were forced to leave the site a number of weeks earlier than they otherwise would have left."

Brown & Root's favorite despot, Saddam Hussein, had gone and invaded Kuwait. And that was going to be bad for business—at least for a little while.

But Brown & Root and Halliburton were resilient. So was Bill Clements.

Chapter 13   "America's Superstate"

Bill Clements was always ambitious, and his years at the Pentagon only whetted his appetite for politics. In 1977, just a few weeks after Jimmy Carter won the White House, Clements returned to Dallas and decided to run for governor. He put up $5 million of his own money and outspent his Democratic opponent, John Hill, by more than two to one. He ran as an everyman candidate, despite the fact that he was worth $100 million or so. He promised to cut taxes and reduce the size of Texas' bureaucracy. It worked. In November 1978, Clements beat Hill by a whisker, becoming the first Republican governor of Texas in 105 years.

Bill Clements was leading a charmed life. His support for Richard Nixon and the Republican Party had paid off in big ways. Clements's stint in Washington had helped him become a better, more electable candidate. He had won the Texas governor's office even though he was a lousy candidate with little speech-making ability, a short temper, and an incurable devotion to plaid sport coats. Clements won despite the fact that Texas was still overwhelmingly Democratic. At that time, Republicans held one of the state's two U.S. Senate seats, two of the 18 seats in the U.S. House of Representatives, just 18 of the 150 seats in the Texas House, and only three of the 31 seats in the Texas Senate.[1]

Clements had won even though nearly all of the other Republicans on the 1978 ballot lost. One of those also-rans was James A. Baker III. Like Clements, Baker had been bitten by the political bug while working in Washington. In 1975, thanks to help from George H. W. Bush, Baker had been offered and accepted a job in Washington at the Commerce Department. Then, in 1976, President Gerald Ford's chief of staff, Dick Cheney, chose Baker to run Ford's 1976 reelection campaign. Ford lost, narrowly, to Jimmy Carter. But Baker loved the game. He moved back to Houston and ran for Texas attorney general. He raised a ton of money from the special interest groups and political action committees. But he still was beaten badly by a Democrat, Mark White.

Baker's defeat didn't really matter. Clements's victory did. Clements's victory marked a critical turning point in Texas—and American—politics. Clements had taken the influence he'd gained in Washington and transferred it to Austin.

Clements's success in politics was followed quickly by the fall of his business partner, the Shah of Iran. In January of 1979, two months after Clements's election, the Shah was forced to flee Iran. Ten months later, on November 4, 1979, Iranian militants stormed the American embassy in Tehran, taking more than four dozen hostages. The militants were praised by the Ayatollah Khomeini for their actions and immediately demanded that the Shah be turned over for trial and that all of his assets be found and turned over to the state. The stalemate continued for 444 days, nearly half of Clements's first term in office. The Iranians also took over Sediran's operations. Clements's ties to the Shah of Iran were largely ignored by the Texas press.

Meanwhile, Clements became a loud—and frequent—critic of America's energy policies. He became one of the most vocal opponents of President Jimmy Carter. He pushed tax cuts and smaller government. He also began changing the Lone Star State's political system through the power of appointment. The Texas governor has to fill about four thousand different positions in the state's government.

He put allies on key boards and commissions. His administration hired a horde of young conservatives to staff the governor's office. Those people quickly recruited others. One of Clements's first hires was a sharp political operative named Karl Rove.

Rove had been intoxicated by politics since he was born, on Christmas Day, 1950. By the 1970s he had become the head of the College Republican National Committee and had an office at the Republican National Committee's headquarters in Washington. There he met the party's chairman, George H. W. Bush. In 1977, he moved to Houston and began working for Bush's presidential political action committee, the Fund for Limited Government. He stayed with Bush's organization for about a year, then went to work for Clements. He rose to chief of staff for Clements, then went out on his own to form Karl Rove + Company, a political consulting firm, in 1980. The original investors in Rove's venture were Halliburton board member Anne Armstrong and her husband, Tobin Armstrong. Karl Rove + Company's very first client was Bill Clements. Rove understood the critical importance of fundraising with direct mail, and his ability to mine his extensive mailing lists for political cash was and is critically important to Republicans in Texas and other states. Rove was also incredibly skilled—and ruthless—at whipping Democrats in Texas and elsewhere.

The newly independent political operative also worked with Clements and Peter O'Donnell, a millionaire Dallas Republican, organizing Ronald Reagan's presidential campaign in Texas. By 1980, that wasn't a difficult task. With George H. W. Bush as Reagan's running mate, Texas voters were ready and willing to get rid of Jimmy Carter and replace him with a Republican. As O'Donnell and Rove began plotting strategy for Reagan, the two shared ideas about how they could rally more Texas voters to the Republican cause. During one of their meetings, according to O'Donnell, Rove came in with a slogan, already printed on a bumper sticker, that he thought would help them in their effort. The sticker read "Texas: America's Superstate."

O'Donnell and Rove didn't end up using the bumper sticker, but the superstate moniker seemed appropriate. It was certainly appropriate when it came to presidential elections. In 1980, Reagan crushed Carter in Texas, taking 55 percent of the vote. The election allowed Texas to send another vice president—George H. W. Bush—to Washington, the second Texan to have that post in 17 years. Reagan's victory also reestablished Texas as a solidly Republican state in the presidential sweepstakes, and one that was likely to remain so for the foreseeable future. The push for Reagan was helped by one of the state's U.S. senators, John Tower. A smallish man with a sharp mind and excellent debating skills, Tower was elected to the U.S. Senate in 1961, taking the spot vacated by Lyndon Johnson when he became vice president. Despite sustained Democratic efforts to depose him, Tower remained in office until 1985. (In 1989, President George H. W. Bush nominated Tower to be his defense secretary, but the Senate would not confirm him owing to rumors about Tower's drinking and womanizing. So Bush nominated Dick Cheney.)

Clements's tenure as governor was a key part of the Republicanization of Texas. But his stint as governor wasn't the only significant development of this period. His residence in the Texas governor's mansion occurred during a time of great change in America's financial institutions. In October 1982, Reagan signed into law a measure that was modeled on Texas' savings and loan regulations. The Texas regulations were far more liberal than the federal S&L rules. They lifted certain restrictions on asset requirements and allowed the state's S&Ls to lend money on commercial real estate.[2]

After Reagan took office, federal regulators began looking at the Texas rules and figured that they were just the recipe for struggling S&Ls across the country. At that time, S&Ls were having difficulty competing with commercial banks because of high interest rates and restrictions on the S&Ls' business. Congress decided to use the Texas laws as the basis for a set of federal S&L regulations called the

Garn–St. Germain Depository Institutions Act, which loosened regulations on what those financially conservative institutions were allowed to do. Reagan was so enamored with the new bill that upon signing it he announced, "I think we hit a home run."

For a short time, the new S&L laws looked like a grand slam. Garn–St. Germain, when combined with OPEC-induced high oil prices, quickly transformed the entire state of Texas into a boomtown. By late 1982, a barrel of West Texas Intermediate crude was selling for nearly $33. Oil production in Texas was starting to decline, but there were still fortunes to be made, if only speculators could get the money they needed to drill. Small, older oilfields—ones that were marginal in times of low prices—could be made profitable by high commodity prices. There were also fortunes to be made in real estate. Fortunately for all of the speculators, the newly deregulated S&Ls had mountains of federally insured money to lend.

Thus began one of the largest transfers of wealth from the rest of the United States to the Lone Star State.

NUMBER OF FAILED SAVINGS AND LOANS, BY STATE

State	Number	State	Number
Texas	237	Oregon	12
California	101	Alabama	11
Illinois	93	Kentucky	11
Louisiana	77	Arizona	10
Florida	63	North Carolina	9
Ohio	40	Nebraska	8
Oklahoma	38	South Dakota	8
New Jersey	37	Utah	8
New York	30	Connecticut	7
Kansas	27	Wyoming	7
Iowa	26	Massachusetts	6
Missouri	26	West Virginia	6
Mississippi	25	Alaska	5
Virginia	24	North Dakota	5
Arkansas	22	South Carolina	4
Colorado	22	Wisconsin	4
Tennessee	22	Idaho	3
Georgia	19	Montana	3
Indiana	18	Nevada	3
Pennsylvania	17	Hawaii	2
New Mexico	16	Maine	2
Maryland	14	Rhode Island	2
Minnesota	13	New Hampshire	1
Washington	13		
Michigan	12	**TOTAL:**	1,169

Source: James Barth, Milken Institute and Auburn University.

Chapter 14   10000 Memorial and the "Texas Strategy"

Sometimes, a big story can be explained by looking at just one small piece of it. To understand the great savings and loan disaster of the 1980s and '90s, you need look no further than a swank nine-story office building called Park Laureate, located in Houston's upscale Memorial neighborhood.

Park Laureate may be Houston's poshest office building. The lobby has acres of polished pink granite, glass, and chrome. A black baby grand piano sits in front of a wall of windows. The piano, its paint faded from too many hours in direct sunlight, is the main prop in a three-story-high glass-walled atrium that looks out over an expanse of ultra-green grass that slopes down toward Spring Branch Creek.

Park Laureate has its own gigantic four-story parking garage—far too big for a building with just nine floors and 52 tenants. And those tenants don't have to expose themselves to the elements as they get to and from their cars, for the garage is connected to the office building by a 200-foot-long, air-conditioned skywalk. The swankienda also boasts a small fitness center, a fountain, a small pond, and a network of asphalt-paved walking trails.

Park Laureate was launched in 1984, at a time when Houston was booming like never before. And that boom was largely due to the price of oil.

Between early 1979—when Bill Clements was sworn into office—and early 1984, the price of oil doubled, to about $29 per barrel. Everyone in the oil business was smart and good-looking. And nearly everyone who lived in Texas was an oil man—or about to become one. Speculators were drilling wells like there was no tomorrow—if they could just get their hands on a drilling rig. The smart money in the Oil Patch was betting that prices would be at $50 in a couple of years. Fortunes were being made.

Of course, all of those new oilmen needed a place to hang their pearl-gray Stetsons, and real estate speculators were only too happy to provide them with acres and acres of new offices, condos, and houses. Construction cranes became the new state bird of Texas. Dallas and Austin were overrun with new developments. Houston went nuts. Between 1982 and 1984, downtown Houston added 11.2 million square feet of new office space, or about five times the space in the Empire State Building.[1] Much of the construction was fueled by an avalanche of capital that was coming from the state's savings and loans. As downtown grew, so, too, did the desire for office space in outlying areas, places like the Memorial section, located about 20 minutes' drive from downtown Houston.

In 1985, workers began building the foundation for the Park Laureate. The money for the project—a $20.5 million loan—came from Commonwealth Federal Savings Association, one of Houston's biggest S&Ls. Commonwealth also took an ownership interest in the deal. As the first concrete on the project was being poured, it was clear that Houston had enough office space. The city's vacancy rate was already 24 percent. But that didn't matter. Oil prices were heading up, up, and up some more. Everyone knew that. The future of the world lay in Texas, a place where people could dream bigger and bolder than any other state. That's why, in 1985, while the champagne was still flowing,

Stanley Adams, the CEO of Austin's Lamar Savings, applied to open a branch office of his S&L *on the moon*.[2]

Alas, Stanley Adams never got to set up his motor bank near the Sea of Tranquillity. His plans—along with those of a battalion of other promoters—got waylaid by cheap oil.

In early 1986, a glut of oil caused oil prices to collapse. Between January and July prices fell from $25 to $11. No one was smart or good-looking anymore. That year, just as the first few tenants were trickling into the freshly painted offices at Park Laureate, Houston's vacancy rate hit 32 percent.[3] Over the next three years, the new building, like many others in the city, had to beg for tenants. The developers couldn't pay their mortgage. The building was just one of many bad loans that began to drag down Commonwealth Federal Savings. In March 1989, the S&L collapsed and was taken over by federal regulators. The failure of Commonwealth cost American taxpayers $1.4 billion.[4]

Multiply Park Laureate and Commonwealth Federal Savings a few dozen times and you begin to have an idea of the scope of the S&L meltdown.

Between 1980 and 1995, 1,169 banks and savings and loans failed in America—and Texas led the failure parade. During that time period, federal authorities rescued or shut down 237 financial institutions in Texas—that's more than two times the number of failures in any other state. And those Texas failures cost American taxpayers dearly. Fully *one half of all the money lost in the S&L disaster was lost in Texas*.

A 1990 study found that the S&L bailout had a net benefit of $4,775 for every Texan. Much of that benefit came in the form of newly built real estate. By comparison, every man, woman, and child in New Jersey lost $1,074. The findings didn't cheer Senator Frank Lautenberg of New Jersey, who complained, "Texas opened the vault of the U.S. Mint, handed the keys to a bunch of crooks and reckless cowboys and said 'Come in, y'all.'"

To pay for the bailout, the federal government sold bonds. By the time those bonds are retired in 2020 or so, the final price tag of the S&L debacle will likely reach a staggering $300 billion. "Even the most conservative estimate makes this the biggest peacetime federal expenditure ever, second only to the cost of World War II," wrote one newspaper man in 1990. "It will surpass the tab on Vietnam. It will more than double the Marshall Plan cost of postwar aid to Europe."[5]

The Marshall Plan for Texas subsidized the greatest American real estate bubble of the twentieth century. By 1986, Dallas had some 38 million square feet of unused office space—an amount equivalent to that of 17 Empire State Buildings.[6] Houston and Austin had massive gluts too. A 1987 study estimated that the Texas S&L industry had funded about $30 billion worth of new construction in the state.

Much has been written about the S&L disaster. But the entirety of the disaster can be summarized very quickly: Crooks looted dozens of Texas S&Ls; Texas politicos protected the crooks; Texas got to keep all the buildings put up during the S&L bubble; and, in 1988, George H. W. Bush of Texas won the White House in part because he and his crony and campaign manager, James A. Baker III, continually denied the magnitude of the S&L disaster and downplayed the contributions that Bush's son, Neil Bush, was making to the S&L disaster.

"The primary goal of the Reagan administration at all times was to cover up the scale of the S&L disaster," says William Black, an attorney who helped clean up the S&L mess while working for the Federal Savings and Loan Insurance Corporation and, later, as the deputy director of the Office of Thrift Supervision. Black contends that James A. Baker III, in particular, purposely downplayed the huge losses occurring in the S&L industry. The Reaganites were "willing to do the most outrageous, unprincipled and dangerous things to maintain the cover up" said Black, and Baker was one of "the centerpieces of this strategy."[7]

★

Like most financial disasters, the S&L disaster began with a relatively simple problem: an "interest rate squeeze." And it was driving S&Ls into financial ruin.

Prior to the passage of Garn–St. Germain, savings and loans were different from banks. They didn't do commercial lending. Instead, they focused on the safest sector of the lending business: home mortgages. The S&Ls attracted deposits by paying interest on those deposits. They then loaned that money to home buyers who took out long-term mortgages. But in the late 1970s and early '80s, interest rates surged. The S&Ls had to match the interest rates paid by other financial institutions. Soon, the S&Ls were paying out more in interest to their depositors than they were earning on loans held by their borrowers. The solution, according to the free-marketeers in the Reagan administration and Congress, was deregulation. By the end of 1982, the administration and Congress had passed a set of laws that:

- Increased the amount of federally backed insurance on deposits from $40,000 to $100,000.
- Removed ceilings on the amount of interest that could be paid to depositors.
- Allowed S&Ls to go beyond home mortgage lending and into lending on oil and gas projects and real estate development.
- Relaxed accounting rules so that even insolvent S&Ls could appear healthy.
- Allowed S&Ls to finance 100 percent of a project, which meant that prospective borrowers didn't have to put any of their own money at risk.
- Drastically reduced the number of S&L regulators.

In short, they built a superhighway to deregulation, cut down the speed limit signs, and fired all but a handful of traffic cops.

Increasing the insurance on deposits and removing the limits on interest rates meant that money brokers in New York and elsewhere could bundle big deposits and shop them around to S&Ls all over the country. The S&Ls began competing for the deposits by offering ever-higher interest rates, a move that allowed them to grow very rapidly. But that growth was unsustainable because the S&Ls simply couldn't afford to pay the interest rates they'd offered. That led them to invest in ever-riskier ventures, like junk bonds, real estate, and other deals in order to make back the money they were losing on the deposits. Although the changes were intended to prove the Republicans' assertion that a deregulated marketplace is the best marketplace, the result was far different. The deregulation of the S&Ls proved that a marketplace without enough rules gets corrupted, quickly.

For instance, an S&L owner could launch a development project, like, say, an office building, give it artificially high valuations, lend all of the money needed to build the project—including interest reserves that could be used to make the payments on the loan for the first several years—and include a 2 to 4 percent developer's fee that could be taken out at the beginning of the project by the deal makers. The scam was perfect for crooks because it assured the project developers got a fat profit up-front, regardless of whether their project was ever built. Within a short time the scam became so common it was known as the "Texas strategy."

Perhaps the easiest way to understand the S&L meltdown is by comparing it to a giant Ponzi scheme. The crooks running an S&L would attract money from out-of-state depositors by offering them sky-high interests rates. They'd lend that money to one of their pals who wanted to build a few condos or offices. The pals would provide a kickback to the S&L owner and then either default on the loan or simply build a substandard project. Meanwhile, none of the bad guys had to worry about the failure of their S&L or about having enough cash to lend or repaying depositors because their entire operation was insured by the federal government. It was, in short, a perfect environment for organized crime.

Don Dixon and Edwin McBirney were just two of many S&L crooks who understood exactly how to execute the Texas strategy and other scams. They just did it bigger than their fellow crooks. The two were more like cartoon characters than businessmen. During the 1980s, the two scalawags led the high life of private jets, expensive cars, mansions, and European vacations—and much of it was paid for with other people's money.

Dixon grew up in Vernon, Texas, a small ranching and farming town of about 12,000 residents located 170 miles northwest of Dallas and just ten miles or so from the Red River, which marks the border between Texas and Oklahoma. Dixon was ambitious and eager to escape. He graduated from high school a year early, and a few years later got a business degree at the University of California at Los Angeles. In 1982, Dixon went back to Vernon and bought control of a hometown S&L, Vernon Savings and Loan.

After the passage of Garn–St. Germain, Dixon and his fellows began looting Vernon for all it was worth. The S&L began offering extravagant interest rates to depositors and those rates attracted money from all over the country. Between 1982 and 1986, Vernon's assets went from about $83 million to $1.3 billion. Over that same time period, Vernon Savings and Loan paid out $23 million in dividends, $22 million of which went to a shell company owned by Dixon. Meanwhile, Dixon was making sure that many of the things he wanted were paid for by his S&L.

In 1983, a Vernon S&L subsidiary bought a Colorado ski chalet for $1.9 million. A Vernon partnership bought a 112-foot long yacht, the *High Spirits*, which was a sister ship to the presidential yacht, *Sequoia*. In the winter, Dixon kept it in Boca Raton, Florida. In the summer, he kept it near Washington, D.C., where he used it to entertain Big Shots like Representative Tony Coelho of California and House Majority

Leader Jim Wright. But the *High Spirits* didn't come cheap. It cost $2.6 million. The flower bill alone was reportedly $800 per day. There were other toys, including six jets and a $2.4 million Texas hunting lodge equipped with $40,000 worth of handmade Italian shotguns. Dixon and his wife took expensive European vacations, at Vernon's expense. The S&L also bought a palatial beach house in California, so that Dixon could live the high life with a bit of sand on the side. He regularly hired prostitutes to entertain some of his friends. He even hired hookers to entertain bank regulators.

Vernon was able to pay for all these perks because it was charging borrowers a healthy fee on every commercial real estate loan it made. It was also charging borrowers to renew their loans. And if the borrower defaulted on the loan? No big deal. Nearly all of their deposits were insured by the feds. The failure of Vernon Savings and Loan cost taxpayers $1.3 billion.[8]

Edwin T. McBirney III apparently attended the same steal-'em-blind-school-of-business-principles that guided Don Dixon. McBirney was the chairman of Sunbelt Savings Association, one of the biggest S&Ls in Dallas. McBirney turned Sunbelt, with about $3 billion in assets, into his personal playpen. He used the S&L's money to fly guests to Las Vegas for lavish parties. In 1984 and 1985, Sunbelt spent over $1.3 million on Halloween and Christmas parties. At one Halloween party, held at his mansion in Dallas, McBirney served broiled lion, pheasant, and antelope. All the while, Sunbelt kept seven airplanes, which McBirney used to fly his friends and clients to meetings in Las Vegas, Hawaii, and Mexico.

Several people witnessed McBirney, after a few too many cocktails, waving blank contracts asking, "Anybody want to borrow a hundred thousand dollars?" On another occasion, Sunbelt Savings financed the purchase of about 80 Rolls-Royces from an Indian guru named Bhagwan Shree Rajneesh, who was living in Oregon. The idea behind the deal was that the cars could be brought to the Lone Star State and sold to the Big Rich.[9]

The failure of Sunbelt, later called "Gunbelt" by regulators, cost taxpayers about $2 billion. Of course, not all of the S&L frauds were so brazen as the ones pulled by Dixon and McBirney, nor were all of them based in Texas. But it was the Texas frauds that got the attention of the top federal regulator, Edwin Gray. And as soon as he saw the scams being pulled in Texas, Gray began cracking down. Or at least he tried to—until he was gunned down by a group of Texas politicos.

Edwin Gray was not qualified to be the head of the Federal Home Loan Bank Board, the agency that regulated America's S&Ls. Gray was a public relations man, not a finance man. He'd once served as Ronald Reagan's press secretary while Reagan was governor of California. Although he had little experience in banking, Gray was honest and he was smart. And those two character flaws got him into trouble.

Gray was appointed to head the bank board in 1983. His appointment was something of a fluke. The leaders of the S&L industry expected him to be a go-along-to-get-along type of guy. Gray would later say that the industry "wanted me in the job because they thought I was going to be their patsy." He wasn't. Despite being the accidental head of one of the most important agencies in the federal government, Gray quickly saw that the Texas S&Ls were out of control. Within a few months of taking over at the bank board, Gray shut down Empire Savings and Loan of Mesquite. Empire had financed thousands of condominiums along Interstate 30, east of Dallas, that never got finished. Instead, the uncompleted shells of the condos were left to rot in the sun. Many had to be torn down owing to the shoddy workmanship. The Empire mess marked the beginning of Gray's education into the fraud that was happening in the Texas S&L industry.

Shutting down Empire cost taxpayers $170 million, and Gray wanted to keep the S&L losses from growing. So he quickly implemented rules that raised the net worth requirement for new S&Ls, imposed limits on the ability of the S&Ls to grow quickly, prohibited the formation of new S&Ls in Texas and California, and transferred the investigative functions formerly held by the Office of Management and Budget to the regional arms of the bank board, a move that allowed the bank board to double the number of personnel examining the books of S&Ls. Plus, Gray began agitating for more money for the Federal Savings and Loan Insurance Corporation, the arm of the bank board that insured deposits held by S&Ls.[10]

Then, in July of 1986, just as world oil prices were reaching their low mark, Gray made a move that really began to frighten the S&L bandits: he rounded up 250 specially trained bank examiners and sent them to Texas to investigate S&Ls that were suspected of being broke. To stop Gray, the S&L bandits turned to Congress, where they got a friendly response from Representative Jim Wright, the populist Democrat from Fort Worth. In 1986, Wright got $240,000 in campaign contributions from S&Ls and real estate interests, which amounted to one fifth of his campaign funds. In September of 1986, Wright asked Gray to meet him in his office. When Gray arrived, three other Texas congressmen were already there: Democrats John Bryant and Martin Frost and Republican Steve Bartlett. For two hours, the Texans verbally assaulted Gray, telling him that the bank board was using "Gestapo tactics" in Texas and that the board's "bullying examiners" had to be brought to heel.

Gray didn't take the hint. Instead, he and his regulators kept charging ahead, investigating people like Don Dixon. By 1986, Gray's bank board regulators were convinced that Vernon Savings and Loan was ready to collapse. Dixon, aware that he was in danger of losing his cash cow, needed help. In late 1986, Wright called Gray and asked him to get his regulators to back off of their investigation into Vernon.

Gray reluctantly agreed to talk to bank board officials, who were ready to close the deeply insolvent Vernon Savings.

In January of 1987, Wright became Speaker of the House, and he made it clear that he opposed giving more money to federal regulators because they would "go out there and close down an enormous lot of institutions."[11] To prevent regulators from being too hard on Texas S&Ls, Wright did some horse trading with Treasury Secretary James A. Baker III.

Wright knew that Baker and the Reagan administration needed Congress to appropriate several billion dollars to the Federal Savings and Loan Insurance Corporation, which had been spending huge amounts of money closing down insolvent S&Ls. "Baker came to me wanting money for the Federal Savings and Loan Insurance Corporation," Wright told me in 2003. "I said 'If you will give a little bit, and [get the regulators] not to foreclose on loans that the borrowers haven't had a chance to repay, then yeah, I'll find some money.'" So Baker and Wright cut a deal: if Wright agreed to pass a bill that raised $10 billion or so for the insurance corporation, Baker would agree to replace Gray with a federal regulator who wouldn't be as forceful. That someone was M. Danny Wall, a bureaucrat who was even less qualified than Gray.

Wright insists he didn't care who replaced Gray. "I didn't argue for Wall. I didn't know Wall from Adam," he told me. "My deal was with Baker. I wanted somebody who was going to give an opportunity to the legitimate businesspeople in Texas to have a chance to pay back their loans."[12]

Baker and the other members of the Reagan administration didn't care that Wall was unqualified. Nor did they care that Wall's only real claim to fame was that in 1982, he'd been the staff director of the Senate Banking Committee. In that job, he'd played a key role in crafting the Garn–St. Germain Depository Institutions Act—the very law that had opened the Pandora's Box of fraud and looting that was causing the entire S&L mess. In short, with Baker's backing, Wall was going to be in charge of fixing the very same S&L mess that he had helped create just five years earlier! The fox was in charge of the hen house. The only thing that mattered to Wright—and apparently to Baker—was that the S&L lobbyists liked Wall. Plus, Wall had made an important promise: he wouldn't shut down the Texas S&Ls.[13]

A few months after Baker and Wright made their deal, Congress agreed to a compromise that provided $10.8 billion for the Federal Savings and Loan Insurance Corporation. And in the summer of 1987, Danny Wall took over as head of the Federal Home Loan Bank Board. Baker was so excited that he even called Wright in Fort Worth to deliver the good news.[14] But Baker's boy at the bank board cost taxpayers dearly. Not only would Danny Wall launch a hyper-expensive rescue program for Texas S&Ls that did little but reward a few Big Rich Texans, he also helped George H. W. Bush and James A. Baker III by continually denying that the S&L mess was a problem.

One of Wall's first actions as head of the Federal Home Loan Bank Board was to create a scheme called the Southwest Plan. The idea was simple: rather than close insolvent S&Ls, the bank board would shore up the faltering S&Ls in Texas and elsewhere by combining them with healthy S&Ls. By the time Wall's Southwest Plan had finished, the bank board had done 15 deals involving 87 insolvent Texas S&Ls. Wall had estimated that his scheme would cost about $7 billion. It ended up costing more than $80 billion.

One of the reasons it cost so much was that Wall gave boatloads of federally backed funds to people who really didn't need them. One of those lucky recipients was Caroline Hunt, Ray Hunt's half sister, whose net worth in 1987 was estimated at $900 million or so. Caroline Hunt owned a Dallas S&L called Southwest Savings Association. In 1988, Southwest Savings was faltering. Hunt was having to pump about $3 million per month into the S&L in order to keep it operating. But the heiress still had plenty of money left over to give to Republican political causes. That year, she gave $10,000 to the GOP Presidential Trust. She also gave another $20,700 to other Republicans, including $1,000 to George H. W. Bush's presidential campaign.

In a deal cooked up by Wall and his regulators, Hunt agreed to provide $25 million in new capital, and her S&L, Southwest Savings, would take over four additional S&Ls. In return, Hunt would not have to contribute any more capital to prop up Southwest Savings. Plus, Hunt got a promise from the Federal Savings and Loan Insurance Corporation that it would cover the cost of the bad assets that Southwest Savings acquired. The deal was so good that Hunt couldn't pass it up. Unfortunately, it didn't help her, or taxpayers. By 1990, Southwest Savings had a negative net worth of $350 million and it had to be taken over by the federal government. As one book on the S&L crisis points out, the only thing accomplished by the Hunt deal was that "one of the richest people in America was bailed out" by the federal government.[15]

Wall's bank board gave an even better deal to an even richer Texan, Robert M. Bass, one of Sid Richardson's grand-nephews. Among the biggest political donors in Texas, Bass was particularly charitable when it came to Republicans. A staunch supporter of George H. W. Bush, Bass would later become a member of Team 100, the group whose members agreed to give $100,000 to the Republican National Committee.

About the same time that Wall's regulators did their deal with Caroline Hunt, the bank board agreed to sell California-based American Savings and Loan to one of Bass's companies. Under the original terms of the deal, Bass agreed to put in $350 million in cash and promised to come up with $150 million within a few years. In return, Wall's negotiators agreed to give the Bass group the right to use $1.5 billion of American Savings' deposits as venture capital that it could then use for takeovers and leveraged buyouts. The cost to the Federal Savings and Loan Insurance Corporation for the Bass deal: $2 billion.

When congressional investigators began looking at the huge subsidies given to Hunt, Bass, and, another zillionaire, Revlon's Ronald Perelman, they were incredulous. In 1989, when Wall appeared before the House Banking Committee, Representative Walter Fauntroy, the outspoken congressman from the District of Columbia, asked him, "Why is it only white folks who get that kind of deal?"[16]

In addition to the subsidies that Wall engineered, he was also constantly minimizing the estimated cost of the S&L crisis—a fact that made him particularly valuable to George H. W. Bush, who didn't want the S&L mess to hinder his race for the White House. Throughout the summer of 1988, Wall insisted that the bailout of the S&Ls would not be disastrously expensive. Wall's giveaways and misrepresentations were egregious enough, but the truly artful deception came from Bush and Baker.

On April 19, 1988, Treasury Secretary Baker appeared before a subcommittee of the House Appropriations Committee. During that appearance, Baker said that the $10.8 billion that had been appropriated to the Federal Savings and Loan Insurance Corporation to clean up the S&L disaster was all that was needed. That amount of money, Baker told the panel, "will provide FSLIC with enough resources to handle the problems of the industry over the next three years." Baker went on to say that the Federal Deposit Insurance Corporation, which insures banks, had plenty of funds. "There are some commercial banks that are having problems, but the FDIC's fund, currently with about $18.6 billion in it, should be able to handle these problems."[17]

It's difficult to overstate the importance of Baker's statement. Few people in America had more information about the troubles facing the nation's financial system than Baker. He had dozens of staffers whose jobs were to monitor and assess the health of the nation's financial systems. As early as 1986, Baker and other Treasury Department officials knew that the cost of the cleanup would be $50 billion or more.[18] In fact, at about the same time that Baker was testifying before the House Appropriations Committee, the Federal Home Loan Bank Board was putting out its own estimate on the cost of repairing the nation's S&L industry. That group estimated that resolving the problems at the 500 worst S&Ls in America would cost $21.8 billion—more than twice what Baker was claiming.[19] Furthermore, by the time Baker testified, America's S&Ls were racking up losses at the rate of *$1 billion per month.*

Even Baker's own deputy, George D. Gould, the Treasury Department's undersecretary for finance and the Reagan administration's top policy maker for banking and finance, was saying more money was needed. In May of 1988, the month after Baker appeared before the House subcommittee, Gould told the Associated Press that $20 billion was "probably not enough."[20]

Baker had access to plenty of other information that should have led him to push for more action on the S&L issue. Baker had spent his entire life around bankers. His grandfather, Captain Baker, had been a founder and board member of Texas Commerce Bank in Houston. Baker himself had served on that very board. Plus, despite being treasury secretary, Baker continued to own significant amounts of bank stock. Baker had significant holdings in Texas Commerce Bank, which in 1987 merged with Chemical Bank (now owned by J. P. Morgan Chase). Baker had dozens of friends in the banking and S&L business in Texas. Surely he was hearing the gossip about how tiny S&Ls were doing huge real estate deals in Dallas and Houston and how they were continuing to build despite huge surpluses of office space. Surely he knew that many banks and S&Ls in Dallas and Houston were teetering on the edge of bankruptcy.

But the key issue for James A. Baker III was not truth, or bankruptcy, or the potential damage being done to taxpayers. The key issue was timing.

Throughout 1987 and most of 1988, Bush and Baker stuck to a simple strategy on the S&L problem: deny, deny, deny. All their efforts were focused on winning the November 1988 election and making George H. W. Bush the forty-first president of the United States. Neither Bush nor Baker could admit that the Reagan administration's grand experiment in deregulating the S&L business had been a colossal failure. They couldn't admit that Reagan's "home run" was actually a franchise-ruining foul ball. Nor could they admit that the worst of the problems were happening in their home state. Furthermore, any attention the two gave to the S&L mess would have added to the travails of one of George H. W. Bush's sons, the hapless oilman and S&L poster boy, Neil Bush.

In 1985, Neil Bush—despite having no experience in the S&L or banking business—was asked to serve on the board of directors of Denver's Silverado Savings and Loan. While on the board, he got into a partnership with two real estate developers, Bill Walters and Kenneth Good. Although Walters and Good didn't know anything about the oil business, they decided that with a last name like Bush, their pal Neil must have a nose for hydrocarbons. So the three men set up a new oil company, JNB Exploration Co.

JNB Exploration's original capital came from three people: Walters put in $150,000. Good contributed $10,000. Neil Bush put in a grand total of $100. Walters then arranged for the new oil company to get a $1.75 million line of credit at Denver's Cherry Creek National Bank, which Walters controlled. Kenneth Good cosigned the note that allowed Bush's new oil company to have the line of credit. While serving on the Silverado board, Bush never disclosed that he was doing business with Good and Walters. Yet, while serving on that same board, he voted to approve deals in which Silverado did $100 million worth of business with Walters. In 1986, Good asked Silverado to restructure $32 million worth of loans he had from Silverado. At the same time, Good agreed to pump another $5 million into JNB Exploration. Bad move.

By 1987, JNB had drilled 30 dry holes. And yet, Good increased Neil Bush's salary from $75,000 to $120,000 per year. Bush even got a $22,500 bonus, presumably for drilling so many dry wells. Furthermore, Good agreed to cover $1 million in loans that Bush had personally guaranteed. Those loans came from Walters's Cherry Creek National Bank.[21] By mid-1988, the vice president's son was up to his gluteus maximus in the S&L mess. And that's when the first details of Bush's unsavory dealings with Silverado began to filter out. That summer, Silverado Savings announced that it had lost $245 million over the previous 12 months.

Which brings us to August of 1988. That month, Neil Bush quietly resigned from Silverado's board of directors. A spokesman for the S&L told a reporter that he didn't know why Bush had resigned except to say, "It has had something to do with his father's campaign."[22] That same month, polls showed that George H. W. Bush's campaign wasn't doing too well. Bush and his running mate, Dan Quayle, were trailing Massachusetts Governor Michael Dukakis and Senator Lloyd Bentsen of Texas by as many as 18 points. Bush realized he needed to overhaul his floundering campaign. He needed someone with lots of campaign experience and lots of organizational savvy.

When the Bush family gets in trouble, they call Baker Botts.

The person needed to revive George H. W. Bush's faltering campaign was obvious: James A. Baker III. When Baker rode in to take over the Bush campaign, the vice president said that Baker's arrival, "will simply enhance this organization ... on schedule, just at the right moment." Bush was right. Baker had the knack. And his handling of Bush's campaign was nearly perfect. The S&L issue—and Neil Bush—remained nearly invisible. Each time the S&L issue came up, the Bush team stuck to a few sacred talking points. They constantly attacked Michael Dukakis. Their most infamous attack focused on the release on furlough of a Massachusetts felon named Willie Horton, who brutalized and raped a woman in Maryland while on a weekend pass. When it came time to discuss the S&L problem, Bush's campaign insisted that the bailout wasn't going to be that big. The other talking point was that taxpayers weren't going to be on the hook for the costs. In mid-October of 1988, just a few days before the election, Bush flatly declared that he "would oppose any costly government bailout" of the S&L industry.[23]

That pledge lasted about a month.

On November 8, 1988, Bush was elected president. And the S&L mess was shuffled off to a new treasury secretary, Nicholas Brady. Victory in hand, the newly elected Bush administration chose to finally admit what Baker and others in the Reagan administration had known for months. On November 30, 1988, William Seidman, the head of the Federal Deposit Insurance Corporation—the agency that Baker had said "should be able to handle these problems"—said that the real cost of the S&L bailout would be far higher than what Baker had told the House Appropriations subcommittee seven months earlier. On that day, Seidman admitted that closing down the 100 worst S&Ls in the United States would cost *at least $30 billion.*[24] Furthermore, he said that the *total cost of the S&L bailout would be $100 billion.*[25] He was wrong, of course. The final tab was much higher.

The S&L scandal ended the careers of Jim Wright and Tony Coelho. In the spring of 1989, the House Ethics Committee released a report that analyzed 69 allegations of ethical misconduct against Wright. The 279-page report said that by acting on behalf of Don Dixon and Vernon Savings and Loan, "Wright could not have picked a more unseemly beneficiary of his influence." But because the S&L corruption involved misdeeds by members of both parties, it represented a political liability to both parties, and the committee members preferred to sidestep it and focused most of their fire not on Wright's S&L dealings, but on a book deal. The allegation was that Wright had written a book that he self-published and then sold in bulk to various buyers in lieu of paying Wright for his speaking services. The criticism over the book deal was too much for Wright. He resigned on May 31, 1989.

Coelho's S&L entanglements were similarly outrageous. He resigned two weeks after Wright, thanks to the discovery that he had purchased a $100,000 junk bond from Drexel Burnham Lambert, the investment firm of the infamous junk-bond king, Michael Milken. Half of the money for the bond had come from the owner of a California S&L who was later indicted. Furthermore, Coelho had failed to disclose it. By jumping into bed with the S&L shysters, they became shysters, too. Wright and Coelho deserved what they got.

But the other Texas Big Shots who played key roles in the S&L mess skated free. On May 31, 1989, the same day that Wright resigned, the newly elected president, George H. W. Bush, was in Western Europe meeting with British Prime Minister Margaret Thatcher and other leaders about the NATO alliance, where he was accompanied by his new secretary of state, James A. Baker III.

For his valiant efforts in helping Bush and Baker downplay the scope of the S&L crisis, Danny Wall was forced to quit. On December 6, 1989, Wall tendered his resignation. Bush, in accepting the resignation, praised Wall for his "hard work" and for his "unselfish recognition that the job of revitalizing the industry demands the complete and undistracted attention of the agency's entire leadership and staff."

Over the next four years, while living in the White House, Bush continued to ignore the S&L disaster as best he could. But in late 1992, after losing his bid for reelection to Bill Clinton, Bush began planning his return to private life. He needed a place to land in Houston. As a former president, he needed an office that would be prestigious, comfortable, and close to his home in northwest Houston. In December of

1992, Bush found just the spot. The location was perfect. Ten Thousand Memorial Drive was just a short drive from the Houston Country Club. Bush would have a custom-built 8,500-square-foot office on the top floor of a luxurious, nearly new, and still largely empty office building...Park Laureate.

According to General Services Administration documents obtained through the Freedom of Information Act, the rent on Bush's office at Park Laureate in 2003 totaled $248,532.[26] Thus, taxpayers are getting billed for Park Laureate in two ways: once for the cost of the failure of the building's former owner, Commonwealth Federal Savings (still being paid for because the federal government sold bonds to pay for the S&L bailout) and again in the form of rent now being paid to the building's current owner by the General Services Administration.

It's a testament to the American public's short attention span—and to George H. W. Bush's political skills—that his role in the S&L disaster has largely been overlooked. Bush's place in American history will be defined not by his role in the S&L mess but by the First Iraq War, and the 100-hour-long ground campaign that he waged against Saddam Hussein. It was a war that he didn't quite finish, and that decision would have major consequences.

Chapter 15   "It's Not About Oil!"—Part I

"It's not about oil! It's about naked aggression!"

—George H. W. Bush, 1991

"The economic lifeline of the industrial world runs from
the [Persian] Gulf, and we cannot permit a dictator such
as this to sit astride that economic lifeline."

—James A. Baker III, 1990

George H. W. Bush never deviated from his script.
In the first few hours after the Iraqis swept
into Kuwait, the White House issued a statement saying that the
United States was seeking the "complete and unconditional withdrawal of Iraqi forces from Kuwait and restoration of the legitimate
government of Kuwait."

For the next six months, that phrase—"the legitimate government
of Kuwait"—was the mantra of the Bush White House. America's
desire to get Saddam Hussein's soldiers out of Kuwait had nothing to
do with oil. America had to intervene, Bush and his loyalists insisted,
because they could not allow Iraq's "naked aggression" against its
smaller neighbor to go unchallenged.

Bush used the "legitimate government" line on September 28, 1990,
when talking to the press on the South Lawn of the White House, right
after he met with the Amir of Kuwait, Sheikh Jaber al-Ahmed

al-Jaber al-Sabah. Of course, Bush didn't bother to remind the reporters that the Amir of Kuwait was a monarchy. Or that women in Kuwait couldn't vote. Or that Kuwait was one of the founding members of the entity that had done more to disrupt the American economy than perhaps any other: OPEC. Instead of acknowledging that history, Bush stuck to his script, conveniently ignoring the fact that ever since Thomas Jefferson wore diapers, Americans have been less than resolute in their support of monarchies and all that they represent.

Regardless of what Bush said in public, it was clear that he knew exactly why America had to throw Saddam Hussein out of Kuwait, and it wasn't because Kuwait exported broccoli. Kuwait had 100 billion barrels of oil—a tenth of the world's known reserves. Bush knew that America couldn't allow Saddam Hussein to control that oil. As a Texas oilman, George H. W. Bush knew the strategic importance of oil better than any of the previous inhabitants of the Oval Office. Throughout Bush's life in business and politics, the Republican Party, the oil industry, and the national interest had been nearly inseparable.

In the 1960s, Bush's company, Zapata Off-Shore Drilling, had drilled for oil in an area off the coast of Kuwait. Once Bush entered politics, he relied heavily on oil industry money and he sought it at every opportunity. His Senate race in 1964 raised huge amounts of oil money. In his 1970 Senate race, the oil industry again flooded Bush with campaign funds.

After Nixon resigned from the presidency in 1974, the oil industry's move toward the right became even more pronounced. Bush was one of the key Republicans charged with keeping the Grand Old Party lubricated with oil money. From 1973 to 1974 Bush was the head of the Republican National Committee, and throughout that period he continued building ties to the energy business.

He didn't have to work too hard. The Democrats were attacking the oil industry like never before. In 1975, a Democrat-dominated Congress repealed the bulk of the oil depletion allowance, the tax dodge that had made the oil business a haven for the Big Rich. And in 1979, when gasoline shortages hit, President Jimmy Carter helped institute the windfall profits tax, which placed an extra levy on the oil industry's enormous profits. "Carter pushed all the oil people into the Republican Party," Chet Upham, an independent oilman and chairman of the Texas Republican Party, told the *Washington Post* in 1983. "There is no question about it: the principles of the Republican Party are more akin to the things that oil and gas people are seeking."[1]

When George H. W. Bush became vice president under Ronald Reagan, he worked long and hard to help his energy cronies. In 1981, President Ronald Reagan signed a bill giving $6 billion in tax breaks to the independent oil producers back in Midland and elsewhere in the Oil Patch. Bush also headed the Reagan administration's task force on rolling back federal controls on natural gas pricing, a move that independent oilmen and pipeline operators had been pushing for decades. Bush's task force succeeded in rolling back many of the federal pricing rules on gas, and that helped bring even more money from the industry into GOP coffers. In 1981 and 1982, more than a quarter of the Big Rich contributors to the national Republican party were in the oil business.

As vice president, Bush was constantly looking out for his pals in the energy business. In 1986 oil prices crashed. In April of that year Bush went to the Persian Gulf to talk to officials in Saudi Arabia, Bahrain, and Oman about energy issues. During his trip, Bush even went so far as to argue for *higher* oil prices. He said that the low prices "have caused a devastation to many people" and that oil prices needed to rally in order to preserve America's domestic oil producers. Bush's complaining about prices didn't find an appreciative audience—particularly among American gasoline consumers who couldn't understand how Bush could utter such heresy.

While in the Persian Gulf, Vice President Bush took a side trip to one of the remotest parts of the Arab world to do a favor for one of his biggest contributors, the independent oilman Ray Hunt.

The son of H.L. Hunt, Ray Hunt had long been one of Bush's biggest backers. In 1979, Hunt and his wife contributed $1,500 to Bush's presidential campaign. In August 1980 they gave $10,000 in soft money to the Texas Republican Party. In the 1984 election cycle, Hunt gave another $20,000 or so to Republican causes. By then, Hunt, who was still in his thirties, was gaining recognition as the savviest of H. L. Hunt's offspring. While his half brothers, Nelson Bunker Hunt and Herbert Hunt, were trying in vain to corner the silver market, Ray Hunt was investing in real businesses. He'd struck oil in the North Sea with the giant Beatrice field. He was investing in insurance, Dallas real estate, publishing, and of course, more oil projects. In 1984, Hunt's company, Hunt Oil, the primary piece of his father's empire, struck oil in the middle of the Yemeni desert, a place so desolate that it is known as the Great Empty Quarter of Arabia. Hunt had found 500 million barrels of oil and he wanted his pal, George Bush, to come see the project. Thus, in April of 1986, shortly after Bush talked with the Saudis, he flew to Marib, Yemen, to see the unfinished refinery being built by Hunt Oil.[2] During his visit to the heavily guarded facility, Bush hailed the refinery as an example of how cooperation between the oil industry and the government of Yemen "can lead to a better life for all the people of this country in the years to come."

After the speech was over, the friendship between the Bushes and Ray Hunt was made even more obvious: Hunt bummed a ride back to the United States aboard Air Force Two with the Bushes. Bush's trip to the Persian Gulf was part of a broader policy shift in the U.S. government, one that acknowledged that America's strategic interests were increasingly being dominated by energy imported from the Persian Gulf.

As the Iranians and Iraqis continued killing each other by the thousands, the Department of Energy released a report that said that a disruption of oil shipments through the Strait of Hormuz during 1987 would have a devastating impact on the U.S. economy. For example, the price of crude oil would increase from $18 to $43 a barrel, and gasoline from 96 cents to $1.54 a gallon. Inflation would increase by nearly 3 percentage points.[3] America's energy-intensive economy couldn't afford to let anybody disrupt the flow of oil through the Strait of Hormuz. And it didn't matter if those people were loyal to the ayatollahs or to Baath Party leaders like Saddam Hussein.

The policy that Reagan had articulated in 1983 in the document that said the United States would "undertake whatever measures may be necessary to keep the Strait of Hormuz open" was put to the test shortly after his vice president, George H. W. Bush, became president.

Bush had been in office for 19 months when Saddam Hussein's troops invaded Kuwait. As predicted by the Department of Energy a few years earlier, energy prices soared. Within days of the invasion, oil prices more than doubled, going from about $15 per barrel to nearly $40. President George H. W. Bush—the man who'd helped formulate the policies that allied the U.S. with Saddam Hussein during the 1980s—was forced to act. In September, Bush ordered the release of oil from the Strategic Petroleum Reserve—the federally owned salt caverns on the coast of Louisiana and Texas that hold about 700 million barrels of oil—in order to stabilize prices.[4] At about that same time, Bush tossed another treat to his pals in the energy industry when he signed into law a series of tax breaks worth $2.5 billion—called "incentives"—for oil producers.[5] The incentives were designed to increase domestic production.

Bush was continually declaring that America's interest in the Persian Gulf wasn't about oil; meanwhile he was secretly approving and signing a document that admitted that oil was, in fact, *the* motivating factor for the First Iraq War. On January 15, 1991—just one day before the U.S. military began launching bombing and missile attacks on Iraqi positions in Iraq and Kuwait—Bush huddled with his national security advisers. That day he signed National Security Directive 54, a top secret document whose heading was "Responding to Iraqi Aggression in the Gulf."

The very first line of the three-page directive declared, "Access to Persian Gulf oil and the security of key friendly states in the area are vital to U.S. national security." It goes on to state that the United States "remains committed to defending its vital interest in the region, if necessary through the use of military force, against any power with interests inimical to our own."[6] The message on the South Lawn of the White House was the importance of putting the Amir of Kuwait back atop his throne. But the true reason for the war was that Persian Gulf oil was "vital" to America's national security.

Bush's main foreign policy adviser, Secretary of State James A. Baker III, was saying much the same thing. But he made the mistake of saying it in public. In the run-up to the First Iraq War, Baker was jetting around the world, exhorting America's friends to join in the battle to evict Iraqi soldiers from Kuwait. On November 13, 1990, Baker held a press conference during which he said that the "economic lifeline of the industrial world runs from the [Persian] Gulf, and we cannot permit a dictator such as this to sit astride that economic lifeline. And to bring it down to the level of the average American citizen, let me say that means jobs. If you want to sum it up in one word, it's jobs. Because an economic recession worldwide, caused by the control of one nation, one dictator if you will, of the West's economic lifeline will result in the loss of jobs on the part of American citizens."

In his 1995 book, *The Politics of Diplomacy*, Baker didn't change his position one iota. He wrote that until his November 1990 press conference, the Bush administration had "done a lousy job of explaining not only the fundamental economic ramifications of Iraq's aggression but also the threat to global peace and stability." Baker wrote getting Iraq out of Kuwait was essential because the United States had "vital national interests at stake, something all prior administrations, Democrat and Republican, going all the way back to FDR [Franklin Delano Roosevelt], had recognized. . . . We had to make sure we could maintain a secure supply of energy." If Hussein had been allowed to stay in Kuwait, Baker wrote, "he would easily be able to influence worldwide oil pricing decisions. Higher crude prices would almost certainly follow, which in turn would likely create not only a global economic downturn but also a recession in the fragile U.S. economy. Inevitably, that would mean the loss of tens of thousands of American jobs."[7]

The battle to protect American jobs didn't last long. The bombing campaign in the First Iraq War began on January 16, 1991. The ground assault, which involved over 500,000 troops from the United States and several other countries, began on February 23. On February 27, just 100 hours after the ground war began, Bush declared that major offensive operations were complete and a cease-fire would be negotiated.

Within days of Bush's announcement, American companies were rushing into Kuwait, looking for lucrative contracts. One of those companies was Halliburton. But even as Halliburton began looking for new work, it was also looking to collect an old debt. Just six days after Bush declared that the First Iraq War was over, lawyers for Halliburton's Brown & Root subsidiary were in the federal courthouse in Houston, filing a lawsuit against their old friends, the Iraqis. At issue was the repair work the firm had done on Mina al-Bakr before Iraq invaded Kuwait.

The case, known as *Brown & Root International, Inc. vs. State Company for Oil Projects of Iraq,* demanded that the Iraqis pay Brown & Root for millions of dollars worth of engineering and construction work it had done on Mina al-Bakr that had not been paid for: "the total amount of $17,833,862.17, together with interest, attorneys fees and costs." The suit asked the court to make a judgment against the Iraqi state company in that amount. Brown & Root's lawyers were from Vinson & Elkins. But the company's lawyers didn't have much luck serving the legal papers on the defendants. Over the next year, the

State Company for Oil Projects failed to respond to all of the plaintiff's court actions. The lawyers sent process servers to the Iraqi embassy in Washington, D.C., but the embassy refused to accept the court documents. They sent process servers to the United Nations in New York City, where they tried to hand the papers to members of Iraq's delegation, but the Iraqis again refused to accept them. Finally, on June 29, 1992, U.S. District Court Judge Kenneth Hoyt signed a final order whereby the Iraq oil company must pay Brown & Root the disputed amount. Further, he ordered that the Iraqis be required to pay 10 percent annual interest on the unpaid balance.[8]

Despite the legal action, the Iraqis were still eager to work with their friends at Brown & Root.

Documents from the court case—which until now have never been published—show that on May 15, 1991, Iraq's oil minister, Osama A. R. Hamadi al-Hiti, sent a telex to Brown & Root officials in Houston. The tone was cheerful and blithely ignorant of the fact that American troops had recently invaded Kuwait and Iraq. "With the situation being back to normal in our area," he wrote, "we would like to resume our previous relationship and to initiate with your company discussions concerning your participation in our rebuilding and reconstructing our oil installations. For this matter we would like to invite you and your representatives to visit us in Baghdad. Please let me have your reply as soon as possible."

Eight days later, Brown & Root's vice president, T. E. Knight, responded with his own cheery note, saying the company was "pleased to hear from you as we have always valued our relationship with SCOP [State Company for Oil Projects] and the ministry of oil. However, at this time, it is not possible for us to accept your invitation because of the legal restrictions imposed by the U.S. government. When the restrictions are removed, we will be happy to meet with the ministry of oil for such discussions."[9]

By the time the Iraqis and Brown & Root exchanged their letters, a raft of Texas companies were at work elsewhere in the Persian Gulf. In the aftermath of the war, Kuwait City became a boomtown as contractors from all over the globe came looking for business. The first thing to take care of was the burning oilfields. When the Iraqis left Kuwait, they set 732 wells aflame. Extinguishing the blazes was left largely to the derring-do hellfighters from Texas, led by the legendary Red Adair and the firm Boots & Coots.

Of course, Halliburton got its share of fat contracts. And just as it had in Vietnam and Iran, the company worked closely with the U.S. military. As soon as the war ended, Halliburton won multi-million-dollar contracts from the U.S. Army Corps of Engineers to repair Kuwait's infrastructure. Another military contract, one worth about $60 million, required Brown & Root to handle 214,000 tons of unexploded ordnance left behind by the American military after the war ended. That project required Brown & Root to hire some 200 Americans, many of them former military officials, and about 1,000 workers from other countries.

One of the biggest contracts won by Halliburton involved rehabilitating Kuwait's oilfields. Halliburton was one of several contractors who were given a share of the $8.5 billion that the Kuwaitis spent drilling new oil wells, fixing pipelines, and installing and upgrading pumping stations in Kuwait's oilfields. Halliburton also won a $450 million contract to build a petrochemical plant for the Kuwaitis in the industrial town of Shuaiba. The biggest payoff for Halliburton, however, came from the Saudis. Six months after the end of the First Iraq War, Brown & Root was given a six-year $1 billion contract to manage the expansion and upgrade of the Saudis' giant refining complex at Ras Tanura, one of the world's largest petrochemical facilities. That contract created about 1,000 jobs for Brown & Root in the United States.

By 1992, Halliburton could scarcely have been doing better. The company's connections to the Pentagon were deep and growing, and its connections to the White House were impeccable. One longtime member of the company's board of directors, the Republican activist Anne Armstrong, a veteran of the Nixon White House, was personal friends with George H. W. Bush. Armstrong was so close to Bush that he had made sure that she was appointed to the President's Foreign Intelligence Advisory Board when he was vice president. Armstrong chaired the intelligence body from 1982 to 1990.[10] Throughout this period Armstrong was also serving on the board of Halliburton.[11]

Halliburton and the Bushes were prospering together. By 1992 it appeared that George H. W. Bush's performance during the First Iraq War would help him win another term in the White House. But the American economy was in the doldrums and Bush's campaign was on shaky ground. Bush needed help. He called Baker. In August of 1992, Baker agreed to a demotion: he quit his job as secretary of state to become Bush's White House chief of staff. From there he would try once again to pull George H. W. Bush's political fat out of the fire.

All Bush and Baker had to do was beat the upstart from Arkansas, Bill Clinton, and the maverick billionaire from Dallas, Ross Perot. The two Texans had plenty of advantages: Bush was the incumbent, he'd be able to raise plenty of money, and the Republican National Convention would be held on Bush's home turf, in Houston's Astrodome.

The 1992 Republican National Convention should have been the scene of George H. W. Bush's great triumph. He'd presided during the fall of the Iron Curtain. He'd taken care of Saddam Hussein (at least temporarily) and restored the royalty of Kuwait to their thrones. Having the convention there meant that the city's big corporations could provide myriad services and hospitality to the Republican visitors.

Not only that, Bush and Baker could rely on their hometown cronies, folks like Enron's Ken Lay, to help pay for the convention. As a matter of fact, Enron owed George H. W. Bush a few favors. With Bush in power, Ken Lay acknowledged, the energy industry has "pretty much gotten what we felt we wanted." Bush had helped repeal the windfall profits tax on oil companies and had rolled back natural gas regulations. He'd given tax breaks to the industry. And more goodies would surely be granted if Bush won a second term in the White House. To show its gratitude, Enron contributed $250,000 to the GOP's convention effort. It also contributed huge amounts of personnel, computers, and other support.

Alas, the convention was to be George H. W. Bush's last hurrah. The combination of Bill Clinton on the left and Ross Perot on the right left Bush stranded in the middle. But it was not the last hurrah of the Bush political dynasty.

Chapter 16

A Pit Bull on the Pant Leg of Cronyville

Geeorge W. Bush knows whence he comes. When asked to explain his remarkably good fortune in the business world, he responded by saying he was a "bulldog on the pant leg of opportunity."[1] That's demonstrably true. No other president in modern American history has humped a richer forest of Brooks Brothers pant legs than George W. Bush.

In 1992, when his father lost his bid for reelection, George W. Bush was living in Dallas. Eager to join the ranks of Texas' Big Rich, he had called on every crony connection he had to get him there. In fact, Bush's entire business career has been the essence of crony capitalism. Although that fact is by now well understood, it is essential to recount the highlights of Bush's career, for the key people who helped Bush—who funded his failing oil ventures, who helped him buy the Texas Rangers and got the government to seize the land and raise taxes to pay for the team's new stadium, and the lawyers who helped him avoid being pursued by the Securities and Exchange Commission—all were richly rewarded once Bush got to the White House.

George W. Bush benefited mightily from his family's ties to the oil business long before he ever began looking for oil himself. In 1968, as

Bush was graduating from Yale, he faced the possibility of being drafted and sent to Vietnam, where the war was raging. Bush was able to avoid serving in Vietnam thanks to the intervention of Sid Adger, a Houston-based friend of his father's who worked in the energy business. Adger called the speaker of the Texas House, Ben Barnes, and asked him to call the head of the Texas Air National Guard about getting Bush a spot in the Guard. Barnes did as Adger requested, and even though there were about 200 applicants ahead of Bush eager to get into the Texas Air National Guard, Bush was given a spot.[2] He spent the next four years or so flying airplanes at Ellington Air Force Base in Houston, far from the harrowing battlefields around Saigon.

After serving his hitch in the Guard (and apparently playing hooky from it for a few months), Bush decided to move back to Midland to try his hand at the oil business. His luck was no better than that of his kid brother, Neil.

George W.'s first company, Arbusto Energy, failed. He changed the name to Bush Exploration Oil Company and quickly got $1 million in new capital from Philip Uzielli, a Princeton classmate of James A. Baker III. Bush ran through Uzielli's money in short order and, with few other options, merged Bush Exploration into another company, Spectrum 7, which was owned by a pair of Ohioans, William DeWitt and Mercer Reynolds. But Spectrum 7 didn't succeed either. So in 1986, Bush merged his outfit with Harken Energy Corporation.

It was clear from the beginning of the Harken deal that Bush's last name was the only real asset that he brought to the table. The former president of Spectrum 7 explained that Harken's management "believed having George's name there would be a big help to them." The Harken management was so convinced of this that it gave Bush a seat on Harken's board of directors and a consulting gig that paid him about $120,000 a year.[3] In addition, Bush was given a chunk of stock in Harken, and that stock, some $600,000 worth, allowed Bush to make an even bigger deal: in 1989, two months after his father was sworn into office, George W. announced that he and a group of investors had purchased the Texas Rangers baseball team for $86 million.

It couldn't have been a sweeter deal for George W. Bush. He financed his share of the club with a loan from a bank in Midland. His total investment was $606,000—the smallest of any major investor.[4] For his money, Bush became a managing general partner of the Rangers, a job that paid him $200,000 per year. He also got an accelerated equity clause in his contract which said that once his partners recouped their investments, Bush's stake in the ball club would jump from about 2 percent to more than 11 percent.

Better still, Bush would be the public face of the Rangers. He would be the one who would talk to the press, pose for photos, sit in the owners' box, and hobnob with the fans. The Rangers job would be his soap box, his launching pad, for an even higher position. He'd even go so far as to print baseball cards with his picture on them to give out as souvenirs. One can imagine some text for those cards—George W. Bush: *Bats right, throws right, leans waaaay right.*

Bush's purchase of the Rangers was a complicated transaction, involving the team's lease on Arlington Stadium as well as numerous other details. Lots of law firms could have handled the matter. But Bush's team drafted lawyers from Baker Botts for the job.

As soon as Bush's group took over the team, they began angling for a new stadium. Arlington Stadium, located in Arlington, a suburb halfway between Dallas and Fort Worth, had been the Rangers' home ever since they were lured away from their old home of Washington, D.C., where they'd been known as the Washington Senators. A former minor-league venue, it didn't have luxury boxes or any of the other fancy amenities that were becoming common in professional sports venues, so the new Rangers owners began agitating for a new stadium. They threatened to move the team if they didn't get what they wanted: a new facility in Dallas, Arlington, or another city in the region. After months of negotiation with the city of Arlington, the group concluded that Arlington was the ideal location.

A new stadium in the city would dramatically increase the value of the Rangers, but that wasn't all that Bush and his investors wanted. In addition to a new stadium and the revenues that came with it, they also wanted to create a major real estate development around the stadium. As Bush put it, "The idea of making a land play, absolutely, to plunk the field down in the middle of a big piece of land. That's kind of always been the strategy."

But there were problems with that strategy: Bush and his owner group didn't want to pay for the stadium, and they didn't own the land on which they wanted to make "a land play." Getting those two things accomplished meant they would have to (a) get taxpayers to pay for the stadium and (b) get the city of Arlington to use its power of eminent domain to condemn land that Bush and his buddies coveted. This was not an easy hurdle to clear. Texas state law still allowed landowners to keep and enjoy their property unless the city or state could prove that it was needed for a public purpose, like a road, fire station, or library. A baseball stadium didn't exactly qualify. Bush needed a special law—one written specifically for the Rangers—that would allow them to condemn the acreage they wanted for their land play. And they needed the law to be pushed through the kindergarten for grownups better known as the Texas legislature.

That task was handled by a Bush family friend and staunch Republican, Ray Hutchison. A lawyer and former legislator, Hutchison had run for governor in 1978 against Bill Clements. His wife, Kay Bailey Hutchison, was an up-and-comer in Republican circles. In 1990 she won a statewide race and became Texas state treasurer. In 1993, she was elected to the U.S. Senate in a special election. A few months before his wife won her Senate seat, Ray Hutchison shepherded a bill through the Texas legislature that allowed the creation of the Arlington Sports Facilities Development Authority, a quasi-governmental entity endowed with the power of eminent domain. About that same time, the new sports authority hired Hutchison's law firm to advise it on strategy, financing, and other matters. One of Hutchison's primary jobs was helping find ways to minimize the amount of cash Bush and his partners would have to invest in the stadium. Before his work for the authority ended, Hutchison's law firm, Hutchison Boyle Brooks & Fisher, had been paid over $488,000.

Bush had other key allies: Mercer Reynolds, Mike Reilly, Tom Schieffer, and Arlington's mayor, Richard Greene. Three of them would be rewarded handsomely by Bush after he went into national politics.

Reynolds was a co-owner of Spectrum 7, the company that bailed out Bush Exploration in 1984. Reynolds was one of several key investors who backed Bush and allowed him to get in on the Rangers deal.

Mike Reilly was a real estate broker and part owner of the Rangers. He was also the Rangers' hatchet man. As the stadium deal was being put together, Reilly was charged with negotiating with recalcitrant landowners who didn't want to sell their property to Bush's group. It was Reilly who wrote a memo (later called the "smoking gun memo") that showed that the owners were planning to use the city of Arlington's eminent domain authority to seize their land, months before the Texas legislature had even approved the creation of the Arlington Sports Facilities Development Authority. In mid-November 1990, the Arlington City Council called for a referendum to decide whether the city should adopt a sales-tax proposal to fund the construction of the stadium. Yet on October 26, three weeks prior to the City Council meeting and a full three months before the referendum went before the voters, Reilly wrote, in a memo to the Rangers owners, of one particular tract, "[I]n this particular situation our first offer should be our final offer.... If this fails, we will probably have to initiate condemnation proceedings after the bond election passes." He went on to say

In 1931, Texas National Guard troops took over the giant East Texas Field, allowing the Texas Railroad Commission to control the supply—and therefore, the price—of world oil for four decades.

The invasion was ordered by Texas governor Ross Sterling. Before becoming governor, Sterling was a founder and first president of Humble Oil & Refining—now known as Exxon Mobil (*left*). George & Herman Brown, founders of Brown & Root, at their Houston shipyard in 1942. Their alliance with Lyndon Johnson resulted in enormous defense contracts for their company, which merged with Halliburton in 1962 (*right*).

Bell Helicopter helped fly Lyndon Johnson to victory in his 1948 Senate campaign. Bell later became a key helicopter supplier to the Pentagon during the war in Vietnam, to the Shah of Iran in the 1970s, and to Saddam Hussein in the 1980s.

John Connally, oil man Sid Richardson, and Lyndon Johnson chat during a dinner in the 1950s. Richardson helped fund Johnson's rise to power; today, his heirs, the Fort Worth-based Bass family, are big donors to the Republican party.

Lyndon Johnson loved his fellow Texan, Speaker of the House Sam Rayburn, almost as much as he loved the depletion allowance. From the 1940s to the 1960s, the two Texans assured that Big Oil's lucrative tax dodge stayed in place.

OPEC-founder Abdullah Tariki was the first Saudi Arabian to be educated at the University of Texas. He modeled OPEC on the Texas Railroad Commission.

Texans loved Republican Senator Joe McCarthy. He raised more money at this 1954 Dallas fundraiser than any other Republican up to that time.

George H. W. Bush and James A. Baker III on the campaign trail in 1964, the first of Bush's two unsuccessful bids for the U.S. Senate.

With former Treasury Secretary Baker managing Bush's 1988 presidential campaign, the two Texans assiduously ignored the burgeoning savings and loan crisis. Bush won the White House. But the S&L crisis would cost taxpayers $300 billion— half of those losses occurred in the Lone Star State.

On Inauguration Day 2001, George H. W. Bush, James A. Baker III, and George W. Bush were all smiles as George W. became America's forty-third president.

The Shah was reinstalled as the ruler of Iran in 1953 thanks to a CIA-engineered coup. After the coup, the Shah quickly opened Iran's oilfields to American and British companies. Clements' company, Sedco, began drilling in Iran in 1958 and stayed there until the Shah was deposed in 1979.

While serving as deputy defense secretary from 1973 to 1977, Texan Bill Clements was business partners with the Shah of Iran.

The son of the billionaire bigamist, H. L. Hunt, Dallas oil man Ray Hunt (*left*) has been one of the Bush family's most reliable sources of campaign cash. In 2003, George W. Bush appointed a Hunt loyalist, Jim Oberwetter, as U.S. ambassador to Saudi Arabia.

Ken Lay delivered loads of Enron cash to the Bushes on a silver platter. By 2000, Enron was George W. Bush's biggest career patron.

This building in northwest Houston was built in the mid–1980s by an S&L whose failure cost taxpayers $1.4 billion. Today, former president George H. W. Bush has his office in the building's penthouse.

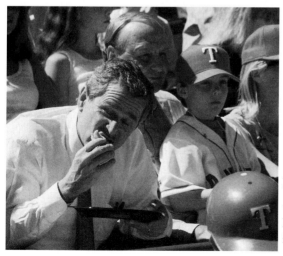

As a lead owner of the Texas Rangers baseball team, George W. Bush lunched on a heaping helping of crony capitalism.

From 1995 to 2000, vice president Dick Cheney was the CEO of Halliburton. During that time, the company paid him about $45 million.

U.S. Coast Guard reservist Taurean Cooper, nineteen, rinses after brushing his teeth on board the Mina al-Bakr oil terminal, April 13, 2003. The terminal, the site of the first military action of the Second Iraq War, was built for the Iraqis by Halliburton in the 1970s.

that the Rangers owners should tell the city to establish development standards for the area around the stadium. "By doing this, *no one* within a certain radius of the ballpark development could get a plat or building permit approval without the City's approval. The 'development standards' established by ordinance would give you a tremendous amount of 'quiet' control over the land parcels you do not own in this area" (italics as in original).[5]

While Reilly was arranging the Rangers' land grab, Richard Greene was helping assure voter approval for the tax package. And even though he was mayor, he went above and beyond the call of duty to get the stadium deal approved. Shortly before the referendum went to voters, Greene personally paid for the printing of 12-page pamphlets that promoted the stadium deal. The materials—printed on green paper—explained why he favored the deal—and why voters should approve the tax increase package for the stadium. The stadium, said Greene, would be of benefit to Arlington. It could help the city pull out of the real estate slump that was hurting it in the wake of the savings and loan debacle.

Greene knew plenty about the S&L mess. He'd been involved in two different Texas S&Ls: Ed McBirney's Sunbelt Savings and The SavingsBanc. Both of them failed. Those failures cost federal taxpayers about $2 billion.[6] When federal authorities sued Greene for his involvement with the failed institutions, he agreed to pay the government $165,000 rather than fight them in court. "It was either pay them or be pursued and made miserable for literally years," Greene later said. "I was watching people who were fighting that process, and they were losing."[7]

Another key Bush ally was a former state legislator, Tom Schieffer. A partner in the investment group that bought the Rangers, Schieffer was, like Bush, a managing general partner of the team. Schieffer gave the Rangers political clout—in spite of his less-than-stellar record in the Texas House. In 1975, *Texas Monthly* named him one of the ten worst legislators in Texas, saying, "What you get is even less than what you see. Arrogant—and what is worse—ambitious . . . he wins his spot by conspicuous lack of merit in every field." The story, which includes a picture of Schieffer sleeping in his chair in the House chamber, went on to say, "The most appalling news of the 64th Legislature may be the fact that Tom Schieffer is soliciting pledges to be Speaker of the House."

Luckily for the people of Texas, Schieffer never rose to that level of power. Instead, with the Rangers, he became a sort of public relations shield for George W. Bush. Whenever there were pictures to be taken, TV interviews to do, or credit to be taken, Bush was always front and center. Whenever there were hard questions about how the mechanics of the deal worked or why the Rangers weren't carrying their share of the tax load, Schieffer fielded the calls.

All of these characters worked together to get the stadium, called the Ballpark in Arlington, built, but their financial finagling didn't prevent them from making some spectacularly poor decisions. In fact, they made one of the worst personnel decisions in baseball history—one that rivals the Boston Red Sox' decision to sell Babe Ruth to the New York Yankees in 1920. In 1989, a few months after Bush and his cronies took over the Rangers, the team traded a skinny, 20-year-old rookie outfielder from the Dominican Republic to the Chicago White Sox. His name was Sammy Sosa. In Sosa's first game against the Rangers, he homered. Sosa, who later moved on to the Chicago Cubs, is the only player in baseball history who's hit 50 or more home runs in four straight seasons. At the end of the 2003 season, he'd hit 539 homers and was one of the most feared hitters in baseball.

Despite their bad decisions, the Ballpark in Arlington was a gold mine for Bush and the other owners. Luxury boxes, club seats, and higher ticket prices sent the value of the Rangers franchise soaring. By 1994, *Financial World* magazine put the value of the team at $132 million—a nearly 50 percent increase in just five years. But while the

Rangers were doing well, Bush's allies with the team couldn't shield him from the calls that came from the Securities and Exchange Commission.

George W. Bush is either incredibly lucky or he's a crook. And if you look at the sale of his stock holdings in Harken Energy, it's hard to tell exactly which.

The facts of the sale are rather straightforward: On June 22, 1990, when Harken's stock was selling for $4, George W. Bush sold 212,140 shares of the company for $848,560. He used most of the money to pay back the money to the bank in Midland that he'd used to buy his share of the Rangers. Eight days later, on June 30, Harken finished its second quarter with a loss of $23.2 million, or more than eight times the loss it had for the year-earlier period. On August 20, when Harken released its second- quarter numbers, Wall Street punished the stock, sending the share price down to $2.37.

The key question is a familiar one: What did Bush know and when did he know it?

As a Harvard MBA and a member of Harken's audit committee, George W. Bush knew—or should have known—Harken's finances inside and out. And by April 1990, it was obvious that Harken was in deep financial trouble. On April 20—almost exactly two months before Bush sold his Harken stock—he received a memo from the company's president, Mikel Faulkner, in which he made it clear to Harken's board that Harken's situation was dire. Low world oil prices, Harken's high debt load, and a soft equity market had put the company on the brink of bankruptcy. The company desperately needed cash to keep it afloat. The company had to find a way of "resolving this liquidity crisis."

Bush attended a meeting on June 11, 1990, during which accountants from Arthur Andersen discussed Harken's plan to sell some of its key assets, a sale that was likely to reduce the value of the company's stock. On June 15, 1990, Harken's lawyers from the Dallas law firm of Haynes & Boone wrote a letter to Bush and the other Harken directors advising them not to sell their stock in the company if they had major negative information about the company's prospects. "Unless the favorable facts clearly are more important than the unfavorable, the insider should be advised not to sell," said the letter. Exactly one week later, Bush sold anyway.[8] He did not file federally mandated insider sales forms.

Ten months later, on April 12, 1991, the Securities and Exchange Commission wrote him a letter, asking for records of his stock sales, copies of his brokerage account statements, and other pertinent documents. The agency also instructed Bush or his lawyer to give them a call.

And when the Bushes need help, they call on Baker Botts.

Within a few days of the arrival of the letter, a Baker Botts attorney, Robert W. Jordan, was working for Bush on the SEC inquiry. But Jordan and Bush didn't supply the SEC with all the documents it asked for. Instead, according to the *Washington Post,* Jordan apparently kept the Haynes & Boone letter until August 22, 1991. That date is important because it was exactly one day after the SEC's investigators decided that there wasn't enough evidence to recommend an enforcement action against Bush for insider trading. By withholding the letter, Jordan prevented the SEC from obtaining evidence that was directly germane to their investigation.

When asked later by the press about the stock sale, Bush used every excuse this side of "the dog ate my homework." He said he didn't know that Harken's financial condition was so bad. He also said he'd received approval to sell the stock from Harken's general counsel. So why didn't Bush file the federally mandated insider sales forms with the SEC? Bush first blamed the SEC, saying that the agency must have lost his paperwork. Then he said the matter was a clerical mistake.

When the case went to the SEC, the agency was headed by Richard Breeden, a Baker Botts lawyer who'd been appointed to his position by

President George H. W. Bush. Breeden had been a key Bush confidant during the discussions about how to overhaul America's financial regulations during the Reagan administration. The SEC's general counsel at the time was James Doty. It was Doty who, while working at Baker Botts, had helped Bush negotiate all the paperwork when his group of investors bought the Rangers in 1989.

Perhaps the involvement of Baker Botts in the Harken inquiry is coincidental. Breeden and Doty both have dismissed any suggestion of malfeasance on their part. But Bush's stock sales at Harken were part of a broader pattern of questionable deals he participated in while on the board. Corporate governance experts frown on boards who give consulting contracts or loans to board members. Bush received both. Bush was a paid consultant for almost his entire tenure on the Harken board. Furthermore, in 1986 and again in 1988, Bush received below-market rate loans totaling more than $180,000 from Harken so he could buy company stock, and he profited handsomely from the loans. In 1989, the company relaxed the terms of one of the loans, a move that effectively guaranteed Bush could not lose. Thanks to the change in terms, Bush was no longer personally liable for repaying the loan. The only collateral he had to provide to guarantee the loan were the Harken shares that he was buying. If the shares declined in value, he could simply return them to the company.[9]

Furthermore, while on the board, Bush apparently approved a deal in 1989 in which Harken sold 80 percent of one of its subsidiaries, Aloha Petroleum, to a group of insiders that included Harken's chairman. The sale price was $12 million, $11 million of which came in the form of a loan from Harken. The sale of Aloha—which occurred while Bush was sitting on Harken's audit committee—allowed Harken to inflate its financial statements. Although the company received just $1 million, it recorded a $7.9 million profit on the transaction. It also gave Bush a window of opportunity during which he unloaded his Harken stock. When the Securities and Exchange Commission investigated the

Aloha deal, it forced Harken to restate its earnings, a move that wiped out $9.3 million in profits.

The jury is still out on whether Bush violated federal laws on insider trading. But it is painfully obvious that Bulldog Bush seized Harken's pant leg and humped it for all it was worth. The Harken deal set the table for the acquisition of the Rangers baseball team. By buying a stake in the Rangers—Bush later sold it for a profit of more than $14 million—he was able to make "more money than I ever dreamed I would make," and join the ranks of the Texas Big Rich.

While Bush hit a financial home run, taxpayers were left holding a mittful of empty promises. When promoting the stadium, Bush and his cohorts promised the citizens of Arlington that the stadium complex would have a 1,500-seat amphitheater and a River Walk. In a flashy eight-page tabloid-size flyer promoting the stadium, the Rangers promised that the amphitheater "will be the site of everything from country western shows, the symphony, plays, musical revues, as well as Easter and Christmas services." The River Walk was to be built along Johnson Creek, a smallish slough that runs a few dozen yards from the main entrance to the stadium. The facility would be designed "after the successful River Walk in San Antonio" and it was "sure to be a winner with its waterfront stroll of festive shops and restaurants."

The Amphitheater was never built. Instead, the site of the project is little more than sun-baked asphalt and parking stripes. The River Walk is similarly unimpressive. There are no restaurants or festive shops. The only residents of the River Walk who showed up during a recent visit were a handful of mockingbirds and the occasional white egret.

But promises made to taxpayers aren't really important. Action is important. George W. Bush was an action guy. The stadium proved that. Almost overnight, he'd transformed himself into a successful businessman—and with that qualification established, Bush knew that he could make a credible run for a major political office. He acknowledged that fact in 1993, as he was launching his campaign against the incumbent governor, Ann Richards. While walking around the stadium with R. G. Ratcliffe of the *Houston Chronicle,* Bush grandly took credit for the entire project. "When all those people in Austin say 'He ain't never done anything,' well, this is it," he said.

The trajectory was becoming clear: The Oil Patch led to Harken. Harken led to the Rangers. The Rangers led to the governor's mansion. The governor's mansion led to the White House. All Bush needed to make the leap was the backing of his buddies in the energy industry. That wouldn't be a problem.

SNAPSHOT: GEORGE W. GOES TO CARLYLE AND CATERAIR

The crony network takes care of its own. And under normal circumstances, the inner dealings of the network stay secret. But in April of 2003, David Rubenstein, a cofounder and managing director of the Carlyle Group, the powerful international investment group, was struck with a brief attack of truth telling. That month he spoke to the Los Angeles County Employees Retirement Association and divulged how the Carlyle Group had given a job to George W. Bush for no other reason than that he was the president's son.

The known details are these: In 1990, just a few months after George W. Bush became a part owner of the Texas Rangers, he was given a spot on the board of Caterair International, a firm that provided food services to the airline industry. It's not clear how much Bush was paid for his work, but he was given 1,000 stock options in Caterair. Caterair had just been purchased by the Carlyle Group, the huge investment group whose most prominent members include James A. Baker III, George H. W. Bush, former Defense Secretary Frank Carlucci, and former British Prime Minister John Major.

George W. Bush's job at Caterair came courtesy of Fred Malek, the former deputy chairman of the Republican National Committee and a longtime friend of George H. W. Bush's.[10] Malek had served in the Nixon administration and was also one of George W.'s cash backers in his bid to buy the Texas Rangers.

In his 2003 speech, Rubenstein detailed the events that led to Bush's hiring. Rubenstein didn't know it, but his comments to the retirement association were being recorded. A few months later, that tape got into the hands of journalist Suzan Mazur. Mazur broke the story in July of 2003 when she posted Rubenstein's comments on the *Progressive Review* web site.[11] Rubenstein's comments:

> When we were putting the [Caterair] board together, somebody [Malek] came to me and said, look there is a guy who would like to be on the board. He's kind of down on his luck a bit. Needs a job. Needs a board position. Needs some board positions. Could you put him on the board? Pay him a salary and he'll be a good board member and be a loyal vote for the management and so forth.
>
> I said well, we're not usually in that business. But okay, let me meet the guy. I met the guy. I said I don't think he adds that much value. We'll put him on the board because— you know —we'll do a favor for this guy; he's done a favor for us.
>
> We put him on the board and [he] spent three years. Came to all the meetings. Told a lot of jokes. Not that many clean ones. And after a while I kind of said to him, after about three years—you know, I'm not sure this is really for you. Maybe you should do something else. Because I don't think you're adding that much value to the board. You don't know that much about the company.
>
> He said, well I think I'm getting out of this business anyway. And I don't really like it that much. So I'm probably going to resign from the board.
>
> And I said, thanks—didn't think I'd ever see him again. His name is George W. Bush. He became President of the United States. So you know if you said to me, name 25 million people who would maybe be President of the United States, he wouldn't have been in that category. So you never know. Anyway, I haven't been invited to the White House for any things.

During the four years or so that Bush served on the Caterair board, the company lost about $263 million. Shortly after Bush quit Caterair's board, Carlyle sold the company.

Chapter 17 Oil for W (and W for Oil)

Once George W. Bush beat the Democratic candidate, Ann Richards, in the 1994 Texas governor's race, his run for the White House was virtually assured.

It wasn't that Ann Richards didn't try to win. She called George W. Bush "Shrub." She made fun of his family. Her campaign hammered Bush on his corporate connections. They brought up the Caterair deal, the Rangers stadium deal, the Harken Energy stock sale, and everything else they could think of. She told the press that it was "difficult to run a race against someone who doesn't have a clue."

Richards was an incumbent. She was smart. She was popular. She even raised $15 million. But still, she didn't stand a chance. Her down-home, just-folks campaign didn't work. Whatever she said, she was always going to be a Democrat and her opponent's last name was always going to be Bush. Plus, she couldn't keep up with him when it came to fundraising. That was due in part, to the cash pipeline Bush had installed in Enron's headquarters.

In 1993, when Bush was just beginning his campaign for governor, he paid a visit to an Enron executive named Rich Kinder. The second-in-command to Enron's CEO, Ken Lay, Kinder was rich and aggressive and knew practically everybody in Houston's energy business. Bush asked Kinder to be his finance chair in Houston, the city that is traditionally the biggest source of political money in the state. Although Kinder barely knew George W. Bush, he quickly agreed. With the help of Kinder and a bunch of other well-connected Republicans, Bush raised more money than any other gubernatorial candidate in Texas history: over $16 million. Bush beat Richards by eight percentage points. The path to the White House was wide open.

Bush's win in 1994 was exceeded by his landslide victory in 1998. That year, Bush crushed his Democratic opponent, Garry Mauro, taking 69 percent of the vote. More important, though, Bush showed that he could raise the kind of money needed to begin his assault on the White House. In the 1998 race, Bush raised a staggering $25.2 million. Mauro raised just $4.8 million. Better still, Bush didn't spend all his money. When the race ended, he had about $13 million in the bank, which he immediately began spending on his presidential bid.

The biggest source of Bush's cash horde was, of course, Texas' Big Rich energy crowd. Between 1994 and 1998, more of Bush's biggest donors came from the energy business than any other sector. Of the top eight corporate donors to Bush's campaigns, four of them came from the energy sector, according to figures compiled by Texans for Public Justice. The biggest cash machine for Bush was Enron. During Bush's stint in the Texas governor's mansion, Ken Lay and other donors affiliated with the energy giant gave him $312,500. The second-largest donor was Bass Family Enterprises, the conglomerate created out of the energy empire built by the wildcatter Sid Richardson, the oil baron who supported Lyndon Johnson throughout his career. In all, the Basses gave Bush just over $221,000 while he was governor. Bush also got significant contributions from his pals on the board at Halliburton. While he was governor, Anne Armstrong and her husband, Tobin, gave Bush's campaign $6,000. Another board member, Ray Hunt, gave the campaign a total of $109,000. During the 1998 race, Bush got $3,000 from Halliburton's CEO, Dick Cheney, and his wife, Lynne Cheney.

Of course Bush did his best to reward his energy cronies when he was governor. In 1995 he tried to rewrite the state's tax code—a move that would have dramatically reduced the tax burden on capital-intensive industries like pipeline companies, refiners, and oil producers. One of the key people who worked on that tax overhaul package (which ultimately failed to pass) was Enron's Rich Kinder. In 1999, among the first bills George W. Bush signed during that year's legislative session was an emergency measure that gave $45 million in tax breaks to the state's small oil and gas producers. Bush was in such a hurry to give the oil folks a tax break that passage of the bill was even deemed an "emergency."

By 1999 Bush had the money. He had the name. And he had the perfect state from which to run. Texas had 32 electoral college votes—nearly 12 percent of the 270 electoral votes needed to win the White House. Rove and Bush could see that if they could just win Florida, where his brother, Jeb, was governor, George W. would have over a fifth of the votes needed to triumph.

Texas has more distinct media markets—geographic areas in which political campaigns and other advertisers buy commercial broadcast time on radio and television—than any other state: 19. (California has 12 media markets; Florida has 11; New York has 10.) With so many different markets, national candidates have to purchase TV and radio time in places like Amarillo, Abilene, Tyler, and Laredo if they want to run a competitive race in the state. Furthermore, they may have to tailor their message to different sectors of the state. "It can be like running a campaign in five different states," says the veteran Texas political strategist Kelly Fero. Knowing that he had Texas in his pocket gave Bush "a huge, huge, huge advantage. The amount of money he saved by not having to advertise in Texas gave him more money that he could then use in other states."

Once Bush finally announced that he was running, on March 7, 1999, he used all of that money and all of those advantages. As soon as

Bush became a serious candidate, he turned once again to his oil industry cronies for help. A clear example of that assistance came in the Iowa straw poll, the first important beauty contest of the presidential campaign. By the summer of 1999, Bush had already raised $37 million. But he wanted to conserve his campaign cash, so he turned to a Texas crony, Ray Hunt, to help fund the Iowa effort. In July of 1999, Hunt was among a handful of Bush supporters who each donated $10,000 to the Iowa Republican Party. In all, the donors came up with $43,500 that was then spent to rent a prime spot outside the venue where the straw poll was being held. There, the Bush campaign set up a lavish air-conditioned tent—complete with wooden floors, performing musicians, giant buffet tables stacked with all kinds of food, and stadium seating—where it wined and dined the awestruck Iowans.[1] Bush went on to win the Iowa straw poll by a wide margin.

The coronation of George II had begun. Over the next few months, Bush steamrolled the rest of the Republican contenders for the party's nomination. Bush had the name, he had the money, and with Karl Rove, he had a Machiavellian political strategist who could put it all together. By the early summer of 2000, his nomination at the Republican National Convention was assured. All he needed was a running mate.

SNAPSHOT: HUNT OIL/HUNT CONSOLIDATED

Headquarters: Dallas

Annual revenues (2002): $1.7 billion (estimated). Hunt Oil is privately held and does not release revenue figures.

Employees: N.a.

CEO: Ray L. Hunt (net worth: $2.3 billion)

What it sells: Oil and gas. Hunt Oil is one of the world's biggest privately held independent oil companies. It has operations in the U.S., Canada, Yemen, Oman, and Peru.

The cash-and-carry story: Ray L. Hunt has long been one of George W. Bush's biggest contributors. He gave $105,000 to W's gubernatorial campaigns in Texas. He was a member of The Pioneers, the elite group of fundraisers who agreed to raise at least $100,000 for Bush's 2000 campaign. The Hunt family has given about $460,000 to Republican campaigns at the state level. The company and its minions have donated more than $1 million to GOP causes since 1995. In 2000, W appointed Hunt to be the finance chairman of the Republican National Committee. As president, Bush appointed Hunt to the President's Foreign Intelligence Advisory Board, the prestigious group that monitors America's intelligence operations. Hunt is also the chairman of the Federal Reserve Bank of Dallas.

The crony factor 1: When George H. W. Bush was in Congress, his press spokesman was James Oberwetter. After working for the elder Bush, Oberwetter went to work for Hunt Oil as the firm's director of public and governmental affairs. In November 2003, George W. Bush nominated Oberwetter to be his new ambassador to Saudi Arabia. Oberwetter replaced yet another Texas crony, Robert Jordan, a Baker Botts lawyer.

The crony factor 2: Ray Hunt has been a Bush insider for years. In 1986, when George H. W. Bush was vice president, he made a special side trip to visit a newly built refinery owned by Hunt Oil in Yemen. Hunt has served on the board of Halliburton since 1998. He serves on Halliburton's compensation committee.

Chapter 18 Halliburton Hires a Crony

George Brown would have been pleased as punch if he had lived to see it. Ever since his first meetings with Lyndon Johnson in the 1930s and 1940s, Brown had been cultivating friends in Washington who could help his company garner federal contracts. In 1995, a dozen years after George Brown's death, Halliburton hired the ultimate Washington insider, Dick Cheney.

Cheney didn't become the CEO of Halliburton because of his expertise in the energy business. He knew squat about drilling for oil or doing complex construction projects. But then Halliburton didn't hire him for *what* he knew, they hired him for *who* he knew. Hiring a man who'd worked in the White House, the U.S. House of Representatives, and then at the top spot in the Pentagon meant that Halliburton—a company that had been mixing business and government for decades—would be able to mine all of Cheney's contacts in Washington. With Cheney at the helm, Halliburton's business and America's business would become inseparable. Cheney would make sure of that.

One of the best descriptors of Cheney's style was the code name assigned to him by the Secret Service when he served as chief of staff to President Gerald R. Ford: "Back Seat."[1] With Back Seat in the driver's seat, Halliburton's fortunes improved rapidly, particularly when it came to making money off the company's longtime client, the Pentagon. While Cheney was defense secretary, the Pentagon paid Brown & Root $8.9 million for a couple of studies on how to privatize the military's logistics operations. Shortly after those studies were completed, the Pentagon gave the very first logistics support contract to Brown & Root.

The trend that Brown & Root started in Vietnam—a war that Cheney avoided by getting student and marital deferments—was coming full circle.[2] In the 1960s in Vietnam, Brown & Root changed the course of American military history when it began doing construction work for the military in a war zone. By the 1990s, thanks in part to Cheney, Brown & Root was the Pentagon's quartermaster-for-hire. Not only was Brown & Root building camps for American G.I.s operating in war zones, it was also cooking their breakfast, doing their laundry, and delivering their mail. With that first five-year logistics contract, Brown & Root began working alongside GIs in Zaire, Haiti, Kosovo, the Balkans, Somalia, and Saudi Arabia.[3]

Although the Pentagon was happy with Brown & Root's work, the General Accounting Office was—once again—less enthusiastic. In 1997, it found that while working for the Army in the Balkans, Brown & Root was charging the Army $86 for sheets of plywood that cost $14 and that the Army was "unable to ensure that the contractor adequately controlled costs."[4] In September of 2000, the GAO again found that the company was overcharging the military for a whole range of things. This time the list included providing twice as much electricity as was needed at army facilities in Kosovo and ordering outlandish amounts of furniture and routinely overstaffing operations. One example: army offices at Camp Bondsteel in Kosovo were cleaned four times a day. The company was so punctilious it was even cleaning the latrines three times a day, no doubt getting paid for each swab of the mop. During Dick Cheney's tenure, 1995 to 2000, Brown & Root's logistics contract in Kosovo cost the Pentagon $2.2 billion, making it one of the most expensive services contracts in the history of the U.S. military.[5]

Halliburton officials have not been shy in discussing the rationale behind the hiring of Cheney. He had the contacts that the company needed. Cheney was able to "open doors around the world and to have access practically anywhere. . . . There was a lot that he could bring in the way of customer relationships," Halliburton's former chairman, Thomas H. Cruikshank, told *Texas Monthly*. Another Halliburton board member involved in the hiring of Cheney, the arch-Republican and long-time chairman of the President's Foreign Intelligence Advisory Board, Anne Armstrong, said, "There was instant backing for Dick when his name was brought to our attention."

Halliburton's bet on Cheney paid off. Cheney's successor at the top spot at Halliburton, David Lesar, said Cheney had the kind of access that corporate bosses can only dream about. When Lesar went to Oman, he "could see the energy minister. But when Cheney and I went to Oman, we would see the sultan. When we went to Kuwait, we would see the emir." In 2004, Lesar told Bloomberg that Cheney was "in effect a celebrity CEO for Halliburton, and he put the name Halliburton on the map in a way that probably nobody else could have."

Cheney had a star-studded Rolodex. He also knew how to vacuum up federal money and federal contracts. Figures from the Center for Public Integrity show that while Cheney was at Halliburton, the company won $2.3 billion in federal contracts—nearly double the amount of the previous five-year period. More important, Cheney helped the company get federally backed loans and insurance from export credit agencies like the Export-Import Bank and the Overseas Private Investment Corporation. In the five years prior to Cheney's arrival, Brown & Root garnered about $100 million in loans and guarantees from those two agencies. During Cheney's tenure, that number increased *15-fold*. The company got backing for a number of developments including a $292 million guarantee to refurbish a major oilfield in Russia owned by

Tyumen Oil Co., a controversial outfit that allegedly had ties to organized crime. It also got funding for projects in countries from Algeria to Angola.

Cheney knew that in Washington, influence comes from distributing cash to the right people. While Cheney was the boss at Halliburton, the company more than doubled its political giving, providing over $1.2 million in soft and hard money—mostly to Republican causes—according to numbers compiled by the Center for Responsive Politics. Halliburton also doubled its lobbying budget. Between 1996 and 1999, the company's lobby spending went from less than $300,000 to about $600,000.

Cheney also hired military types to reinforce the company's ties to the Pentagon. He hired Joe Lopez, a retired admiral who was his military aide while he was defense secretary. Lopez became the chief operating officer of Brown & Root, a position that allowed him to work on the company's many military contracts. He also hired Dave Gribbin, his former chief of staff at the Pentagon. Gribbin became one of Halliburton's main lobbyists in Washington.[6]

While Cheney was filling Halliburton with former military types, he was also railing against U.S. government sanctions, which were hampering Halliburton's business overseas. In a 1998 speech at the Cato Institute, Cheney made it clear that the needs of America's energy business shouldn't be constrained by the desires of the American government. "The good Lord didn't see fit to put oil and gas only where there are democratically elected regimes friendly to the United States. Occasionally we have to operate in places where, all things considered, one would not normally choose to go. But, we go where the business is." Cheney went on to claim that the United States has "become 'sanctions-happy,'" and that it is "very hard to find specific examples where they [sanctions] actually achieve a policy objective."[7] That same year, Cheney personally lobbied U.S. Senator Phil Gramm in an effort to get a waiver from the Iran-Libya Sanctions Act, a federal law passed overwhelmingly by Congress in 1996, which prohibits American interests from doing major business deals in those countries.[8]

Cheney had a good reason to seek relaxation of the sanctions; Halliburton was actively doing business with three countries that had been declared enemies of the United States: Libya, Iran, and Iraq.

During Cheney's tenure, Brown & Root continued its long association with the Libyan strongman, Muammar al-Qaddafi. Since 1984, Brown & Root has done more than $100 million worth of engineering work on the Great Man-Made River Project, a massive, $20 billion pipeline project that will bring water for Tripoli and other Libyan cities. To get around the U.S. sanctions, Halliburton transferred the engineering work to Brown & Root's overseas offices.

Cheney oversaw a similar deal that skirted American regulations so that Halliburton could do business with the theocratic regime running Iran. Ever since the Iranians took Americans hostage in 1979, Iran and the United States have been at odds. And yet, despite a ban on trading with Iran, Halliburton provided the country with an undisclosed amount of oilfield equipment while Cheney was the company's CEO. Cheney defended the trading Halliburton did with Iran because, like the Libyan work, it was done through foreign subsidiaries. In fact, in June of 2000, he gave a speech arguing that the United States should relax its sanctions against Iran so that American firms could invest there.[9]

And of course, the deals with Saddam Hussein's corrupt regime in Iraq continued. While Cheney was the CEO of Halliburton, the company sold $73 million in oil production equipment and spare parts to Iraq. Like the Libyan work, the goods were sold through subsidiaries in Europe. To get the goods to Iraq, Halliburton diverted them through affiliated companies in France. Halliburton did business with Iraq even though Cheney insisted that he had imposed a "firm policy" against trading with Saddam's regime, which was under a skein of U.S. trade sanctions. "Iraq's different," Cheney insisted—though he never said exactly how it was "different."[10] In addition to the equipment and spare parts, Halliburton also worked in Iraq's oilfields. In the late 1990s, Halliburton did some $23.8 million worth of work to repair damage done to the oilfields during the First Iraq War.[11]

Halliburton had many other deals in the Persian Gulf. In 1999, it signed a 25-year deal with Saudi Aramco to do oilfield logging operations in Saudi Arabia.[12] (Logging is the process of measuring the physical qualities of a well.) The size of the deal was not revealed. But it added to the huge contracts that Halliburton got from the Saudis in the wake of the First Iraq War.

Cheney also worked to increase the size of Halliburton. In 1998, he arranged the $7.3 billion merger of Halliburton and Dresser, the second-largest oilfield services company in Texas. Dresser—the outfit that had first employed George H.W. Bush when he moved to West Texas in the late 1940s—made oilfield equipment and provided many of the same services as Halliburton. Also like Halliburton, it had a big construction and engineering outfit, M. W. Kellogg. On the surface it looked like a great deal. It wasn't. Cheney's merger included the liabilities associated with a Dresser subsidiary that had manufactured asbestos products. Between 1998 and 2001, asbestos-related litigation exploded. In 1998, Halliburton was a defendant in about 70,000 asbestos lawsuits, a figure that mushroomed to 274,000 by the end of 2001.[13]

But none of that really mattered to Dick Cheney. He was a corporate boss. In addition to the paychecks he got from Halliburton, Cheney also got paid to sit on the boards of three other companies, the railroad giant (and former Baker Botts client) Union Pacific; Ross Perot's old company, EDS; and Procter & Gamble. In 1999, those three outside jobs paid him $282,500.

His wife, Lynne, became a diva of the corporate world. She was working for the American Enterprise Institute, a conservative think tank in Washington, the same place that had hired Dick Cheney immediately after he left the Pentagon in 1993. She also had jobs serving on the board of directors of the defense behemoth Lockheed Martin, a company that was doing tens of billions of dollars worth of contracting for the Pentagon. And like Dick, she was in the energy business. She served on the board of Union Pacific Resources Group. In 1999 alone, Lynne Cheney was paid more than $300,000 to serve on various corporate boards.

Dick and Lynne Cheney's migration from the political world to the corporate world was absolutely seamless. By serving on the boards of America's biggest companies, the Cheneys further cemented their ties to America's corporate titans. And those corporate Big Shots could provide the money needed to further the Cheneys' political goals. Plus, by serving on other corporate boards, Dick Cheney got even closer to two other longtime members of the Texas Big Shot club: Ray Hunt and James A. Baker III.

In June of 1996, Cheney, Baker, and Hunt joined the board of Dallas-based EDS, as the computer systems company was being spun off from General Motors. And all of the men made the most of it. During their service on the board, they made sure to reward both themselves and EDS's new boss, Dick Brown, who was named chairman and CEO in January of 1999.

For their work on the EDS board, Cheney, Baker, and Hunt were all paid $35,000 per year, as well as $2,500 for each meeting they attended. Plus, they were each given stock options on 1,500 shares of the company's stock. While the three men were getting paid to look out for EDS, Baker was also looking out for his own interests. In 1999, the EDS board apparently approved a deal under which Baker's law firm, Baker Botts, would do legal work for the company. Thus, Baker, the man who has always prided himself on his moral rectitude, was put in the position of being both an independent board member and a consultant to EDS—a position that is considered a no-no by corporate governance experts. The same year that the board approved the hiring of Baker Botts, it also approved an enormous compensation package for the newly hired CEO, Richard H. Brown. (Brown would later be fired after EDS discovered accounting irregularities that took place under Brown's aegis.)[14]

The cozy relationship among Cheney, Hunt, and Baker was reinforced yet again in 1998, when Cheney and his fellow board members at Halliburton decided to bring on a new director, Ray Hunt. At Halliburton, Hunt was appointed to serve on the company's compensation committee, which oversaw the pay for the company's executives, including Hunt's buddy, Dick Cheney.

By joining the Halliburton board, Hunt got a key position from which to watch over the company that was doing a substantial amount of work for him. Hunt's exploration and production company, Hunt Oil, was using Halliburton crews at its operations in Yemen. (The year before Hunt joined Halliburton's board, Yemeni bandits had kidnapped a Halliburton employee working for Hunt Oil.) Hunt Oil was also developing the huge Camisea gas field in Peru. Hunt would later hire Halliburton to do engineering work on a controversial pipeline associated with the project, which cuts through a prime Peruvian rainforest.

Of course, Hunt had plenty of other reasons to be on Halliburton's board. His oil company was among the biggest privately held companies of its type on the globe. In addition to oilfields in Canada, Texas, and elsewhere, he owned a refinery in Alabama that bought crude from various suppliers, including the Saudis.

Hunt's enormous wealth—and of course, his connections with Cheney and Baker—made him attractive to George W. Bush, too. In May of 2000, Bush named Hunt the finance chairman of the Republican National Committee.[15] Pulling Hunt into W's presidential campaign solidified the longstanding ties between the Bush family and the Hunts. George H. W. Bush's former press secretary, Jim Oberwetter, had been working for Ray Hunt for nearly three decades.

Just a few weeks before naming Hunt for the finance job, Bush had named Dick Cheney to head the search for a suitable running mate. Cheney's job was to find an appealing vice presidential candidate, someone with gravitas, someone with sterling credentials, someone who could raise a ton of money from corporate America, someone a lot like Dick Cheney.

By the end of July, Bush had made up his mind. Thanks in part to lobbying by George H. W. Bush, the younger Bush decided that Cheney was the Halliburton man of the moment. In announcing the merger, George W. Bush said "the person most qualified to be the vice-president has been working by my side." The announcement sent Halliburton's stock on a wild run. The prospect of having a former Halliburton boss as the vice president of the United States led to premium pricing. Stock investors assumed that Cheney could help steer fat federal contracts to his old company in Texas. In the days before Cheney emerged as the front-runner for the VP spot, Halliburton's stock was selling for about $42 per share. By early September, with Bush and Cheney hard on the campaign trail, Halliburton's stock had risen nearly 30 percent, to over $54.

Nevertheless, when he was named as Bush's running mate, Cheney insisted that he was making a big sacrifice. Asked how the move would affect his finances, Cheney said he would take a "financial bath." In the end, Cheney's "bath" was a retirement package worth $33.7 million.[16] His total pay during his tenure of less than five years at George Brown's old company: $45 million.

Dick Cheney had made a ton of money by traveling through the paved-with-gold revolving door between government and business. But it appears that Cheney's take was minuscule when compared to what his old pal, James A. Baker III, was making.

SNAPSHOT: CARLYLE GROUP

Headquarters: Washington, D.C.

Employees: 500

Type of enterprise: Privately held partnership

Total invested capital: $14 billion (2002)[17]

CEO: Louis Gerstner. Carlyle does not release pay figures. Gerstner is the former chairman and CEO of IBM. While at IBM, Gerstner's total pay exceeded $366 million.

Carlyle's Notable Big Shots: George H. W. Bush, James A. Baker III, John Major, Frank Carlucci, Arthur Levitt.

The firm's business: Buys stakes in various industries, including defense, energy, health care, and telecommunications. Its best-known holdings are in United Defense, the company that makes the Bradley Fighting Vehicle.

The Carlyle–bin Laden connection: On September 11, 2001, the Carlyle Group's Big Shots were meeting at the Ritz Carlton in Washington, D.C. One of the attendees was Shafiq bin Laden, brother of Osama bin Laden. Other attendees were former Secretary of State James A. Baker III and George H. W. Bush.

The cash-and-carry story: Fred Malek, a Carlyle cofounder, gave $1 million to the George Bush Presidential Library.

Chapter 19   Baker Cashes In

When I left office they loved us. Today America is not as respected by its allies and feared by its adversaries as it was in January 1993. . . . [Now the United States is] perceived as an arrogant bully.

—James A. Baker III, Princeton University, March 2000

Just 33 days after leaving the first Bush administration, James A. Baker III had the revolving door spinning so fast it created a sonic boom. On February 22, 1993, he went to work for Ken Lay, the chairman and CEO of Enron. Announcing the move, the Enron boss gushed that his company was "delighted" that Baker would be joining the company to promote "the development of natural gas projects around the world."

Baker's work as a lobbyist/fixer began a few weeks later when he hopped on a flight aboard a Kuwait Airways jet. Sitting next to him was his buddy, former President George H. W. Bush, who was going to collect an honorary medal from the Kuwaitis. The Kuwaitis wanted to show their appreciation to Bush for rescuing their country from Saddam Hussein. Baker was tagging along to score a fat contract for Enron. The former secretary of state, who just a few months earlier had been discussing military and political strategy with the Kuwaitis, was now trying to persuade the country's just-back-from-exile royal rulers on the merits of a 400-megawatt power plant that Enron wanted to rebuild at Shuaiba, an industrial zone south of Kuwait City. Baker's lobbying for Enron didn't stop in Kuwait. The former secretary of state also pushed Enron projects in Turkey, Qatar, and Turkmenistan.

Baker also wrote a paper for Enron on the political risks of investing in the Dabhol power plant project 50 miles south of Bombay, India. (Ignoring warnings from the World Bank, Enron went ahead with the $3 billion project, which was canceled by the Indian government in early 2001.) Although it's not clear how much Baker was paid for his work for Enron on the Dabhol project, in Kuwait, and elsewhere, sources at the now-bankrupt energy trading company say that Baker demanded a king's ransom for his services on a particular deal in 1994.

That year, Enron was having trouble negotiating a deal with the Indian government over an oil and gas concession. So the company called Baker to see if he would intercede on their behalf with one of the ministers in India. They were shocked when they heard the price tag. "If they wanted to use Baker, it would cost five hundred thousand dollars to sign the contract and five hundred thousand to make the phone call," says a former Enron employee who worked on the deal. "That's for one phone call."

Enron decided not to use Baker on the India deal, but the $1 million he demanded for his services is indicative of the kind of money Baker expects while working as an international lawyer-lobbyist-fixer.

Sixteen days after Baker began working for Ken Lay at Enron, he signed on to work as "senior counsel" with the Carlyle Group, the arms-focused investment firm. When the announcement was made, the *Washington Post* theorized that Baker's main value to Carlyle was likely to be "his high profile and his global contacts, which could help Carlyle raise additional money from investors in the United States, the Middle East and elsewhere.... His close ties to many chief executives of American companies also could provide Carlyle with opportunities to buy and sell businesses and make new investments."[1]

By joining Carlyle as a partner—meaning he would share in the private investment firm's profits—Baker became the highest-profile Big Shot to sign on with the firm. Of course, Carlyle was already filling up with Big Shots eager to travel the revolving door between government and business. One of the main Big Shots at the firm was Frank Carlucci, Ronald Reagan's secretary of defense, who had become Carlyle's managing director.

Baker's job at Carlyle was to help the firm reach into deep pockets, and it appears that he did just that. When Baker joined Carlyle in 1993, the firm had stakes in 10 companies and had about $2 billion under management. The companies it owned had total revenues of about $5 billion. By 2000 Carlyle had grown into a juggernaut. Its money under management had quintupled, to about $10 billion, it owned stakes in dozens of companies, and its defense businesses alone had annual revenues of $5 billion.[2]

One of Baker's tasks at the Carlyle Group was raising money from rich people in general and the Saudis in particular. For that job he hooked up with George H. W. Bush, who signed on to work at Carlyle in 1995. Bush is reportedly paid about $100,000 for each speaking gig he does on behalf of the Carlyle Group. Bush and Baker traveled together to Saudi Arabia to help the Carlyle Group solicit funds. The two "would meet with all the big guys in the royal family," says a source quoted in *Vanity Fair* in October of 2003. "Indirectly, the message was 'I'd appreciate it if you put some money in the Carlyle Group.'" The message got across. Baker's longtime pal and hunting buddy, Prince Bandar bin Sultan, the longtime Saudi ambassador to the United States, invested money in Carlyle. So did two sons of a wealthy Saudi banker, Khaled bin Mahfouz, who'd previously gone into business with John Connally and had invested money in Harken Energy, George W. Bush's failed oil company.[3] A few million more came from the family of Osama bin Laden.

While Baker and Bush were seeking cash for Carlyle, the investment group was doing plenty of work for the Saudis. One of its subsidiaries, Vinnell, was providing training for the Saudi National Guard, which was overseen by Crown Prince Abdullah bin Abdul Aziz. Vinnell was reportedly connected to the Central Intelligence Agency and its work for the Saudis was closely tied to the Pentagon. Carlyle owned Vinnell from 1992 until 1997. In addition to the Vinnell contract, another Carlyle company, United Defense Industries, was making big money in Saudi Arabia. United Defense, which went public in December of 2001, makes the Bradley fighting vehicle, a 25-ton tank that has been a mainstay of the American military. Each Bradley costs about $3.1 million. Saudi Arabia is the second largest buyer of the Bradley, after the Pentagon.[4]

Carlyle's work with the Saudis was very good for Baker's bank account. Although Carlyle doesn't reveal its internal financial information, the *Guardian* newspaper estimated that Baker's ownership interest could be worth as much as $180 million.[5]

About the same time that Baker signed on with the Carlyle Group, the lawyers at Baker Botts decided that they could suspend their antinepo-

SNAPSHOT: INTERVIEW WITH JAMES BAKER

In the fall of 2003, this reporter briefly caught up with Baker at a fundraiser for the James A. Baker III Institute for Public Policy at Rice University.

RB: What about the Carlyle Group? There have been reports that your interest there is worth $180 million.

JB: That's bullshit. [*yelling*] You print that.

RB: What is it worth?

JB: That's for me to know [*still yelling*] and you to NOT know.

Baker refused to answer any other questions.

tism rule long enough to hire an unemployed former secretary of state with an Astrodome-sized Rolodex. Sources say Baker's salary at the firm exceeded $1 million per year.

For the firm, that was money well spent. Baker's political connections apparently helped his firm get lucrative legal contracts in the oil-rich regions of the Caspian Sea. In 1997, Baker Botts was chosen by an international consortium of 11 oil companies known as the Baku-Tbilisi-Ceyhan Pipeline Company, to represent its interests with the countries of Azerbaijan, Georgia, and Turkey.[6] The stakes are huge. The oil companies, led by BP, which owns a 30 percent share, are building the Baku-Tbilisi-Ceyhan pipeline in order to export oil and gas from the landlocked Caspian Sea. The pipeline, which will cover more than 1,000 miles and cost about $3.5 billion, is among the biggest energy development projects on earth. Scheduled to be completed in 2005, the pipe will achieve a decades-long goal of oil producers in the oil-rich Caspian region: a direct link between Baku, the Azerbaijani capital and the oil industry's hub, and the shipping lanes of the Mediterranean Sea. The U.S. government hopes that the pipeline, which will carry about 1 million barrels of crude per day, will help reduce global dependence on hydrocarbons from the Persian Gulf.

Baker Botts was charged with writing the rules governing everything that might affect the pipeline, including land acquisition, security, and the tax code. These rules have been designed to be a binding international treaty that will supersede all conflicting domestic laws in Azerbaijan, Georgia, and Turkey. Once agreed to by the three countries, the rules will also govern how human rights and environmental policies will be adjudicated.

It was surely no coincidence that Baker Botts won the contract. One of the original partners in the pipeline consortium (formed in 1994) was a Baker Botts client, Hugh Liedtke's company, Pennzoil. Pennzoil had been working to get into the Caspian region for years, and Baker Botts had been handling the firm's legal efforts.[7] Furthermore, when Baker was secretary of state, he worked closely with former Soviet foreign minister Eduard Shevardnadze.

After the disintegration of the Soviet Union, Shevardnadze went back to his home, and become president of the newly independent Republic of Georgia. Baker Botts insisted that it didn't win the contract in the Caspian solely because of Baker's friendship with Shevardnadze, but the firm's lead partner for energy affairs, George Goolsby, in a 2002 interview with journalist Daphne Eviatar, made it clear that Baker's presence is very good for business. "I've got to think our association with him has helped in ways we're not even aware of," Goolsby said.

Indeed, Baker Botts touts Baker's experience to help garner clients throughout the world, particularly in the Middle East, where the firm has an office in Riyadh, Saudi Arabia, and an alliance with a firm in the United Arab Emirates. On the law firm's web site, Bakerbotts.com, it says it can provide clients with the "perspective and experience of James A. Baker III, 61st U.S. secretary of state," a person who can give "the firm's clients an additional resource on which to rely regarding their activities in the region."[8]

Baker's connections have been transformed into cold, hard cash for Baker Botts. According to a story in *American Lawyer*, written by Eviatar, the firm billed the pipeline consortium for more than 40,000 hours of work between 1997 and 2002.[9] At $200 per hour (probably a low figure for Baker Botts), that's $8 million in fees.

All of his connections made Baker the most powerful former secretary of state in America. Henry Kissinger may have been on TV more, gone to more Big Shot parties, and had more clients for his consulting firm, Kissinger Associates. But he was also less discerning. Kissinger has shown a willingness to represent practically any client, as long as they can write a big enough check.

Baker is more subtle than Kissinger. He is more selective and far more judicious. That makes him more valuable to clients and therefore more influential. He is also apparently a lot richer. In 1982, when Baker was working in the Reagan administration, he estimated his family's net worth at about $5 million. During his stint in Washington he couldn't do much to add to that sum. But between 1993 and November of 2000, Baker made an absolute killing. The lobbying for Enron, the rainmaking for Baker Botts, the Carlyle Group job—gave him more money than he needed. Speaking gigs paid him $100,000 per throw. He was 70 years old and was happily insulating himself from the world, doing the deals that interested him, and traveling when he wanted to. He was living in a lavish home on a heavily wooded lot in the exclusive Memorial section of Houston valued by the Harris County Appraisal District at $1.1 million. He owned ranches in Wyoming and in South Texas, where he hunted and relaxed. Baker's time was his own. He could do as he pleased. He could work as much or as little as he wanted. He very rarely talked to the media. And he never, never, talked about his work for the Carlyle Group—or anyone else.

That wouldn't be "Bottsian."

You see, in addition to his other attributes, James A. Baker III had been trained from the crib in the code of omertà that comes with being a corporate lawyer. Baker Botts had become an enormously valuable legal franchise. The firm—founded in 1840 and the second-oldest law firm west of the Mississippi—had built its reputation on a buttoned-down-starched-white-shirt belief in its absolute innate superiority. An integral part of that attitude was known inside the firm as the "Bottsian Way." The term is shorthand for thoroughness and rectitude. Being "Bottsian" means staying away from any kind of criminal cases, divorce proceedings, or any type of personal damage litigation. "You don't sue another law firm," says a former lawyer at Baker Botts. "You don't sue a corporation on behalf of an individual. That wasn't Bottsian. You could only sue a corporation if you were suing on behalf of another corporation." There are other rules. "You couldn't leave the office or the building without wearing coat and tie. You couldn't grab a sandwich in shirt sleeves. Also, you don't talk to the press, that's not Bottsian."

Baker is the Obi-Wan Kenobi of the Bottsian Way. He is the quintessential crony, the loyal soldier who doesn't talk. In his book, *Politics of Diplomacy*, which came out in 1995, he could have settled some scores with his rivals in the Reagan and Bush administrations. But he didn't. Baker could have used the book to smack around his enemies, people like Lyn Nofziger, the Reagan press aide, who, in his book, *Nofziger*, barbecued both Baker and the elder Bush. Among other salvos, Nofziger wrote that it seemed appropriate that "a guy with III after his name is working for a fellow with two middle initials. If nothing else, they are doing the country club set proud."[10] Baker doesn't mention Nofziger in his book. Nor does he take the opportunity to slap Dan Quayle, Bush's famously inept vice president. Quayle's name doesn't even appear in Baker's book. That's the essence of the Bottsian Way: get even by showing the other side doesn't exist.

By the fall of 2000, Baker's stint as secretary of state, his wealth, his contacts, and his influence made him a Big Shot of the first order. And he was still taking the time to hunt. In mid-November, he was scheduled to go on a pheasant-hunting trip in England with George H. W. Bush, retired Army general Norman Schwarzkopf, former national security adviser Brent Scowcroft, and Dick Cheney. Their host was to be one of their longtime pals, Saudi Arabia's ambassador to the United States and one of Baker's cronies, Prince Bandar bin Sultan.[11]

Baker never went on that trip. In early November instead of hunting pheasants in England he suddenly found himself in Florida, in charge of the team that was hunting the biggest trophy in world politics: the presidency of the United States.

Headquarters: Houston (additional offices in Austin, Baku, Dallas, London, Moscow, New York, Riyadh, and Washington, D.C.)

Revenues: $365 million (2002)

Employees: 612 lawyers; several hundred more support personnel[12]

Type of enterprise: Privately held partnership

Top lawyer: James A. Baker III (net worth estimated to be $180 million)

What it sells: Legal services, influence

Clients: Looters, polluters, and plutocrats

The cash-and-carry story: In the 2000 election, Baker Botts was George W. Bush's ninth-largest campaign contributor, giving his campaign $116,121. During the 2000 election cycle, Baker Botts also gave $20,000 to the Republican National Committee.

How Baker Botts's business became America's business: Can you say "Florida recount"? In the end, Bush won the presidency because he had James A. Baker III and his lawyers from the Baker Botts offices in Washington and Houston slug it out with Al Gore's legal team. The result was a knockout.

The Baker-Saudi connection: Baker Botts represented Prince Sultan bin Abdul Aziz al-Saud, the defense minister of Saudi Arabia, in the $1 trillion class-action lawsuit brought against dozens of Saudis by survivors of the victims of the September 11 attacks. Arguably the single most corrupt member of the House of Saud, Sultan was dismissed as a defendant in the case in November 2003.

The crony factor: George H. W. Bush and James A. Baker III have been best friends since they became tennis partners at the Houston Country Club in the 1950s. Baker Botts represented Bush's company, Zapata Off-Shore Drilling, throughout its early years. In return, Baker Botts did favors for the Bushes: George W. Bush's first summer job was in the mailroom of Baker Botts.

Notable cronyism: Robert L. Jordan, a Baker Botts partner, was appointed America's ambassador to Saudi Arabia by George Bush right after his election. Jordan had never been to Saudi Arabia. (Jordan quit that post in October 2003.)

Notable cronyism 2: J. Bruce McDonald, a partner in Baker Botts's Houston office, was tapped by the Department of Justice to head the department's antitrust division with oversight of energy issues in June of 2003.

Notable cronyism 3: Halliburton signed up Baker Botts in 2002, after dropping Vinson & Elkins, which had been representing it for decades.[13]

BAKER BOTTS (PARTIAL) CLIENT LIST

Exxon Mobil Corporation

Reliant Resources

Dynegy Inc.

ConocoPhillips Company

Dow Chemical Company

Occidental Petroleum Corporation

Halliburton

Valero Energy Corporation

Cisco Systems, Inc.

Fleming Companies, Inc.

Goodyear Tire & Rubber Company and Subsidiaries

Dell Computer Corporation

Waste Management, Inc.

Texas Instruments, Inc.

EDS (James A. Baker III served on the board of EDS from 1996 to late 2003. Corporate governance experts frown upon directors who have direct business relationships with the companies on whose boards they sit. Baker left the EDS board after George W. Bush appointed him the debt czar for Iraq's foreign debt.)[14]

Chapter 20

2000: Lawyers, Airplanes, and Money—Part II

I t was 1948 all over again.

When the ballots were counted on November 7 and 8, 2000, less than 1,000 votes separated George W. Bush and Al Gore in the key state of Florida. Gore had won the popular vote in the rest of the country. He'd won more votes than any presidential candidate in American history except for Ronald Reagan. He'd beaten Bush by over 500,000 votes. But those votes didn't matter. Only the votes in Florida mattered—the electoral votes, that is. The candidate who won Florida's popular vote would take the state's 25 electoral votes, and the presidency. To win the White House, Gore had to win Florida. The same was true for Bush.

Every day, every minute, was critical. On election night, as November 7, 2000, turned into November 8, a cold rain was falling in Austin. George W. Bush had to make several decisions. He knew he had to get his lead campaign people down to Florida, and he had to do it quickly. He needed someone to handle the media, oversee the lawyers, and bully or bluff his way through any difficulties that arose. He needed someone with stature, someone who was comfortable being in the Klieg lights and who knew how to assert power and do so forcefully. George W. Bush knew there was only one choice.

When the Bushes need help, . . .

The telephone call to James A. Baker III was made by Bush's oil patch pal, Don Evans, the CEO of Tom Brown Inc., a Denver-based oil and gas company. By pulling in Baker to lead the Republican attack in the Florida recount battle, George W. Bush knew that he was getting more than just a former secretary of state. With Baker in charge, the Bush campaign would have a real general, someone whom campaign staffers, local politicians, and reporters would respect and listen to. Baker had jousted with some of the smartest, most ruthless politicians on earth. He was rich, smart, tough as nails, and a devout believer in the primacy of the Bush family. But Baker, the Bush family's consigliere, was even more than this: he was also the ultimate insider, both in Washington and in Texas. He commanded a brigade of some of the smartest lawyers in America, a corps whose members were ready to do whatever he said at a moment's notice.

When Evans called him on the morning of November 8, 2000, Baker had arrived over his life's course at the enormously lucrative intersection of business, legal work, politics, and diplomacy. He was a grand master of presidential campaigns and a sixth-degree black belt in insider Washington politics. He'd been a key player in five presidential campaigns—one for Gerald Ford, three for George H. W. Bush, and one for Ronald Reagan. He'd been chief of staff in the White House, treasury secretary, and secretary of state. He was one of the most accomplished leakers in Washington—his talents in this department had given him cozy relationships with key members of the national press. The result was a complete dearth of negative stories about Baker. For a high-profile politico who'd spent about two decades in the District of Columbia, Baker's ability to avoid negative press was one of his most remarkable achievements.

But charity is not one of Baker's skill sets. In Florida, he also had his own business interests at stake. Like Alvin Wirtz, who was the key lawyer for Lyndon Johnson during his 1948 race for the U.S. Senate,

James A. Baker III and his law firm represented Big Oil. If Bush lost to Gore, it would very likely mean bad things for Baker and Baker Botts. Al Gore wasn't from the oil patch. Sure, Gore owned a significant chunk of stock in Occidental Petroleum, but he'd also made it clear that if he won the White House, it wouldn't be business as usual for the oil companies or anybody else. In his book *Earth in the Balance* Gore wrote, "We must make the rescue of the environment the central organizing principle for civilization." Gore was also strongly in favor of the Kyoto Protocol, which if ratified by the Senate would force the United States to reduce the amount of greenhouse gases it releases. Baker knew that his clients didn't want to rescue the environment and they hated the idea of the Kyoto Protocol.

The other attraction for Baker was obvious. He was at the end of his political career. The Florida recount would probably be his last big rodeo. By going to bat for George W. Bush, Baker would secure his legend. So James A. Baker III went into action. Like Alvin Wirtz 52 years earlier, the corporate lawyer was charged with coordinating a network of lawyers, airplanes, and money—a network that Al Gore, vice president though he be, simply would not be able to match.

From the get-go Baker stuck to the same script. Appearing at a jammed news conference on November 11, 2000, Baker said, "As I said yesterday, the vote in Florida has been counted, and then recounted. Governor George W. Bush was the winner of the vote. He is also the winner of the recount." From a purely spin standpoint, it was a good message: concise and to the point.

There was only one problem with Baker's statement: it wasn't true. And Baker knew it. The day before Baker delivered his favorite sound bite, the Gore campaign had requested recounts in at least four counties, but only two of them had actually begun recounting their ballots.[1] That fact didn't matter to James A. Baker III. He had one message, and it became the Bush camp's mantra: *Stop counting. Our boy Bush won. Gore's a sore loser. Get over it.*

Of course, many factors swung the final result to Bush. First and foremost, the fact that Bush consistently maintained a lead, though slim, over Gore in the ballots that had been counted was a tremendous tactical advantage. It allowed the Bush team to push for an end to the recount and to argue repeatedly that their man was the legitimate winner. The conservative leaning of the U.S. Supreme Court, which ultimately sealed the victory for Bush, was also, of course, critically important. It was the five-member majority, led by the Reagan appointee Antonin Scalia and George H. W. Bush's appointee, Clarence Thomas, who stopped the Florida recount and awarded the White House to the younger Bush.

Some observers have argued that the makeup of the Supreme Court is the *only* factor that needs to be discussed when talking about the outcome of the 2000 presidential race. But many important events occurred before Bush's team took its case to the Supreme Court, and they were handled better and more forcefully by Bush's team. As Jeffrey Toobin wrote in his book *Too Close to Call,* the Republicans were "more organized and motivated, and also more ruthless, in their determination to win."[2]

The ruthlessness came straight from Baker. "James A. Baker's personal presence, experience, strategic foresight, de facto authority and unflinching commitment to winning maintained an astonishing degree of discipline among the numerous elite lawyers and other professionals that made up the Bush legal team and contributed to the efficiency and effectiveness of that team," writes Steve Bickerstaff, an Austin-based lawyer who was not involved in the recount. "There was no equivalent figure to enforce discipline on the Gore legal team."[3] That was demonstrably true. The Gore team relied on Warren Christopher, who, like Baker, was both a corporate lawyer and a former secretary of state. But Christopher was no match for Baker when it came to the killer instinct.

Furthermore, Christopher didn't have a brigade of lawyers who worked for him and were loyal to him. Sure, David Boies worked with Christopher. Boies is a very skilled lawyer. But he is also independent. He has his own law firm, and his loyalties were not necessarily to Christopher. Baker had a fleet of lawyers who had been schooled in the Bottsian Way. Baker's name appeared on every one of their paychecks. Those lawyers were experienced and very, very sharp. Two of the firm's best litigators, Irvin Terrell and Daryl Bristow, who played key roles, had been asked by Baker himself to come to Florida to take on various duties. Both had plenty of trial experience. In the mid-1980s, Terrell, along with a Houston lawyer, Joe Jamail, had represented Pennzoil in a mammoth lawsuit against Texaco in which the trial court awarded Pennzoil $11 billion. Pennzoil was the company headed by George H. W. Bush's longtime business partner, Hugh Liedtke. Bristow, at that time with a different Houston law firm, had also worked on the Pennzoil case, but on the losing side.

Other top Baker Botts lawyers played pivotal roles: Robert Jordan, a partner in the firm's Dallas office who had defended George W. Bush on the Harken case, joined the recount team in Florida. Another partner, Kirk Van Tine, was the legal team's Washington D.C. "field general," coordinating the movement of personnel and strategy and helping write some of the legal briefs.[4] Thus, at least five of the firm's most experienced partners worked directly on the Florida recount. In addition, a whole platoon of other lawyers and personnel from Baker Botts gave them support.

Just as Alvin Wirtz had done in 1948 when he led a group of lawyers to the U.S. Supreme Court in Washington to argue on behalf of his client, Lyndon Johnson, so James A. Baker III led a group of lawyers to the U.S. Supreme Court on December 11, 2000, to argue on behalf of his client, George W. Bush.

Although Baker wasn't the one standing before the justices arguing the case, it was clear that he was the one behind the strategy. From the very first hours of his involvement with the Bush campaign, Baker had been predicting that the election would be decided by the Supreme Court.[5] And so it was. On December 12, 2000, by a 5–4 vote, the court ended the Florida recount, deciding that to continue with the recount would somehow violate the equal protection clause of the Fourteenth Amendment, though they didn't say exactly how.

But it took more than kicking Democratic butt in the courtroom to win the White House for George W. Bush. It took a lot of jetting around the country, preferably in the style to which corporate Big Shots are accustomed. Indeed, before and during the recount, the Bush campaign was flying around in style on airplanes provided by Halliburton, Enron, and other corporate players.

The Bush campaign's use of corporate aircraft during the 2000 presidential campaign and the Florida recount has no precedent in American political history. During the 2000 election cycle, Bush and his campaign workers flew on corporate jets no less than 367 times![6] And the key suppliers of those planes were, of course, Texas companies. In addition to jets owned by Halliburton and Enron, the campaign used planes owned by energy companies such as Texas Utilities Co., Occidental Chemical, and Tom Brown Inc., the Midland-based oil company headed by Don Evans. At least three of the companies who provided planes to Bush's campaign were also Baker Botts clients: Halliburton, Occidental, and Reliant Resources.

The biggest provider of planes was W. W. Tichenor & Co., a San Antonio–based company owned by Warren Tichenor, a media magnate with interests in more than a dozen Spanish-language radio stations. Tichenor had also been a key provider of airplanes during both of Bush's gubernatorial races.

During the normal part of the presidential campaign, the corporate jets provided convenience. During the five-week-long Florida recount—when time was of the essence—they provided a critical strategic advantage. Key campaign officials flying on corporate jets were able to avoid cooling their heels in airports, checking baggage, and waiting for all of the tray tables in the coach section to be placed in their full upright and locked position. According to the Bush campaign's filings with the Internal Revenue Service, Bush and his staffers flew on corporate aircraft at least 17 times during the Florida recount. Seven of those flights were taken on jets owned by Texas-based energy companies: Enron, Halliburton, Tom Brown, and Anadarko Petroleum Corporation.

Of those energy companies, it appears that Enron was by far the most amenable to the campaign's wishes. That's not surprising. Enron was Bush's biggest career patron, giving him a total of $736,800 to his gubernatorial and presidential campaigns.[7] During the campaign and the recount, Enron wanted to make sure that Bush had all the transportation he needed, and on more than a dozen occasions the Bush campaign used Enron's jets. The campaign paid Enron about $73,000 for this perk, but those payments were a bargain. Federal election laws only require candidates to reimburse jet owners the equivalent of a first-class ticket for the route flown. And given that a jet can cost several thousand dollars per hour to fly, the cost of a first-class ticket is usually a fraction of the real cost of operating a corporate jet. Plus, the value of the time saved during the Florida recount by using the corporate jets was impossible to measure.

According to former Enron employees, providing planes to the Bush campaign was merely part of the anything-for-the-Bushes attitude at Enron. The company's CEO, Ken Lay, dictated that Enron's fleet be made into the equivalent of Bush Family Airlines. Enron jets flew Laura Bush to campaign appearances across the country on about 10 different occasions during the 2000 campaign. Ken Lay also made sure that the corporate fleet was available to the candidate's parents,

George H. W. Bush and Barbara Bush, who used the planes to fly between Houston and their summer place in Kennebunkport, Maine.

Of course, the Gore campaign had access to jets, too. And one of those jets, *Air Force 2,* carries with it more prestige than any other aircraft—except for *Air Force 1.* And of course the cost of flying Gore to campaign events in *Air Force 2* was borne primarily by American taxpayers. Traditionally, incumbents have always had tremendous advantages when it comes to winning the White House, but the advantage was neutralized by Bush's 2000 campaign. In fact the Gore campaign only used corporate jets a handful of times. In effect, Bush's corporate support infrastructure was broader and deeper than that of the vice president of the United States.

The GOP's corporate gravy train in the sky continued flying high through December of 2000. That month, yet another huge Texas corporate player provided air taxi service to the Bush campaign. The Dallas-based carrier American Airlines provided a brand-new, specially outfitted Boeing 737–800 for use by the Bushies. A few days after Bush prevailed over Al Gore in the Supreme Court, the airplane flew Bush, White House chief of staff Andrew Card, Karl Rove, and National Security Adviser Condoleezza Rice and others from Dallas to Washington, D.C. According to a report by Holly Bailey of the Center for Responsive Politics, American Airlines fed the Big Shots shrimp Caesar salads and chocolate chip cookies. For this luxury travel, the Bush campaign paid American just the cost of one first-class plane ticket per person.[8]

Oh, by the way, the chairman emeritus of American Airlines was the company's former CEO, Robert Crandall, a Dallas industrialist. And Crandall had his own ever-so-cozy ties to the incoming Bush-Cheney White House. In 1995, Crandall was on the board of Halliburton when the company hired Dick Cheney as its CEO.[9] In fact, Crandall chaired the company's compensation committee, which came up with Dick Cheney's princely pay package. The Crandall-

Cheney connection shows, again, that in Texas, politics and business are merely two sides of the same tortilla.

Although the lawyers and the airplanes were invaluable to the Bush Recount effort, they wouldn't have been usable if they hadn't been lubricated by a river of money. The Bush campaign had plenty of that. During the 2000 election cycle, Bush raised more than $191 million.[10] That figure is impressive enough, but the truly astounding fundraising happened during the recount. In the three weeks following the November 7 election, the Bush campaign raised a total of $13.8 million, a quarter of it from just 651 donors, all of whom gave $5,000 (the maximum allowed by the Bush campaign), or $3.255 million. Bush raised more money from those donors than Al Gore raised for his entire recount effort: a total of just $3.2 million.

Not surprisingly, Bush's backers in Texas made up the biggest group of high-dollar donors. Of the group that gave Bush $5,000 apiece, 149 were from Texas, and many of them were Bush intimates from way back: William Stamps Farish, the heir to the Exxon fortune; Ken and Linda Lay of Enron, each of whom gave $5,000; J. Landis Martin, president and chief executive officer of NL Industries Inc., and Bush's oil business buddy, Ray Hunt, both of them members of Halliburton's board of directors; Peter O'Donnell, the Dallas Republican who was a key backer of George H. W. Bush in his 1964 race for the U.S. Senate, and his wife, each of whom gave $5,000; so did Nancy Kinder, the wife of former Enron executive Rich Kinder; the Bass family, those heirs of the oilman Sid Richardson gave a total of $15,000—$5,000 each from Lee Bass and Mr. and Mrs. Perry Bass.

Gore's donors were far fewer and made far bigger contributions. Jane Fonda gave Gore $100,000; Stephen Bing, a Hollywood producer, gave $200,000; Steven Kirsch, a philanthropist, gave $500,000.

Where Gore's fundraising appeared lackadaisical and haphazard,

Bush's was professional and ran with machine-like efficiency. That was no accident. Bush's avalanche of money was the product of years of work by the political genius Karl Rove. Ever since he was first hired by Bill Clements two decades earlier, Rove had been building computerized mailing lists of Big Rich GOP donors, a key element of the highly sophisticated direct-mail operation at Karl Rove + Company. Rove had used his mailing lists and computers to raise tens of millions of dollars for GOP candidates all over the country. In 1999, as Bush began his race for the White House, Rove sold the business to two of his protégés, Todd Olsen and Ted Delisi. The two operatives were loyal to Rove and Bush and had done more than $1 million worth of work for the Bush campaign by the time the recount began. They had the lists of donors who they knew could write big checks and would do so quickly.

Immediately after the recount began, Olsen & Delisi was charged with collecting money. The firm sent out fundraising letters, all of them written by Don Evans, on three different occasions during the recount. They brought in millions. When asked about the fundraising effort, Benjamin Ginsberg, one of the Bush campaign's lead attorneys said, "I think we were a little bit stunned by the amount we received."

The money that poured out of Rove's mailing lists paid for everything that made Bush's recount victory possible: the airplanes, the hotels, the office space—and, of course, the lawyers. So how much were the lawyers actually paid? What was James A. Baker III worth to the Bush campaign? And what were the others worth? When Enron asked Baker to represent them in the 1990s, he demanded a fee of $1 million for work that might have taken him a few hours at the very most. Given that history, how much might Baker have charged a client if he knew that the prize wasn't a drilling contract in India, but was instead the presidency of the United States?

Many of the best lawyers in Houston charge $500 to $1,000 per hour. So let's assume that Baker could charge at the upper end of that scale, $1,000 per hour. Let's assume, further, that during the five weeks of the Florida Recount, Baker worked six days a week for 10 hours per day, for a total of 300 hours. At that rate, Baker's bill alone would have totaled $300,000. But recall that a phalanx of top Baker Botts attorneys was also working on the case.

Yet according to federal filings, Baker Botts was paid just $561,461 for its work on the campaign. In other words, it appears that Baker Botts gave the Bush campaign a cut-rate deal for its work on the recount. The Baker Botts fee was the second-highest amount paid to the Bush campaign's various law firms. The largest sum, $892,000, was paid to the powerhouse Los Angeles–based law firm Gibson Dunn & Crutcher. Ted Olson, a lawyer from that firm, argued the case before the Supreme Court.[11] (After the election, Bush appointed Olson his solicitor general).

Baker Botts officials, following the omertà provision of the Bottsian Way, refused to discuss any aspect of their work for the campaign. So perhaps the proper question is not how much Baker was paid, but rather what was the Bush campaign work worth to Baker and Baker Botts? The answer, it appears, is that Baker Botts ended up getting something far more valuable than plain old legal fees. They got access to the Bush White House.

Lots of access.

Chapter 21　The President from Baker Botts
...and Halliburton, and Exxon Mobil

You can call George W. Bush many things. But you can't call him ungrateful. Even before Bush was sworn into office as America's forty-third president, the former mailroom boy at Baker Botts launched what can best be described as a corporate coup de état. And the beneficiaries of Bush's corporate coup were, of course, from the energy business and Baker Botts. He even remembered to give a tax break to his Big Rich buddies.

Nine days before Bush was inaugurated, a group of high-powered energy industry lobbyists met at the American Petroleum Institute's offices in Washington, a few blocks northeast of the White House. And even though it was after Christmas, the lobbyists were writing a wish list. One participant recalled later that the tone of the meeting was "Okay, what do you guys want? You are going to have the ear of this White House." It didn't take long to come up with a list of energy industry wants: easier rules for drilling on federal lands, opening up more drilling in Alaska and the Gulf of Mexico, and lower royalty payments for offshore oil discoveries.

The group finalized their list and sent it off to Bush's transition team. That group included Hunter Hunt, son of the oil baron and Halliburton board member Ray Hunt. The younger Hunt was Bush's "primary Policy Advisor responsible for energy issues" during the transition.[1]

Shortly after Bush was sworn into office, the lobbyists' list was sent to the Interior Department, where it was likely handled by the agency's newly appointed second-in-command, J. Steven Griles. Griles was certainly familiar with the list. He was one of the leaders of the group that had written it a few weeks earlier. An energy industry lobbyist and staunch anti-environmentalist, Griles was appointed deputy interior secretary by George W. Bush. When his appointment was made, an executive at the National Mining Association called him "an ally of the industry."[2] Another veteran of the meeting at the API office was the lawyer-lobbyist Thomas Sansonetti. Like Griles, Sansonetti had lobbied for the coal industry. Shortly after Bush named Gale Norton as his interior secretary, Sansonetti said approvingly that Norton—who'd done legal work for the mining industry—was a good choice because she wouldn't allow any biologists or botanists "to come in and pull the wool over her eyes." Sansonetti's own energy industry credentials made him a shoo-in for the Bush administration's choice to become the head of the environmental division at the Justice Department.

There were plenty of other appointments for the oil and gas industry. One of Bush's first moves was to name his close friend Donald Evans his commerce secretary. Bush needed to give Evans some type of plum. As the chairman of Bush's campaign, Evans was a key player throughout the campaign. No other member of Bush's inner circle had closer ties to the oil industry than Evans, the head of Denver-based Tom Brown Inc. who also sat on the board of a drilling company, TMBR–Sharp Drilling.

Bush's pick for national security adviser was Condoleezza Rice. The provost at Stanford University, Rice had also spent a decade serving on the board of directors at the oil giant Chevron, another major funder of the GOP. During the 2000 election cycle, the company gave $758,588 to Republican causes. While Rice was serving on the com-

SNAPSHOT: BALLPARK PAYBACK

The cronies who helped George W. Bush put the Ballpark at Arlington deal together got more than peanuts and hot dogs for their efforts.

Tom Schieffer, a former Texas legislator and Bush's partner in the Texas Rangers, was named U.S. ambassador to Australia.

Mercer Reynolds, the rich Ohioan who bailed out Bush's failing oil business, Arbusto, by merging it with his own company, Spectrum 7, also got a plum. Reynolds was named ambassador to Switzerland, a job that the *Wall Street Journal* calls "one of the cushiest diplomatic assignments." Reynolds's job in Bern apparently involved sampling various types of chocolate. Reynolds quit the job in 2003 so that he could raise money for Bush's run in 2004.

Richard Greene, the former mayor of Arlington and an S&L executive, who played a key role in getting the Ballpark in Arlington project approved by voters, was named the regional administrator for Region 6 of the Environmental Protection Agency in early 2003. The job gives him authority over federal environmental programs throughout Arkansas, Louisiana, New Mexico, Oklahoma, and Texas. The EPA press release touting Greene's experience did not mention his career in the Texas S&L business. Jim Runzheimer, a lawyer and accountant in Arlington who has been a longtime critic of the Ballpark in Arlington deal, says the Greene appointment made perfect sense. "We had to wait ten years to see what Greene would get back in return for all his support of the ballpark deal. And now we know."

Craig Stapleton, a Big Rich easterner who married Bush's cousin, was named ambassador to the Czech Republic. Stapleton was an investor in the Rangers. He works out of the Schoenborn Palace, a 140-room seventeenth-century landmark in Prague.[3]

Ray Hutchison, the Big Shot lawyer who advised the Rangers and the city of Arlington on the sale of the bonds for the Ballpark at Arlington, didn't get any notable favors from the White House after George W. Bush's election. He really didn't need any. His wife is in the U.S. Senate and he works for Vinson & Elkins. Hutchison has had at least one notable invite: he—along with his wife, Senator Kay Bailey Hutchison—were among the chosen few who attended the very first White House dinner held by George W. and Laura Bush, the September 5, 2001, event honoring President Vicente Fox of Mexico.

pany's board, Chevron was so enamored of her that it even named an oil tanker after her. (In 2001 Chevron renamed the 129,000-ton *Condoleezza Rice* the *Altair Voyager*.)[4]

The Bush administration's friendliness to the energy industry was so extraordinary and unmistakable that *Newsweek* magazine wrote: "Not since the rise of the railroads more than a century ago has a single industry placed so many foot soldiers at the top of a new administration."[5]

Of course, the president didn't forget his pals from Baker Botts. As one of George W. Bush's first appointments, in March of 2001 he named a former Baker Botts lawyer, Patrick Henry Wood III, to America's most powerful energy body, the Federal Energy Regulatory Commission. Wood had been recommended for the job by Enron boss, Ken Lay. Wood had become a Lay favorite during his tenure at the Texas Public Utility Commission, a job for which Lay had also recommended him. With this appointment Bush was following in the footsteps of Richard Nixon, who named a Baker Botts attorney, Rush Moody, to the powerful FERC post in 1971.

Another key government position, the ambassadorship to Saudi Arabia, went to Robert Jordan, the Baker Botts lawyer who'd defended Bush when the Securities and Exchange Commission investigated his alleged insider trading shenanigans at Harken Energy. Jordan had worked for a spate of big corporations such as GTE, Bell Atlantic, and Reliance Insurance. He knew little about energy or Saudi Arabia, but his personal work for Bush on the Harken deal and the Florida recount were the only qualifications needed. In announcing the selection, Bush said that Jordan "understands the important relationship that exists between the United States and Saudi Arabia, and I am confident he will be an outstanding ambassador." Apparently, it didn't matter to Bush that Jordan had never been to Saudi Arabia.[6]

Another Baker Botts lawyer, Kirk Van Tine, who'd worked on the Florida recount, was named general counsel of the Department of

Transportation. The new position gave Van Tine and Baker Botts extraordinary levels of influence. If only James A. Baker III's great-grandfather were alive to see it: one of the firm's lawyers overseeing the legal affairs of an agency that regulates every major railroad in America as well as airlines, trucking, and maritime transport. Yet another Baker Botts lawyer, Bruce McDonald, was appointed by Bush to be a deputy assistant attorney general in the antitrust division of the Justice Department.

While Baker Botts put many of its lawyers in the Bush Administration, the energy companies that gave big donations to Bush's presidential campaign were getting lots of access to Dick Cheney, who was charged with writing the nation's energy policy. The Cheney task force—officially known as the National Energy Policy Development Group—had an enormous challenge: provide a blueprint for America's energy policy for the coming decades. The group met for about three months, planning and meeting—mostly with people in the energy business who'd given big contributions to Bush's campaign.

For instance, Enron's CEO, Ken Lay, got a special private meeting with Dick Cheney to discuss electricity issues in California. In all, Enron officials met with Cheney's task force five times and chatted with them on the phone at least six other times. Enron was just one of dozens of energy-related outfits that got extraordinary access to Cheney and the task force folks. Given all that access, the result was an energy plan that includes the following measures:

- Opens more public lands to oil and gas drilling.
- Provides for the creation of a national electricity grid, a measure that Enron desperately wanted.
- Calls on the U.S. to back the construction of the Baku-Tbilisi-Ceyhan oil pipeline (a project represented by Baker Botts) "as it demonstrates its commercial viability."
- Invests $2 billion in "clean coal" technologies.

- Supports "the expansion of nuclear energy in the United States as a major component of our national energy policy."[7]

The plan was a clear reflection of Cheney's worldview, which he once summed up by saying that "conservation may be a sign of personal virtue, but it is not a sufficient basis for a sound, comprehensive energy policy." Cheney's statement is true. Conservation alone is obviously not the answer to America's future energy needs. But it can be part of a broader, sounder approach to American energy policy that embraces renewable energy, efficiency, and new energy sources alongside the development of traditional carbon-based energy sources.

The Cheney report echoes a long-held belief among Republicans in general and Texas-based Republicans in particular. It was a belief best summarized in 1973 by Richard Nixon's political adviser and hatchet man, John Ehrlichman, who told another Nixon policy maker, "Conservation is not the Republican ethic."

The entirety of Cheney's energy policy can be summarized in one sentence: *We can produce our way out of this mess.* The fundamental approach of Cheney and his minions began by casting aside any discussions about efficiency, conservation, renewables and fuel cells, and focusing solely on how America's major energy companies could produce ever-increasing amounts of fuel. It was an energy policy written by, and for, America's Big Energy companies. That's not surprising. Those were the people that Cheney was listening to throughout the development of the energy policy. In August of 2003, the General Accounting Office released a report that found that one of Cheney's lead advisers on the energy policy plan "solicited detailed energy policy recommendations from a variety of nonfederal energy stakeholders, including the American Petroleum Institute, [and] the National Petrochemical and Refiners' Association." The GAO found that these same officials met with industry representatives from "the American

Coal Company, Small Refiners Association, the Coal Council, CSX, Enviropower, Inc., Detroit Edison, Duke Energy, the Edison Electric Institute, General Motors, the National Petroleum Council, and the lobbying firm of Barbour, Griffith & Rogers."[8] That lobbying firm is run by the former chairman of the Republican National Committee, Haley Barbour, who was an early backer of George W. Bush's presidential campaign. Barbour was a lobbyist for the Southern Company, a major electric utility. In November 2003, Barbour was elected governor of Mississippi.

Shortly after the report came out, the General Accounting Office asked the White House to provide a list of all the entities that met with Cheney's task force. The White House refused. The GAO sued. And lost, thanks to a judge who said it didn't have standing. But other legal challenges, filed by Judicial Watch and the Serra Club, are going forward. Those suits may ultimately force Cheney to release more documents that will show exactly who the National Energy Policy Development Group met with and what they discussed.

While the Bush administration was doing exactly what the energy industry wanted with regard to developing new resources, it was also singing from the same hymnal regarding global warming. Indeed, when it comes to the global warming issue, George W. Bush is keeping his head firmly up his tailpipe.

When Bush got to the White House he refused to consider pushing for the ratification of the Kyoto Protocol, the agreement that would require the United States to dramatically reduce the amount of greenhouse gases it emits. In June of 2002, the Environmental Protection Agency issued a report that said that the climatic changes "observed over the last several decades are likely mostly due to human activities.... There is general agreement that the observed warming is real and has been particularly strong within the past 20 years."

Bush prefers to ignore the consensus view on global warming—

even when it's produced by an official agency of the U.S. government. When asked about the EPA report, he dismissed it with a wave of the hand, saying, "I read the report put out by the bureaucracy."

Bush was—once again—doing the bidding of his big supporters at Exxon Mobil and the American Petroleum Institute. Both entities have led the charge to discredit theories about global warming. Both API and Exxon Mobil have been key financial supporters of the group of flat-earth scientists who have worked to cloud the evidence that supports the belief regarding the warming trend in the earth's atmosphere. Exxon Mobil has provided backing for the Center for the Study of Carbon Dioxide and Global Change in Tempe, Arizona, one of the leading groups that has tried to refute the overwhelming scientific evidence regarding global warming. Exxon Mobil was also a major funder of the Global Climate Coalition, a group funded by the oil and coal industries that lobbied against America's participation in the Kyoto Protocol and other climate change actions during the 1990s. The American Petroleum Institute was another key member of the Global Climate Coalition.

George W. Bush and his father, George H. W. Bush, both have long-standing ties to Exxon Mobil. One of the Bush family's oldest friends is William Stamps Farish III. Perhaps the world's biggest individual holder of Exxon Mobil stock, Farish is the grandson of William Stamps Farish, who, along with Ross Sterling and several others, founded Humble Oil & Refining. In 1933, the elder Farish became president of Standard Oil of New Jersey. During World War II, Farish used his position at Standard Oil to do business with the Nazis. Farish provided a technology for synthetic rubber manufacturing to the German industrial giant I. G. Farben, but refused to make the process available to the United States and Britain. In 1942, he was fined $5,000 by the federal government for trading with the enemy.[9] Farish's other grandfather, Robert E. Wood, was Sears, Roebuck & Co.'s CEO.[10]

These days, Williams Stamps Farish III is a horse breeder worth several hundred million dollars who controls at least $80 million worth of Exxon Mobil stock. He's been a Bush family insider for decades. In the early 1960s, George H. W. Bush tried to get Farish to buy Zapata Off-Shore Drilling. In 1964, when Bush ran for the Senate, Farish was Bush's aide-de-camp, making coffee, preparing speeches, doing legwork. When the elder Bush became vice president, Farish was the administrator of his blind trust. When the elder Bush became president, he often went to Farish's sprawling ranch in south Texas to hunt quail. When George W. Bush ran for the White House, Farish gave $5,000 to Bush's Florida recount fund and another $100,000 to Bush's inaugural fund. When Bush got to the White House, he appointed Farish to be his ambassador to Britain. The Farish-Bush connection can also be inferred from a visit to the Park Laureate office building in Houston. Three tenants have offices on the ninth floor of Park Laureate: George Bush, the Secret Service, and the William Stamps Farish Fund.

While Farish and Exxon Mobil were apparently helping determine the Bush administration's stance on global warming, Bush's brother Jeb was helping determine how to spend a couple hundred million dollars worth of taxpayers' money.

On page one of Cheney's energy policy plan, there's an unequivocal statement. It says that America "must also increase our supply of domestic oil, natural gas, coal, nuclear, and renewable energy sources." An entire section of the report, chapter 5, details how the U.S. should be working to accomplish increases in domestic energy production. And yet, despite these clearly stated goals, George W. Bush decided in May of 2002 to trade BTU's for votes.

That month, as the Bush administration was continuing its saber-rattling campaign against Saddam Hussein, the Interior Department announced that it was going to pay a group of oil companies $235 million *not to drill for oil and gas* in one of the biggest, fastest-growing states in America.

It didn't matter to Bush that the oil companies, which included ConocoPhillips and ChevronTexaco, believed that the already-discovered fields contained at least 700 billion cubic feet of natural gas—enough fuel to supply a million families for three decades or so. What mattered to George W. Bush and the rest of the GOP was that the gas fields were located just off the coast of Florida, the state that had shoehorned Bush into the White House. All that was necessary to get at the gas was to erect an array of rigs easily accessible from the shore.

Perhaps it's a coincidence, but in 2002, the year the White House decided to pay the industry not to go after that gas, the president's brother, Jeb Bush, was up for reelection as Florida's governor.[11] Thus, nearly a quarter billion dollars of taxpayers' money was spent to assure that voters in a critical swing state—Florida—would not have to look at offshore drilling rigs when they go to the beach. The Bush administration apparently decided that offshore drilling is okay in states like Louisiana and Texas, states that can easily be won by Republican presidential candidates. States like Florida, however, shouldn't be drilled for fossil fuels because they must be mined for votes.

Furthermore, it appears that the Bush White House realized that there was no reason to drill off of Florida when there was plenty of oil to be had in Iraq.

THE LEAVE-NO-BILLIONAIRE-BEHIND TAX CUT

Looking for the biggest beneficiaries of George W. Bush's 2003 dividend tax cut? Well, look no further than Rich and Nancy Kinder. Rich, the former president of Enron, and Nancy, the former secretary of Enron's CEO, Ken Lay, are laughing all the way to the bank.

Rich Kinder left Enron in 1996, married Nancy, and now heads Kinder Morgan, three separately traded but interconnected Houston companies that carry about 12 percent of the natural gas and about 15 percent of the gasoline used in America every day. His stake in the Kinder Morgan companies is worth a cool $1.25 billion. In 2003 those companies paid the Kinders about $39 million in cash dividends. Yet their marginal income tax rate on that fortune—thanks to the Bush tax cut—was a mere 15 percent, or about half the rate paid by a middle-class worker making $70,000. Before the Bush tax cut, the Kinders would have paid about 37.6 percent of their income—about $14.8 million—to Uncle Sam. But the tax cut meant they paid just $5.9 million. Thus, the Kinders saved about $8.9 million in taxes.

Between 2000 and 2002, the Kinders, who live in Houston's ritzy River Oaks neighborhood, gave $490,000 to the Republican National Committee. During the Florida recount in 2000, Nancy Kinder was one of 149 Texans who gave the George W. Bush campaign the maximum donation of $5,000. In the summer of 2003, after hosting a fundraiser in Houston for Bush, Nancy Kinder was the very first Texan to join one of the most exclusive clubs on earth when she became a "Ranger"—an appellation reserved by the Bush-Cheney reelection campaign for people who have raised $200,000 for the president's reelection effort.[12]

For most people, $200,000 is a lot of money. For the Kinders, it's about four days' pay.

Chapter 22

Dreaming War

D ick Cheney's 2001 national energy plan contains just one substantive mention of Iraq and its oil reserves. It was made in an attempt to justify the administration's efforts to drill for oil in the Arctic National Wildlife Refuge. If oil is allowed to be taken from the refuge, that production, says the Cheney plan, "could equal 46 years of current oil imports from Iraq."

But Cheney and the Bush White House had another, far less public, report done that could help them justify not the avoidance of dependence on Iraq oil, but the invasion of Iraq. In April 2001, the James A. Baker III Institute for Public Policy at Rice University and the New York–based Council on Foreign Relations completed their report, titled "Strategic Energy Policy Challenges for the 21st Century." The report recommended a number of very reasonable things. In particular, it said the Bush administration should get serious about energy efficiency, conservation, and greenhouse gases. It also said the United States had to get serious about creating an integrated energy policy that was forward-looking and sensible.

But the most remarkable parts of the 107-page report are the parts where it discusses the problem that vexed Texas governor Ross Sterling way back in 1931: controlling the supply of oil. And the critically important oil, according to the report, was the oil coming out of Iraq.

The section of the report dealing with Iraq was written primarily by the Baker Institute's energy expert, Amy Myers Jaffe. It said that global oil markets had grown very tight in the years prior to 2001. And those "tight markets have increased U.S. and global vulnerability to disruption and provided adversaries undue potential influence over the price of oil. Iraq has become a key 'swing' producer, posing a difficult situation for the U.S. government."[1] The report claimed that Iraq had been "turning its taps on and off when it has felt such action was in its strategic interest to do so."

The report goes on to say that "Saddam Hussein is trying to recast himself as the champion of the Palestinian cause to some success among young Palestinians. Any severe violence on the West Bank, Gaza, or Southern Lebanon will give Iraq more leverage in its efforts to discredit the United States and U.S. intentions. A focus on the anti-Israeli sympathies of some Arab oil-producing countries diverts attention from the repressive nature of the Iraqi regime. Instead it rewards Iraq in its claim to Arab leadership."

The report says that the United States should immediately review its policies toward Iraq and that the goal should be to "set the groundwork to eventually ease Iraqi oil-field investment restrictions." Iraq is a "destabilizing influence to U.S. allies in the Middle East, as well as to regional and global order, and to *the flow of oil to international markets*" (emphasis added). It goes on to say that Saddam Hussein has shown "willingness to threaten to use the oil weapon and to use his own export program to manipulate oil markets.... The United States should conduct an immediate policy review toward Iraq, including military, energy, economic, and political/diplomatic assessments."[2]

Old Ross Sterling himself couldn't have made a better case for taking control of Iraq's oilfields. Iraq was a destabilizing influence. And worse yet, Saddam Hussein was a threat to the flow of oil to world oil markets.

But was Iraq really a serious threat to the flow of oil to international markets? Mike Ameen doesn't think so. An expert on Middle East oil, Ameen, a retired executive who lives in Houston, says that Jaffe and her coauthors "were exaggerating the danger of Saddam to world oil markets. He didn't control anything but Iraqi oil and it wasn't much when compared to the broader market." An American-born son of Lebanese immigrants, Ameen worked in the Middle East oil business for 35 years. During his career, he worked for Aramco and Mobil. He speaks, reads, and writes Arabic and met directly with Saddam Hussein twice over the course of his career. "Sure, Saddam could cause a few problems. But not major problems. He wasn't a threat where he'd go out and damage Kuwait or Saudi Arabia," or the other oil-exporting countries of the region, Ameen told me.

Furthermore, Ameen points out that the Iraqis were smuggling huge amounts of oil on the black market despite the United Nations' restrictions of the sale of Iraqi oil. "Saddam was selling every barrel he could under the table, over the table, and everywhere else. He was smuggling oil out every chance that he had," says Ameen. And that smuggling was serving to lower the price of oil in the region. In February of 2000, the *Chicago Tribune* carried a front-page story that estimated that Saddam's government was smuggling out 200,000 barrels of oil per day. The article, by reporter John Diamond, even quoted a State Department official who acknowledged that the United States was "loath to intervene" to stop the smuggling because so much of the Iraqi oil was going into countries that were getting American military aid, including Turkey, Qatar, Bahrain, Oman, and the United Arab Emirates.[3]

While Hussein was smuggling oil, he was also bucking the restrictions imposed by the United Nations' Oil for Food program—which closely monitored and controlled Iraq's oil exports. On several occasions, Hussein *did* withhold Iraqi oil from the U.N. program, and those actions *did* apparently affect world oil prices. There were also news reports that suggested that Hussein or his agents were playing the oil futures markets in order to profit from the price fluctuations that occurred thanks to his decision to withhold oil.

Both Jaffe and Ed Morse, the chairman of the task force, who worked in the Carter administration and is the former publisher of *Petroleum Intelligence Weekly,* told me that there was no disagreement among the three dozen members of the Baker Institute / CFR task force that produced the report (Enron CEO Ken Lay was one of them) concerning the sections that dealt with Iraq. But several members of the bipartisan task force told me that they were not aware of the sections in the report that dealt with Iraq. One of them, Ed Rothschild, the former energy policy director at the consumer group Citizen Action, told me that he was only consulted about matters relating to energy efficiency and renewable energy. "I would never have considered Iraq a threat," he said.

Jaffe, in an e-mail, defended the task force, saying that it was "not a Republican or neo-conservative group." And she added, "It is my personal opinion that Iraq's manipulation of the oil market is NOT the reason that the Bush Administration went to war in Iraq."

Although the report may not have been written by the neoconservatives, its conclusions about Iraq and its oil were in line with the thinking of a right-wing group of hot-for-war-against-Saddam-Hussein stalwarts known as the Project for the New American Century. Created in 1997, the group consisted of neoconservatives, or "neocons," who believe that the United States must eliminate or intimidate any entity that poses a threat to this country's predominance in economic and military power. The founding members of the group included Dick Cheney, Donald Rumsfeld, Paul Wolfowitz, and Jeb Bush. On January 26, 1998, the hawks from the Project for the New American Century sent a letter to President Bill Clinton. The third sentence declares that America must "enunciate a new strategy that would secure the interests of the U.S. and our friends and allies around the world. That strategy should aim, above all, at the removal of Saddam Hussein's regime from power."[4]

Remember, this letter was written in 1998. And it was signed by men who joined the highest levels of the U.S. government upon George W. Bush's victory in 2000. The signers of the letter included Donald Rumsfeld, who became defense secretary; Paul Wolfowitz, who became deputy defense secretary; Richard Perle, who became a member of the Defense Policy Board; Richard Armitage, who became deputy secretary of state; John Bolton, who became undersecretary of state for disarmament; and Zalmay Khalilzad, who became the White House's liaison to the Iraqi opposition. (Dick Cheney did not sign the 1998 letter.)

After the deadly attacks of September 11, 2001, the calls from Rumsfeld and the other signatories of the 1998 letter grew louder still and they began to press their agenda. The Bush administration quickly decided that it was going to invade Iraq. And it was going to attack regardless of whether Saddam Hussein had anything to do with the terrorists or not. The propaganda war would be fought by accusing Saddam of holding weapons of mass destruction, of funding the terrorists that launched the September 11 attack, and by claiming that Saddam was conducting a nuclear arms program—as Bush did in his State of the Union address on January 28, 2003, with the now-infamous 16 words: "The British government has learned that Saddam Hussein recently sought significant quantities of uranium from Africa."

As the Bush administration's drumbeat for war grew ever louder, the Baker Institute produced another report. The think tank, again in cooperation with the Council on Foreign Relations, wrote a paper recommending strategies for dealing with Iraq and its resources after the war. Prominent among the report's recommendations were suggestions on how the Americans should deal with Iraq's oil resources after the war. Specifically, the report said that the U.S. should try, before the war, to "identify the assets that could, if severely damaged or destroyed during military hostilities, substantially delay resumption of the Iraqi oil export program."[5]

The two lead writers of that report were Edward Djerejian, the director of the Baker Institute, and Frank Wisner. Both had close ties to the oil industry. Djerejian, an Arab specialist and former ambassador to Israel and Syria, is on the board of the third-largest oilfield services company in the world, Houston-based Baker Hughes. He's also on the board of directors at Occidental Petroleum, which is a participant in a massive natural gas pipeline project in Qatar and the United Arab Emirates known as the Dolphin Project. Much of the engineering work on the Dolphin Project is being done by Halliburton.[6] Both Baker Hughes and Occidental have been active in the Persian Gulf for decades.

Frank Wisner has long ties to the American intelligence business and to Enron. The son of a well-known CIA officer, Frank Wisner Sr., he worked at the Agency for International Development in Vietnam from 1964 to 1969 and later served as ambassador to Egypt, then to the Philippines, and then to India. Upon retiring from the ambassador's job in India, Wisner was hired by Enron Corp. to help push the company's investment in the Dabhol power plant, the ill-fated project that ended up costing Enron about $1 billion. Since 1997, Wisner has been on the board of directors of EOG Resources, a publicly traded oil and gas company that used to be known as Enron Oil and Gas.

Thus, while Djerejian and Wisner were paid directors of major energy companies—and no doubt advising them about their foreign operations—they were also telling the U.S. government that it needed to seize Iraq's oilfields as soon as the shooting started, if not sooner.

The challenge of taking over Iraq wasn't going to be easy. The military planners in the Pentagon realized that if they were going to take over the second-largest oil reserves on earth, they were going to need help. They'd need an entity that could manage and repair oil wells, pipelines, refineries, and ports. They'd also need an outfit that could do construction, build roads, and handle logistics for the military.

They needed an outfit like Halliburton.

By 2002, no other corporation in America was more closely wired into the Pentagon power structure than Halliburton. The company's employees were maintaining bases and feeding soldiers at military sites in the Balkans, Africa, Afghanistan, and Kyrgyzstan. The company built the legal-no-man's-land detention camps in Guantanamo Bay, Cuba—the locale that houses alleged members of the Taliban and al-Qaeda who were captured during America's invasion of Afghanistan, as well as alleged terrorists who were handed over to the U.S. by other countries.

All of that work had been lucrative. The company was building the new $100 million U.S. embassy in Kabul, Afghanistan. It had a five-year $300 million logistics contract with the U.S. Navy and a 10-year logistics contract with the U.S. Army. That Army contract had no dollar limit and was reportedly the only logistics deal the military agreed to that didn't have an estimated cost. Halliburton was seeing the potential war as a growth opportunity. In its 2002 annual report, the company wrote that demand for its services are "expected to grow . . . as governmental agencies seek to control costs and promote efficiencies by outsourcing." It continued, "We also expect growth due to new demands created by increased efforts to combat terrorism and enhance homeland security."

That growth became a reality in November of 2002, when the Pentagon asked Dick Cheney's old company to come up with a contingency plan for cleaning up Iraq after the U.S. military had chased Saddam Hussein out of his mink-lined lair. On March 8, 2003, the U.S. Army Corps of Engineers quietly signed a contract with Halliburton

that called on the company to extinguish any oil well fires, to rehabili-
tate Iraq's oilfield infrastructure, and to provide motor fuel and other
supplies to the citizens of Iraq. The contract with Halliburton, which
had a potential value of $7 billion, was not put out for competitive
bids. Details about the contract—including the profit margins, personnel numbers and other details—were not revealed.

In the weeks after the contract was awarded, Halliburton's ties to
the U.S. military were being questioned by most major media outlets
in America. In April of 2003, CBS-TV's *60 Minutes* said, "The early winners in the sweepstakes to rebuild Iraq have one thing in common: lots
of very close friends in very high places." One of the Halliburton
employees interviewed about the Iraq contract was Chuck Dominy,
the company's vice president for government affairs and its chief lobbyist in Washington. Cheney's influence had "absolutely zero impact"
on the Army's decision to award the contract to Halliburton, Dominy
said.

Perhaps Cheney didn't "impact" the contract. But Dominy might
have. He was hired to work at Halliburton in 1996, during Cheney's
tenure at the company. His previous job was as a three-star general in
the U.S. Army. And one of his last jobs in the military was as a commander at the U.S. Army Corps of Engineers—the very agency that
was awarding contracts to Halliburton.[7]

The war business was good business for Halliburton. It was so
good that in the summer of 2003, *Business Week* magazine could write,
"All in all, no corporation has played as central a role in America's
global anti-terrorism campaign—or profited as handsomely from it" as
Halliburton.[8]

Chapter 23

"It's Not About Oil!"—Part II

The oil revenues of that country [Iraq] could bring between fifty and one hundred billion dollars over the course of the next two or three years.

—Deputy Defense Secretary Paul Wolfowitz, testifying before Congress about the Second Iraq War, March 27, 2003

Twelve years after the end of the First Iraq War, George H. W. Bush was still reading from the same script.

On March 25, 2003—five days after the Navy SEALs stormed aboard the Mina al-Bakr oil terminal to start the Second Iraq War—the former president gave a speech at the Marriott Rivercenter Hotel in San Antonio. His audience: the National Petrochemical and Refiners Association.

Bush Senior was a little peeved. Not at his allies in the oil and chemical industry, of course. The National Petrochemical and Refiners Association, a group whose membership includes "virtually all U.S. refiners and petrochemical manufacturers," was a friendly audience. He was angry at those misguided protesters who were staging huge antiwar rallies all over the country. Those demonstrators had gotten under Bush's skin. He was particularly inflamed by the signs that the demonstrators were carrying that said "No war for oil." Bush said he'd seen similar protests and similar signs prior to the First Iraq War. And now that the Second Iraq War was under way, he was still contending that the protesters were mistaken. "This is not about oil," he told the refiners.[1]

At about the same time the elder Bush was delivering that message, U.S. and British troops were in a furious battle with Iraqi tank companies for control of the Rumaila, Majnoon, Qurnah, and Nahr Umr oilfields near Basra. Those four fields contain an estimated 51 billion barrels of oil. As Bush was speaking to the refiners, firefighters from the Kuwait Oil Company were snuffing out the flames at one of the seven oil wells near Basra that had been set aflame by forces loyal to Saddam Hussein. At about the same time, 1,000 troops from the 173rd Airborne Brigade were being airlifted into northern Iraq. Their task was to capture the oilfields around Kirkuk. The troops were being backed up by American warplanes, which were beginning to bomb Iraqi strongholds around Kirkuk. The oilfields around Kirkuk hold about 16 billion barrels of oil.

While U.S. troops were invading the oilfields, the younger Bush, from his perch in the White House, refused to even discuss the oil question. Instead, the president's focus was on the evils of Saddam Hussein and his alleged weapons of mass destruction program. Bush talked about Saddam's "nucular" weapons and claimed that the Iraqi dictator had huge stashes of VX, sarin, and mustard gas that had to be found and destroyed. And while George W. Bush continued his stream of rhetorical attacks on Iraq, his key aides were looking at Iraq's oil and seeing it as a massive piggy bank. They dreamed of a type of drive-through-pay-for-itself-car-wash type of war.

On March 27, two days after Bush Senior spoke to the refiners, Deputy Defense Secretary Paul Wolfowitz testified before Congress about the rapidly progressing war. Wolfowitz, one of the leaders of the neoconservative movement, told Congress that the Second Iraq War wouldn't be overly expensive for American taxpayers. "We're dealing with a country that can really finance its own reconstruction, and relatively soon," he told Congress. Asked how much the Second

Iraq War would cost, Wolfowitz stuttered out: "And my—a rough rec-
ollection—well I'm—the oil revenues of that country could bring
between $50 and $100 billion over the course of the next two or three
years."[2]

Alas, Wolfowitz hadn't done his homework. Even the most opti-
mistic oil experts were projecting that Iraq's oilfields would be ham-
pered for some time to come as a result of a lack of investment in
infrastructure. At best, they estimated that Iraq's oilfields were capable
of producing revenues of only about $10 billion per year.[3]

But Wolfowitz couldn't trouble himself with learning the facts.
Instead, he and his fellow neoconservatives were figuring out how
they could divvy up the spoils of war. Within a few days of his outlandish estimates of Iraq's oil wealth, other pro-Israel hawks inside the
Pentagon began talking to the Israelis about building a pipeline from
the Iraqi oilfields near Kirkuk to the Israeli port of Haifa. A small
pipeline had operated along that route in the 1940s, and the neocons
apparently believed that it was time to build a pipeline from the heart
of Arabia to the heart of the Zionist homeland.

Ensuring a reliable supply of oil to its ally Israel had been one of
America's main obligations in the region for nearly three decades. In
1975, Henry Kissinger signed an agreement that requires the U.S. to
guarantee the flow of oil to Israel during times of crisis. Kissinger was
also a key architect of the plan, pushed by Donald Rumsfeld when he
met with Saddam Hussein in 1983, to build a pipeline from Iraq to the
Jordanian port of Aqaba.

America's oil supply agreement with the Israelis has been renewed
every five years. The deal requires the United States to supply oil to
Israel even if it causes domestic shortages of oil in America. Although
the U.S. has not ever had to make good on the agreement, a pipeline,
reasoned the neocons, could help secure Israel's energy needs, and
provide another way to ship Iraqi oil to the markets and shipping lanes

on the Mediterranean Sea.[4] The pipeline would have huge economic benefits to the Israelis, lowering their oil import bills by as much as 25 percent. The Israelis even began estimating what the pipeline would cost.[5] Unfortunately, a pipeline from Iraq to Israel also would have been a diplomatic disaster. For decades, the Arab oil-producing countries have been objecting to America's ongoing support of the Israelis. And the idea of running a pipeline through Jordan (nearly impossible from a political standpoint) or Syria (absolutely impossible politically) so that the Israelis could have cheap Arab oil, would have been met with outrage by Arab leaders—and a fusillade of terrorists' bombs in their countries.

When news about the pipeline project began surfacing in the British media in April of 2003, James Akins, a former U.S. ambassador to Saudi Arabia, said the plans laid bare America's real motives. "It just goes to show that it is all about oil, for the United States and its ally," he said.[6]

At the same time that the United States was chatting up the Israelis about a pipeline, American troops had subdued Baghdad. But the soldiers made only token efforts to secure Baghdad's cultural treasures and stop the looting that started as soon as the city fell. The result was horrifying. Government offices were ransacked. Stores were looted. Saddam Hussein's palaces were stripped of furniture and fixtures. The National Library of Iraq, the National Archives, and the central libraries of the Universities of Baghdad and Mosul were all looted and burned. Priceless manuscripts, documents, and books were lost. The National Museum of Antiquities was also looted. Assyrian marble carvings, Babylonian statues, and clay pots thousands of years old were all smashed to bits.

The Oil Ministry building, however, wasn't touched. That was not a coincidence. One of the first sites secured by American troops after they got to Baghdad on April 8 was the Oil Ministry building. For the next few days, as the looting continued all around the city, a detachment of American G.I.s with a half dozen assault vehicles stood guard at the Oil Ministry building. On April 13, 2003, the *Washington Post* quoted one Iraqi citizen who asked why the looting was allowed in other buildings and not in the Oil Ministry: "Why just the Oil Ministry?" he asked. "Is it because they just want our oil?"[7] Three days later, Agence France Presse reported that some four dozen U.S. tanks were guarding the ministry building and that "sharpshooters are positioned on the roof and in the windows."

By early June of 2003, Halliburton's technicians were clambering all over Iraq's oil facilities, assessing the damage and making repairs. One of their first stops was Mina al-Bakr.[8] Halliburton did its job well. In late June 2003, about eight weeks after George W. Bush's May 1 "mission accomplished" declaration aboard the USS *Abraham Lincoln* that "major combat operations in Iraq have ended," the country's black gold began to flow.

On June 28, 2003, the first super tanker to load Iraqi crude in the post-Saddam era began filling up at Mina al-Bakr. The buyer of the oil was Condoleezza Rice's old employer, ChevronTexaco. A few dozen hours later, the tanker, loaded with two million barrels of crude known as Basra Light, left Mina al-Bakr and headed straight for refineries—in the United States.[9] Over the next few months, dozens of other supertankers begin filling their holds with Iraqi oil, and the majority of those tankers headed for the United States.

With U.S. troops guarding the Iraqi Oil Ministry in downtown Baghdad and Halliburton employees manning the controls at Mina al-Bakr and other oil facilities, the Bush administration had achieved its goal: the second-largest oil reserves on earth were under the control of the United States. Nearly 30 years after OPEC shut off the flow of oil to America in retaliation for its support of the Israelis, the U.S. had gained a measure of control over Persian Gulf oil supplies. And it had done it behind the barrel of a gun.

Governor Ross Sterling of Texas would have understood the situation perfectly. There were key differences, however, between the American invasion of Iraq and Sterling's 1931 takeover of the oilfields of East Texas. Sterling's operation came cheap: just 1,200 National Guardsmen were needed to control the region's oilfields. The cost of the campaign was less than $30,000 per week (about $357,100 in 2002 dollars).[10] There were no casualties—in fact, not a single person was hurt. The Texas Rangers made only a handful of arrests. And the action was quick: all of the Guardsmen were back home with their families by December of 1932, a mere 16 months after the action began. The only casualty of the campaign occurred several months after the Guardsmen went home. In the summer of 1933, a Texas Ranger, Emmett White, was killed outside of Kilgore in an accident involving an oil truck.

Seventy-two years after Sterling's forces invaded East Texas, another Texas governor was having a far harder time gaining control of a critically important oil-producing area. To win the Second Iraq War, George W. Bush deployed some 140,000 American soldiers and 21,000 soldiers from Britain and other countries to Kuwait and Iraq.

The costs were extraordinary: during the war, an estimated 10,000 Iraqis were killed.[11] Between the start of hostilities in March 2003 and mid-January 2004, more than 500 American GIs were killed and another 9,000 had been injured in battle, hurt in accidents, or had become seriously ill.[12] Sabotage, snipers, and almost-daily car bombings were testing the will and patience of America's soldiers and their commanders.

The financial costs were mind-numbing. By the end of 2003, the occupation of Iraq was costing American taxpayers about $1 billion per week, and that figure was only part of their financial burden. Rebuilding Iraq and maintaining the peace were costing even more. Those costs were going to be huge, even though none of George W. Bush's stated reasons for going to war—Saddam's "nucular" weapons, his stashes of poison gas, and his links to al-Qaeda and terrorism—had been found. By early 2004, despite months of frantic searching, American investigators had not found any evidence that Iraq had weapons of mass destruction. Even after Saddam Hussein was found on December 14, 2003, and questioned by U.S. interrogators, no weapons of mass destruction were found.

In September of 2003, George W. Bush asked the U.S. Congress to approve an $87 billion spending package to pay for the war and for reconstruction efforts in Iraq. Not surprisingly, a big chunk of that money was going to Dick Cheney's old company, Halliburton.

When Bush went to Congress, Halliburton had already been paid about $2 billion for its work in Iraq. The company had 4,500 people on its payroll, and it was hard to tell the Halliburton employees from the U.S. military. Some were working at oil installations like Mina al-Bakr. Others were delivering mail to U.S. troops. Others were cooking meals, doing laundry, and building military bases. Like the soldiers, Halliburton employees were dying. By January 2004, more than a dozen Halliburton workers or subcontractors had been killed while carrying out their duties in Iraq.[13]

For his part, Dick Cheney went on television in September of 2003 to defend his ongoing payments from Halliburton. Cheney insisted that he had "no financial interest in Halliburton of any kind." This was incorrect: when Cheney made that statement, he still had options on about 433,000 shares of Halliburton stock. He was also in the second year of a five-year deferred-compensation deal with Halliburton. In 2002, Cheney received deferred compensation payments from Halliburton that totaled $162,392. That sum was on top of the $205,298 in deferred compensation that Cheney received in 2001.[14] As vice president, Cheney's annual salary is $198,600.

Cheney also defended his old employer, saying he had "no idea" why Halliburton got the no-bid oilfield-repair contract. But he did say that there are "few companies out there that have the combination of the very large engineering construction capability and significant oil field services." In other words, after decades of getting closer and closer to the U.S. government and the U.S. military, Halliburton had become the Pentagon's only choice. It could feed troops, build camps, fix pipelines, repair oil wells, and do everything else America's army of occupation needed. In Iraq, Halliburton became example 1A of what the economist James Kenneth Galbraith has called the "military-petroleum complex."[15]

In Iraq, the U.S. government, the military, corporate America, and the oil business became one.

Chapter 24   Minister of Nondisclosure

Although the Second Iraq War ensured that the United States would control the flow of oil out of Iraq for the foreseeable future, the war also created a global diplomatic mess. In his rush to invade Iraq George W. Bush strained relationships with countries all over the world. None of the countries of "Old Europe"—such as France and Germany—had believed the United States' claims about the immediate need to wage war against Saddam Hussein.

As the major fighting ended in Iraq, Bush realized he needed help. Once again he turned to James A. Baker III for assistance in straightening things out. Baker was quick to oblige. After all, doing favors for the president was good for Baker and what was good for Jim Baker was definitely good for Baker Botts. Thus, Baker became George W. Bush's proxy for two major oil-related problems: the growing unrest in the Republic of Georgia, and Iraq's $120 billion foreign debt load. We'll look at Georgia first.

On July 3, 2003, Bush named Baker his special envoy to the Republic of Georgia. Baker's task in that role was to discuss "ways to advance political and economic reform in Georgia through free and fair Parliamentary elections this fall." The very next day, Baker, armed with his special-envoy status, was in Tbilisi, meeting with his old pal, Georgia's president, Eduard Shevardnadze. The two men had been acquainted for more than 15 years. They'd talked frequently when Baker was secretary of state and Shevardnadze was the Soviet Union's foreign minister. After the collapse of the Soviet Union, the two men became friends. In 1999, Shevardnadze traveled to Houston, where he and Baker held a "town hall" meeting at which they discussed the peaceful end of the Cold War. After their discussion, the James A. Baker III Institute for Public Policy conferred upon Shevardnadze the Enron Prize for Distinguished Public Service.

But by mid-2003, Shevardnadze's political standing in Georgia had become tenuous. Demonstrations against his administration were frequent, and it was not clear that he could continue to stay in power.

Baker, meanwhile, was more powerful than ever. At the same time that Baker was meeting with the Georgian president as an official of the U.S. government, he also had the opportunity to attend to the needs of a few Baker Botts clients.

- Baker Botts is the law firm for the Baku-Tbilisi-Ceyhan Pipeline Company, making sure that the $3.5 billion pipeline project, which depends on cooperation from the Georgian government, stays on track.
- Baker Botts represents Halliburton, which has huge interests in the region. Just before Baker's meeting with Shevardnadze, Halliburton was named a lead engineering contractor for the development of the giant 4.3 billion–barrel Azeri-Chirag oilfield, one of the biggest fields in oil-rich Azerbaijan.
- Another Baker Botts client, the Azerbaijan International Operating Company, is a major oil producer in and around the Caspian Sea. AIOC is keenly interested in using the Baku-Tbilisi-Ceyhan pipeline to ship its oil to market.

- Yet another Baker Botts client, Exxon Mobil, is one of the principal investors in AIOC. Exxon Mobil is involved in more deals in Azerbaijan than any other American oil company.

It's not immediately clear why Bush needed to appoint a special envoy to Georgia. The U.S. ambassador to Georgia, Richard Monroe Miles, could have conveyed any important messages from the White House to Shevardnadze. Miles, a career diplomat who'd spent 36 years in the Foreign Service, working at postings from Moscow to Belgrade, was well qualified to do just that. And he'd already spent 15 months at the U.S. embassy in Tbilisi, getting acquainted with his Georgian counterparts.

Miles may have been a diplomat, but he wasn't an oilman. Baker knows the oil business, and he has made it clear that when it comes to the Caspian region, America's security interests revolve around energy. In 1997, Baker wrote an op-ed for the *New York Times* in which he discussed Georgia's importance to America. Georgia, Baker wrote, "is poised to be a principal outlet for bringing the oil and gas resources of the Caspian Sea to international markets. Caspian oil may eventually be as important to the industrialized world as Middle East oil is today. Georgia's future security, therefore, is important to America's security."[1]

In the fall of 2003, when I caught up briefly with Baker to ask him about his visit to Georgia, he insisted that he didn't know that the Baku-Tbilisi-Ceyhan Pipeline Company was a client of Baker Botts's, even though the firm had been working for the pipeline for six years. He also denied discussing anything with Shevardnadze other than election reform. But Baker, irritated by the question, said it would not have been improper for him to raise the pipeline issue with the Georgian president. "It would have made sense for me to talk to him about it [the pipeline] if I'd known about it. Wouldn't it? And there wouldn't have been any conflict of interest or anything—would there?" snapped Baker.

The timing of Baker's meeting with Shevardnadze is important because the Georgian government has balked at several provisions of the pipeline agreement and the country's environment minister has opposed the routing of certain sections of the pipe. The pipeline is critically important to Georgia, which could get nearly half of its future revenue from the massive project.[2]

While Baker may have wanted free elections, that's not what happened. One report said that there was "spectacular" fraud during the November 2003 election. In one case, 95 percent of the voters cast their ballots for a key Shevardnadze ally.[3] Although Shevardnadze was reelected, the election fraud led to his downfall. On November 23 he resigned, culminating what has since become known as Georgia's "Rose Revolution." In January 2004 Georgia elected a new president, Mikhail Saakashvili, a U.S.-educated lawyer who was the former opposition leader.

Despite the unrest, construction on the massive pipeline project has stayed on schedule—a fact that is surely comforting to Baker and his fellow lawyers at Baker Botts as well as to BP, Exxon Mobil, and the other major oil companies who have invested billions of dollars in the region.

Shortly after Shevardnadze's fall from power, Bush turned to Baker again. This time it was to negotiate with lenders about Iraq's huge foreign debt. Without debt relief, the leaders of the Bush administration knew, it would be impossible for Iraq's economy to recover. There was simply no way that Iraq's oil production could pay back the country's debt and also pay for the massive infrastructure-rebuilding program that would be needed for Iraq to become a country with a viable economy. Someone was needed who could persuade creditor nations to forgive the loans or accept significantly reduced repayment.

In mid-December of 2003, President Bush appointed Baker to be the Iraq debt "czar," and thus, in the wake of the Second Iraq War, Baker became one of the most powerful and important international representatives of the United States. In some ways Baker occupied a more important position than Colin Powell, the secretary of state. For weeks Baker traveled all over the world, meeting with bankers and politicos to convince them that they should forgive all or part of the loans they had extended to Saddam Hussein's corrupt regime in Iraq. And Baker was successful. The former secretary of state—while carefully avoiding talking to reporters—got leaders from Germany, France, Saudi Arabia, Kuwait, the United Arab Emirates, Qatar, and Japan to agree to reduce the amount of their outstanding loans with Iraq. The amount of debt each country agreed to forgive was not made public.

The public also was not allowed to learn about Baker's personal interests. Baker—the man who helped convince the Saudis to invest in the Carlyle Group—was able to convince some of those same Saudis to forgive part of the debt racked up by Saddam Hussein. Were there any quid pro quos with the Saudis or any of the other people Baker met with to discuss Iraq's situation? Were any financial incentives given to Carlyle or big American banks or Baker himself in return for these countries' easing their demands for repayment of loans? That's impossible to say. No information has been made public on any special agreements made by governments and private corporations or banks.

Furthermore, the Bush administration has arranged things so that Baker need never disclose anything about his personal finances in connection with his "Iraq debt czar" activities. Shortly after Bush appointed Baker to the post, the White House released a statement that Baker would not be paid for his work and that he would "comply with all applicable ethics laws and rules including the filing of a financial disclosure form, disclosing his assets and incomes, liabilities and outside positions." It appears that Baker filled out the forms. But the White House quietly made sure that Baker's disclosure was actually no disclosure at all.

You see, the White House used a rather obscure federal statute that was designed to exempt "less senior, executive branch employees" as well as "special government employees" from disclosure laws. The Bush White House used this statute (5CFR 2364.901) to designate Baker a special government employee and thus to ensure that his financial disclosure form would not be released. Thus, the public cannot know who Baker's clients or what Baker's business interests are.

According to a White House spokesman, Baker's financial disclosure form was filed with the White House general counsel's office. The White House did not say who reviewed Baker's financial disclosure nor what standards were applied to determine what might be considered a conflict of interest between his role as a government envoy and his professional relationship with clients or his interest in certain investments. All of Baker's financial interests can remain secret even while he functions as a high-profile representative of the U.S. government.

For the record, the section of the federal law that covers financial disclosure in Baker's case states that the statute was created in order to "guarantee the efficient and honest operation of the Government."

Chapter 25   A Black-Tie Affair

There was more oil money sloshing around than there'd been in Prince William Sound after the grounding of the *Exxon Valdez*. But Dick Cheney, the guest of honor and keynote speaker, didn't mention oil, or energy, during his 20-minute speech. Not once.

It just didn't seem right. The October 17, 2003, black-tie gala—with its minimum entry donation of $750 per person—was a celebration of Houston as a first-tier city in world affairs. It was a celebration of the tenth anniversary of the James A. Baker III Institute for Public Policy at Rice University, the favorite think tank of the Bush administration. It was an event celebrating Houston, the energy capital of the world. Energy money was paying for the jazz quintet, the 10,000 pink roses flown in from florists across the nation, the 77 dining tables, the massive tent, the chandeliers, the brigade of waiters, the cops on horseback, and lots more.

The gala was also a celebration of the Texas nexus—the place where energy money, political power, lobbying, and government are all combined into one big cocktail. And the chief bartender for the evening was the vice president of the United States. Dick Cheney was there as a personal favor to Baker, his longtime political ally. The two had been pals for nearly 30 years. Cheney had given Baker his first opportunity in national politics when, as Gerald Ford's chief of staff, he got Baker involved in running Ford's unsuccessful effort to stay in the White House in 1976. Years later the two were key architects of the First Iraq War, Cheney as defense secretary and Baker as secretary of state. They served on corporate boards together, hunted and fished together, and throughout, fought off the pesky Democrats. They stood shoulder to shoulder during the Florida Recount. In fact, on November 7, 2000, after the polls closed and the ballots were being counted, Baker and Cheney shared a hotel suite in Austin where they monitored the dramatic tallying of the votes.

After Baker helped the Bush campaign secure its victory in Florida, Cheney owed him a favor. And by agreeing to be the keynote speaker at the Baker Institute's gala, Cheney was doing him one.

The gala was one of the biggest events of Houston's social season. Before dinner, liveried waiters in white gloves served hors d'oeuvres: foie gras, salmon tartar, and lemon mousse. Others carried around bottles of wine, eagerly refilling empty glasses. Three open bars served cocktails. The quintet played standards like "All of Me" and "Route 66."

Security was tighter than Dick's hatband. Dozens of uniformed cops patrolled the Rice campus. Police on horseback were stationed at regular intervals along a temporary perimeter fence that had been erected in a three-block circumference around the Baker Institute. All guests were required to walk through a metal detector.

The Big Shots who wrote big checks for the event included Exxon Mobil, ConocoPhillips, and Shell Oil Company (combined market capitalization on the day of the event for those three companies: $396 billion), all of whom paid $100,000 to be "tenth anniversary cohosts" of the soiree. The Baker Institute got another $100,000 from Prince Bandar bin Sultan, the longtime Saudi ambassador to the United States and a crony of James A. Baker III's. (He's also the son of Prince Sultan, one of Baker Botts's many clients.) Bandar did not attend the gala.

The biggest donor to the gala was an energy guy. And he provides a link between modern Texas and the halcyon days of the Shah of Iran. Hushang Ansary, who was the Shah's economics minister and, after that, Iran's ambassador to the United States, gave $250,000 for the honor of being a "tenth anniversary host" of the gala. Ansary fled Iran in 1979. And it appears that he left the country with a bit of money in his pocket. After moving to the United States, Ansary got into various penny stock schemes while living in a huge mansion on Long Island.[1] Later, Ansary got into the oilfield equipment business and became a major donor to the GOP. In 1998 he gave $100,000 to the Florida Republican Party, money that helped Jeb Bush win the state's gubernatorial race. Asked about his big donation, Ansary told the *Washington Post,* "I am a great believer in Republican causes." He wasn't kidding. Between 2000 and mid-2003, he gave $550,000 or so to Republican causes, including more than $500,000 to the Republican National Committee. He also gave $4,000 to George W. Bush's presidential campaigns and $5,000 to Bush's Florida recount effort in 2000. Ansary is the largest individual shareholder of Houston-based National Oilwell, Inc. On the night of the gala, Ansary's stake in that company was worth about $16.7 million.

By giving $100,000 or more, Ansary and the other folks who wrote big checks were invited to attend a "private VIP reception with illustrious dignitaries" (read Dick and Lynne Cheney) before dinner began. They also got a "prime table for 10 guests" at the event. The prime tables were located on a riser in the middle of a 40-foot-high white tent that had been erected for the gala next door to Baker Hall, the home of the Baker Institute. The Cheneys and the Bakers, along with Shahla and Hushang Ansary, sat at the head table on the riser. Employees from the companies that gave $50,000—a list that included Aramco Services (an arm of the giant Saudi oil company), Marathon Oil Corporation, and BP—also got to sit on the riser with the Cheneys and the Bakers.

Dick Cheney's old employer, Halliburton, gave $25,000, and this allowed the company to have a special table at the gala. Other Halliburton types were on the guest list, too, including Anne Armstrong, the longtime Halliburton board member and adviser to Richard Nixon. Another special guest was the former Halliburton CEO Thomas Cruikshank, the man who recruited Cheney to work for the firm.

The guest list had a strong whiff of Enron, too.

In November of 2001, just days before the energy trading company went bankrupt, the institute had provided the forum for the awarding of the Enron Prize for Distinguished Public Service, endowed by Enron and awarded every year by the James A. Baker III Institute for Public Policy. The prize, which was presented by Enron's CEO, Ken Lay, and James A. Baker III, went to the chair of the Federal Reserve, Alan Greenspan. That was one of the last times that Ken Lay got to be a Big Shot in Houston. It was also apparently the last time anyone on the Rice University campus has mentioned anything having to do with the Enron Prize.

The Enron Prize may be defunct, but the Enron refugees are still in Houston. Two former members of Enron's board of directors, John Duncan and John Mendelsohn, were part of the "honorary committee" for the Baker Institute gala. Harry Reasoner, one of Enron's key lawyers and Ken Lay's longtime pal, was also on the list. Reasoner was the managing partner of Vinson & Elkins, the law firm that handled Enron's legal affairs during the company's rise into the stratosphere.

Promptly at 7:30, the guests were ushered to their tables, which were decorated with mounds of roses and candles. Only when all the guests were seated—and all of the 160 waiters working the event were ushered out of the tent—did the Cheneys enter the room.

After the obligatory opening remarks and introductions, Baker got to the podium to introduce his pal. He advised the crowd that he and Cheney had been friends for 30 years; that it was Cheney who'd helped him get into national politics; and that he and Cheney both love the outdoors. When they go hunting or fishing together in Wyoming, Baker announced, Cheney washes the dishes, Baker dries them. A few seconds later, Cheney was at the podium, expounding on the virtues of James A. Baker III. Cheney called him a "'hundred-percenter,' a person of ability, judgment, and absolute integrity. My own career has brought many opportunities, and there's none that I prize more than being in the company of a man like James A. Baker of Houston, Texas." He didn't mention the Carlyle Group.

After the mutual backslapping ended, Cheney went into his well-rehearsed script. His speech at the Baker Institute mimicked one he'd given a week earlier to the conservatives at the Heritage Institute. Filled with justifications for America's invasion of Iraq, it including multiple unsubstantiated inferences that Saddam Hussein was tied to the September 11 attacks on America. "In Iraq," said Cheney, "we took another essential step in the war on terror. The United States and our allies rid the Iraqi people of a murderous dictator, and rid the world of a menace to future peace and security."

Cheney said that Saddam Hussein "had an established relationship with al-Qaeda—providing training to al-Qaeda members in areas of poisons, gases and conventional bombs. He built, possessed, and used weapons of mass destruction. And he refused or evaded all international demands to account for those weapons. . . . Today, because we acted, Iraq stands to be a force for good in the Middle East. In that region and beyond, we will continue to encourage the advance of free markets, democracy, and tolerance—because these are the ideals and aspirations that overcome violence, and turn societies to the pursuit of peace."

He ended with a rhetorical waving of the Stars and Stripes, saying, "A watching world is depending on the United States of America. Only America has the might and the will to lead the world through a time of peril, toward greater security and peace."

When it was over, Cheney took his seat. But at least one member of the audience was disappointed that Cheney had passed up the opportunity to talk about oil or gas, or anything having to do with energy. One oilman who attended the event was a tad dismayed. "He's in Houston, you'd think he might just mention the oil business once," he told me.

Cheney's speech left the crowd hungry. After the Secret Service allowed the waiters to come back into the tent, dinner was served: pumpkin bisque with cilantro crème fraîche (presented in miniature pumpkins), poached lobster with Creole vinaigrette, Cheyenne tenderloin, and breast of quail and, for dessert, Louisiana bread pudding *and* chocolate gateaux, served with champagne. It was all *just* so. Each guest was given an imitation-pewter cup (made in China) and a commemorative program from the James A. Baker III Institute for Public Policy.

The event raised $3.2 million for the Baker Institute. As the speechifying ended, Edward Djerejian, the director of the Baker Institute, told the crowd that the institute now had some $43 million in its endowment. And with Cheney's visit, the White House had once again given its stamp of approval to the Baker Institute.

About two weeks before the gala, Djerejian had delivered to the White House a report on how the Muslim world saw America. He'd been appointed by George W. Bush to head a newly created body called the United States Advisory Group on Public Diplomacy for the Arab and Muslim World. The group's 13 members were charged with investigating how the United States could promote its views to the world's 1.5 billion Muslims. The short version of Djerejian's findings: "They hate us." The report, released on October 1, 2003, said, "Hostility toward America has reached shocking levels. . . . What is required is not merely tactical adaptation but strategic, and radical, transformation." Djerejian's group recommended that the White House spend more money in the Muslim world, building libraries, translating books into Arabic, providing more Internet access, and generally increasing America's profile.

However sizable America's problems were in the Muslim world, they weren't going to overshadow the success that Djerejian and the Baker Institute were having. Thanks to the oil money and the Bush White House, the Baker Institute was giving Houston yet another reason to be proud of itself. James A. Baker III and Dick Cheney were cutting a wide swath. Their friendship was making Houston the place to be. Whether the issue was medicine or energy or foreign policy, Houston was in the middle of things. The Baker Institute and Rice University were in the middle, too. As Baker wrote in a personal note included in the program, the institute's "voice is now being heard."

Partial Guest List at the Baker Institute's Tenth Anniversary Dinner, October 17, 2003 (honorary titles per event program)

His Excellency Hushang Ansary and Mrs. Ansary. Ansary was the minister of economics and finance of Iran under the Shah. After moving to the U.S., he became a penny stock trader, then went into the oil equipment business.

Donation to Baker Institute: $250,000

Donation to George Bush Presidential Library: $1 million

Their Royal Highnesses Ambassador Bandar bin Sultan and Haifa el Faisal. Bandar is the longtime Saudi ambassador to the U.S. and a hunting buddy of Cheney's, Baker's, and George H. W. Bush's. His wife, Haifa el Faisal, has been accused of giving money to Islamic charities that had links to terrorist groups.[2] Bandar and Baker have known each other for nearly two decades. Baker helped convince Bandar to invest money in the Carlyle Group.

Donation to Baker Institute: $100,000

Donation to George Bush Presidential Library: $1 million

James A. Baker III and Susan Baker. The ultimate Bush loyalist, Baker has been pals with George H. W. Bush for five decades. The elder Bush's secretary of state and the younger Bush's savior in the Florida Recount, Baker has made a fortune from being a former secretary of state.

Donation to Baker Institute: $100,000

Donation to George Bush Presidential Library: $10,000

Corporate Donors

ConocoPhillips. A Baker Botts client, ConocoPhillips has oil interests all over the Persian Gulf. It was recently one of the main bidders for a giant natural gas concession in Saudi Arabia. The deal fell through.

Donation to Baker Institute: $100,000

Donation to George Bush Presidential Library: $250,000

Exxon Mobil. The world's largest oil company, Exxon Mobil's ties to the Republican Party are long and deep. A client of Baker Botts's, the company was a bidder for a giant natural gas concession in Saudi Arabia. One of the largest individual shareholders in Exxon Mobil, William Stamps Farish III, is a longtime family friend of the Bushes' and is now ambassador to Great Britain.

Donation to Baker Institute: $100,000

Donation to George Bush Presidential Library by Farish Foundation: $1 million

Corporate Donors (*cont.*)

Shell Oil Company. A domestic subsidiary of Royal Dutch/Shell Group, the Dutch oil giant.

    Donation to Baker Institute: $100,000

    Donation to George Bush Presidential Library by Shell Oil Foundation: $250,000

BP. The British oil giant, formerly known as British Petroleum, is one of Baker Botts's biggest clients. The company chose Baker Botts to represent it on the $3.5 billion Baku-Tbilisi-Ceyhan pipeline project.

    Donation to Baker Institute: $50,000

    Donation to George Bush Presidential Library by BP domestic subsidiary: $100,000

Baker Botts, LLP. The Baker family's law firm, it claims to represent "more than half of the Fortune 100 companies." Its lawyers played a key role in the Florida recount of 2000.

    Donation to Baker Institute: $50,000

    Donation to George Bush Presidential Library: $0

Aramco Services Company. The services arm of the Saudi oil giant Aramco.

    Donation to Baker Institute: $50,000

    Donation to George Bush Presidential Library: $0

Marathon Oil Corporation. Houston-based Marathon has operations all over the world and is particularly active in West Africa.

    Donation to Baker Institute: $50,000

    Donation to George Bush Presidential Library: $0

Halliburton. Dick Cheney's former employer. The Houston-based oil-services giant has garnered enormous federal contracts in Iraq.

    Donation to Baker Institute: $25,000

    Donation to George Bush Presidential Library by Halliburton Foundation: $50,000

Brown & Root. Now owned by Halliburton, Brown & Root is the company whose bosses, George and Herman Brown, paved Lyndon Johnson's road to power in 1937 and 1948. They created the Brown Foundation.

    Donation to Baker Institute: $0

    Donation to George Bush Presidential Library: $10,000

    Donation to George Bush Presidential Library by Brown Foundation: $500,000.

Chapter 26   The United States of Texas

None of the residents of Houston's predominantly African American Third Ward attended the Tenth Anniversary Celebration at the Baker Institute. About the only black faces in the crowd at the gala belonged to the people who were carrying trays.

The Third Ward is only a few miles east of the overwhelmingly white neighborhoods that surround Rice University, but it is light-years away from the privileged affluence displayed at the gala. Block upon block of tiny wood-clad "shotgun" houses sit on postage stamp–sized lots in a quarter that has long been neglected by the city and the state. The Third Ward neighborhood is among the poorest in the state. The average family income in the Third Ward is just over $19,000—less than half the average for the rest of Texas.[1] During the 1990s, infant mortality rates in Houston's poorest neighborhoods exceeded those of countries like Jamaica and Chile.[2] Drugs, crime, and despair are the primary commodities of the Third Ward.

The crushing poverty of inner-city Houston and the growing underclass in the rest of the Lone Star State provide a strong argument against the belief that Texas can continue to dominate American society and provide a model for it. Among the 50 states, Texas ranks . . . :

- ...first in number of citizens incarcerated.
- ...first in the number of prisoners executed.
- ...first in the percentage of adults without health insurance.
- ...first in the percentage of children without health insurance.
- ...first in the overall number of firearms deaths and the number of children killed by guns.
- ...first in the amount of toxic substances dumped into the air, land, and water.
- ...first in smog (with Houston surpassing Los Angeles in 2000 as the city with the worst air quality in America).
- ...second in the number of households who suffer from hunger.
- ...sixth in percentage of population living below poverty level.
- ...forty-fifth in percentage of population who have graduated from high school.

It could be predicted that all of these factors would lead to a decline in Texas' power as the corrosion caused by a growing underclass of low-skilled workers erodes the state's ability to stay solvent and govern itself.

However, it is unlikely that they will.

Texas has always had a substandard educational system. That lack of quality education contributes to the increasing stratification of Texas society. And that disparity will continue. In 1958, the economist John Kenneth Galbraith wrote about the dangers of the United States' becoming a nation dedicated to "private affluence and public squalor." That's a perfect description of Texas, a state in which the poor are wretchedly poor and the rich are wretchedly rich and getting richer. And the state's politicians have little apparent desire to deal with either extreme. The state's inequitable tax system assures that the poorest citizens will continue to pay state and local taxes at rates four times those paid by the state's wealthiest citizens. And with no state income tax, there is no way for the state to wring more tax dollars out of the Big Rich.

The inequities of Texas' tax structure and crumbling social services system have yet to hurt the state's political and business elite. And it's doubtful that they will. Texas will continue dominating America—and the world—and now it's exporting its low-tax, low-service model to the rest of America.

On July 6, 2004, George W. Bush will celebrate his fifty-eighth birthday. About four months later, American voters will decide whether Bush serves a second term in the White House. And given Bush's name, his status as the incumbent, and his ability to raise huge piles of cash—by January 2004, Bush's campaign had raised over $130 million—he may well be reelected.

In the 2004 election, Texas will have 34 electoral college votes (it had 32 in 2000). That means that in 2004, the Lone Star State will have more than 12 percent of the electoral votes needed to win the White House. That fact immediately gives Bush a big head start on whoever opposes him.

But even if George W. Bush loses the White House in 2004, he won't go far. Bush will still be in his political prime. He could attempt a comeback run for the White House in 2008, when he'll be 62. If he loses then, he could even run again in 2012. Or, he might decide to let his brother, Jeb Bush, make a run at the White House. The younger Bush has raised huge amounts of money in Texas and he'd be likely to win the state, given his familiar last name and the state's long tilt toward the GOP.

Plus, George W. and Jeb will undoubtedly rely on the services of the Bush family's resident Svengali, Karl Rove. As the single most powerful and most successful political adviser in America, Rove can tap the money, the networks, and the personnel needed to make a candidate into a winner—and that includes presidential candidates. Rove's power base has always been Texas and the demographic trends in the Lone Star State will help him produce yet more winners.[3]

By 2025, the U.S. Census Bureau expects the state to have over 27 million residents, a 30 percent increase over the 2000 figures. Over the same time period, the federal agency expects that the populations of five other states that have, for decades, played key roles in American politics—Illinois, Michigan, New York, Ohio, and Pennsylvania—will remain essentially flat. That shift in population, and the increased political power that comes with it, will concentrate even more clout within the confines of the Lone Star State as it continues to get additional seats in the U.S. House of Representatives and votes in the Electoral College.

Regardless of whether Bush wins the White House in 2004 or his brother runs sometime in the future, the Texas flag will continue to be carried in Congress by another superconservative Texas Republican, the House majority leader, Tom DeLay. Over the past decade or so, DeLay has become the single most powerful figure on Capitol Hill. Dennis Hastert may be the Speaker of the House, but the place is run by DeLay, who controls more money, lobbyists, and votes than any other politico on Capitol Hill. Hastert himself owes his job to DeLay, who in 1998 pulled strings to make sure that the job was given to the Illinois Republican.

Given his clout, DeLay is likely to be the next Speaker of the House. But even if he doesn't become Speaker, he will undoubtedly continue pushing his right-wing agenda. DeLay is a pro-gun, anti-abortion, antigovernment, born-again Christian zealot who sees his mission in life as the protection of small business and, of course, pork barrel projects for his home state. DeLay is the type of politician who believes pettiness is a virtue. For instance:

- DeLay has passed legislation that prevents the city of Houston from spending any of its federal transportation dollars on mass transit projects like light rail.
- The shutdowns of the federal government in 1995 and 1996 occurred largely because DeLay and his allies in Congress wanted to have a showdown with President Clinton. When Republicans in the Senate wanted to settle the conflict with the Clinton administration, DeLay responded by saying, "Screw the Senate. It's time for all-out war!"
- In the mid-1990s, DeLay allowed lobbyists from the American Petroleum Institute—*is anyone starting to see a pattern here?*—to write major sections of legislation that he was pushing. That legislation, which didn't pass, would have eliminated broad swaths of America's health, safety, and environmental rules. He also tried—and failed—to repeal the Clean Air Act, the federal law that requires industrial plants to minimize the pollutants that they emit into the air. It's probably a coincidence that DeLay's district included numerous petrochemical plants including a Dow Chemical plant that is reportedly the largest complex of its kind in North America.
- It was DeLay who almost single-handedly forced a vote in the House on the impeachment of President Bill Clinton. "Everyone thought impeachment was dead," said a Republican Congressman who opposed impeachment. "He really, in just a matter of weeks, mobilized a base that almost brought down the president of the United States." DeLay mobilized the House to vote on impeachment by threatening moderate Republicans. If they didn't get in line, DeLay told the holdouts, he and his conservative apparatus would find, and provide funding to, a more conservative Republican to run against them in the next election. The threats against the moderates worked. In December 1998, DeLay got his wish. The House,

voting along party lines, impeached Clinton and sent the matter to the U.S. Senate, which in February of 1999 acquitted Clinton. The Senate was nowhere close to having the two-thirds majority needed to remove the president from office. But DeLay had achieved his goal: to embarrass Clinton and weaken the Democrats.

- Americans need not worry about fundamentalist theocrats who live in foreign countries. Instead, they might want to worry just a little about Tom DeLay. In 2002, while preaching at a Baptist church in Pearland, Texas, DeLay told the congregation that God Himself was using him to promote "a biblical worldview." He also said that he'd forced the vote on Clinton's impeachment because the president had "the wrong worldview."

DeLay's divine guidance could be dictating American policy for years to come. Like Bush, DeLay is still relatively young. DeLay, who has been in the U.S. House of Representatives since 1985, the year he turned 38 years old, could hold office until 2020, or even longer. Sam Rayburn served in the House for nearly half a century. DeLay may not serve that long, but his clout and his impact on Congress may ultimately rival that of Rayburn.

DeLay has been a major force on Capitol Hill since 1995, when the Republican Revolution, led by Newt Gingrich, took over the House. That year, DeLay put together a list of the 400 largest political action committees and the amounts of their contributions to each party. DeLay then invited the heads of those PACs to his office, where he showed them how their outfit—and their lobbyists—were classified by the new rulers of the House of Representatives. There were two groups: "friendly" and "unfriendly."

DeLay was playing hardball. And he wasn't shy about it. "If you want to play in our revolution you have to live by our rules," announced the man whose nickname is The Hammer. Those rules included purging all known Democrats from trade associations, political action committees, and lobby firms that work on Capitol Hill. DeLay's "K Street Strategy," named for the Washington street where many lobby firms are located, allowed the Republicans to consolidate their power. More important, it allowed them to begin choking off the flow of money to the Democratic Party. DeLay himself has been the key beneficiary of that choke hold.

In 2002, DeLay raised $1.35 million for his reelection campaign. His political action committee, Americans for a Republican Majority, raised another $3.3 million, which he then doled out—in the same manner that LBJ did while he was in the House and Senate—to his political allies. DeLay also coordinates the flow of millions of dollars through the National Republican Congressional Committee. According to the Center for Responsive Politics, DeLay gave more campaign cash to other Republicans in the 2002 election than any other member of the House. That means that DeLay can help elect more Republicans like himself.

DeLay's money and power give him an extraordinary ability to meld business and politics. In 2003, Nicholas Confessore, writing in *Washington Monthly,* summed up the situation concisely: "The emerging GOP machine" headed by DeLay "is premised on a unity of interests between party and industry."[4]

Put more simply, that "unity of interests" is the merging of business and government. Putting it more simply still, it's crony capitalism of the first order. And as DeLay and Bush become more powerful, their brand of government—*based largely on which donors and special interests are giving money to the Republicans*—will become even more widespread, more pernicious, and more corrosive to our system of democratic capitalism.

The Texas crony network that began its rise with a young congressman named Lyndon Johnson and a little paving company called Brown & Root is poised to radically change the American landscape. From the 1940s to the 1960s, Texans Lyndon Johnson and Sam Rayburn ruled Capitol Hill. Today, Capitol Hill—and Washington—are being ruled by Bush and DeLay, and an army of archconservatives eager to roll back every facet of government and hand it over to their corporate cronies.

Lyndon Johnson and Sam Rayburn were men of a different time. They were not perfect men. They steered contracts to their friends and promoted policies that enriched the already rich. They were staunch supporters of the depletion allowance, a dodge that helped Texas oilmen avoid paying income taxes. But they also passed myriad legislation that changed the face of America—and changed it for the better. Rayburn passed laws that led to rural electrification and soil conservation, put limits on monopolies, and assured proper regulation of railroads and securities. Johnson's wrong-headed support for the Vietnam war ripped the American electorate apart and cost tens of thousands of lives. But he also pushed through some of the most important legislation of the twentieth century, including the Civil Rights Act and the Voting Rights Act. The Civil Rights Act changed the country. It and the Voting Rights Act of 1965 finally—a century after Abraham Lincoln freed the slaves—extended full citizenship to black Americans and other minorities who'd been denied the right to vote.

Johnson signed into law another measure that transformed the relationship between the government and the governed. In 1966, he signed into law the Freedom of Information Act, a truly revolutionary measure that allows ordinary citizens to see the documents that are produced by its government. In signing the law, Johnson said he did so with a "deep sense of pride that the United States is an open society in which the people's right to know is cherished and guarded."[5]

Bush and DeLay are also Texans. But they are cut from a wholly different cloth. Their thirst for power comes not from their desire to help the disenfranchised and the weak, but to strengthen the already strong. Where Johnson and Rayburn believed that government was a tool with which to help mold society, Bush and DeLay believe that government is the enemy. It was DeLay who once called the Environmental Protection Agency "the Gestapo of government." Where Johnson and Rayburn pushed for the improvement of civil rights for all Americans, Bush and DeLay have overseen the biggest rollback of American civil liberties since the Bill of Rights was adopted in 1791. The Patriot Act, passed into law in 2001 by the DeLay-led Congress, repealed big chunks of the Fourth Amendment, which prohibits unlawful searches and seizures. Under the new law, federal police and intelligence agencies can get secret wiretaps on citizens by merely claiming that there is a "significant" foreign intelligence purpose, obtain citizens' phone, bank, and email records, credit card bills, and other documents without having to obtain a subpoena, search homes without notifying the homeowner or showing them a warrant, and even obtain a list of the books a citizen has checked out of the local library or purchased at a local bookstore.

Where Lyndon Johnson believed that the United States is an "open society" and Americans have a right to request and inspect government documents, George W. Bush believes in secrecy. In November of 2001, he signed an executive order that gives him and former U.S. presidents the right to veto any requests to open presidential records. Even in cases where a former president wants his records to be made public, the executive order allows Bush to use executive privilege to stop the release. Furthermore, it gives him and former presidents an indefinite amount of time to consider requests for the release of documents.[6]

The Bush administration also works to limit access to ordinary government documents. In late 2001, Attorney General John Ashcroft sent a memo to federal agencies that directs them to search for and use any legal authority they have to deny access to documents requested by citizens under the Freedom of Information Act.

In 2002, more documents were classified as secret than in any previous year in American history.[7] Bush's secrecy agenda has been so extreme that even Phyllis Schlafly, the longtime conservative Republican and head of the Eagle Forum, blasted the president, saying, "The American people do not and should not tolerate government by secrecy.... Voters aren't going to buy the sanctimonious argument that the Bush Administration has some sort of duty to protect the power of the presidency."[8]

The Bush-DeLay agenda of secrecy and increased power for corporations is in perfect sync with the values of the Texas crony network. Not only are contracts and political money tied together, but the discussion of major policies and big government contracts is done in private, away from the eyes of the press. The cronies are following the Bottsian Way—they're staying quiet and out of the news.

The top Bottsian, James A. Baker III, doesn't have to answer questions from the press about how his work as special envoy to Georgia and as Iraq's debt czar aligns with, or conflicts with, the interests of American taxpayers.

The work that Baker does for the White House, the Carlyle Group, the Saudis, and his other corporate clients is all for him to know and us mortals to NOT know. Baker's law firm, Baker Botts, doesn't discuss how much it was paid for its work in the Florida recount, why it got key appointments from the Bush administration, or what lies behind the contracts it gets from companies like Exxon Mobil and the hyper-corrupt rulers of oil-rich countries such as Azerbaijan. Baker Botts is a law firm. All of its information is privileged. And when it puts its lawyers into positions of power in Washington and elsewhere—well, that's just because they're good lawyers.

When Baker Botts attorneys help set things up so that American taxpayers—through the Export-Import Bank or other federal agencies—are providing loans on financing for the oil companies building the Baku-Tbilisi-Ceyhan pipeline, once again, they're just being good lawyers.

Dick Cheney doesn't have to give information to outfits like the General Accounting Office, when it wants a listing of the people he met with during the formulation of the national energy policy. Cheney has a right to keep all of that information secret, he says, because he's part of the executive branch of government.

George W. Bush's White House has adopted the PR strategy used by corporations: Don't talk to anyone who might be critical. The Bush White House doesn't have to answer questions from the press unless it wants to. Hell, it doesn't even have to provide photographs to authors who are writing books. When the publisher of this book asked for a simple photo of the president and vice president, the White House press office—despite two months of nearly constant phone calls—stonewalled the publisher.

The overriding message from Bush, DeLay, and the entire Texas crony network, it appears, is that all this secrecy is good for us, that all is well in America. *Don't worry*, we're told, *the people who are in power are all Boy Scouts: loyal, honest, brave and hardworking. Furthermore, the fact that we are helping business is good for America. Government needs to run more like a business.*

As America's energy needs continue to grow, that business is increasingly tied to the Persian Gulf—an area that Texas has been colonizing for decades. According to the Energy Information Administration, some 318 American energy companies were doing significant amounts of business in the Persian Gulf in 2003. Of that number, 138 were from Texas—far more than any other state. Texas companies are particularly active in Saudi Arabia. In 2000, Texas companies exported more goods and services to Saudi Arabia—about $1 billion worth—than any other state. That trade accounted for 15 percent of all American exports to the kingdom. In return, the port of Houston takes in about 10 million tons of Saudi crude oil per year, worth about $1.5 billion.

While Saudi crude flows into Houston, Texas companies—led by

Halliburton—are going to be working in Iraq, Saudi Arabia, and other countries in the region for years to come. Whether it is Halliburton, its subsidiary, Kellogg Brown & Root, or another company doesn't really matter. Texas energy companies are going to be in the Persian Gulf because they cannot stay away. Over 60 percent of the world's proven oil reserves are in just five Persian Gulf countries: Iran, Iraq, Kuwait, Saudi Arabia, and the United Arab Emirates. And that oil is essential to world markets and the American economy. Between 2000 and 2020, the amount of Persian Gulf oil imported into the United States will double, to more than four million barrels per day.

Ray Hunt, the Texas crony who helped bankroll the Bushes' rise to power, is investing about $20 million in an exploration program off the coast of Oman. That investment is on top of the tens of millions Hunt has invested in Yemen. Anadarko Petroleum, one of the Texas companies that provided corporate jets to George W. Bush's presidential campaign during the Florida recount, is investing tens of millions of dollars in Qatar, where it recently struck oil in an offshore concession. Anadarko is rapidly expanding its operations in that country.

It's not just lust for oil that's driving the Texas colonization of the Persian Gulf. It's also about slaking America's growing thirst for natural gas. Nine countries in the Persian Gulf contain more than one third of the world's proven natural gas deposits. Qatar alone contains more than 500 trillion cubic feet of gas—enough to supply all of the United States' gas needs for two decades. Iran holds another 800 trillion cubic feet—that's more than three times the combined proven reserves of the United States, Canada, and Mexico.

Texas companies are investing enormous amounts of money to bring that gas home. In July 2003, ConocoPhillips announced a $5 billion deal with Qatar Petroleum to deliver liquefied natural gas (LNG) from Qatar to the United States. Three months later, Exxon Mobil announced a 25-year $12 billion deal to bring Qatari LNG to America. By 2010, Qatar will be the world's biggest exporter of LNG, and that fuel will be increasingly important to global energy markets. Images of tankers carrying huge spherical tanks filled with super-cooled gas could become as common as the familiar oil-carrying tankers of the present.

Given the enormous investments being made by Texas energy companies in the Persian Gulf and the corresponding importance of that energy to the American economy, those companies will need protection that can only be provided by the American military. It's a situation that one American energy executive calls a total "blurring of national energy interests with national security interests." America's energy needs and its national security needs have, he said, "become indistinguishable."

That means that the U.S. Navy will be patrolling the waters of the Persian Gulf, the Gulf of Oman, and the Red Sea for decades to come. The 82nd Airborne Division and the First Marine Expeditionary Unit will remain on call to quell any uprisings and invade any regions that cause trouble. Those commitments will be in addition to the Pentagon's commitments in Iraq. By early 2004, it was clear that the U.S. military is facing a long, bitter, bloody fight in Iraq that will last a decade or more. And the Bush administration, through former Chevron tanker gal Condi Rice, has made it clear that they believe America must make a "generational commitment" to democracy in the Middle East.

While American soldiers promote democracy with M–16s in Baghdad and Bahrain, much of the LNG and crude from the Persian Gulf will be shipped straight to Texas. There, the gas will likely go through LNG terminals and gas pipelines owned by Texas companies. The crude oil will probably be refined at a facility on or near the Houston Ship Channel, which has one of the densest concentrations of petrochemical facilities on earth.

Those plants, worth tens of billions of dollars, cannot be replicated anywhere else in America and the companies that own those facilities—some 125 petrochemical operators are in the Houston area—are going to continue providing huge campaign contributions to politicians like George W. Bush and Tom DeLay. And those laissez-faire Texas Republicans have the exact same worldview as the refiners—that is, a view of the world with cheap, plentiful hydrocarbons, a Hummer in every garage, few (or no) environmental restrictions, easy access to markets, and low taxes.

That's the Texas ethos—and it's coming to your neighborhood.

SNAPSHOT: TEXAS COMPANIES ACTIVE IN THE PERSIAN GULF REGION AND THE MEDITERRANEAN RIM

In 2003 about 318 American companies were doing business in the Persian Gulf, North Africa, and the eastern Mediterranean. Forty-three percent of them, or 138, were from Texas, a tally no other state even approaches. Here are a few of the more recognizable names:

ALGERIA
Anadarko
Burlington Resources
Exxon Mobile
Halliburton
National Oilwell

AZERBAIJAN
Baker Botts
BJ Services
ConocoPhillips
Halliburton

BAHRAIN
Halliburton

DUBAI
Baker Botts
ConocoPhillips

EGYPT
Apache
BJ Services
GlobalSantaFe Corp.
Halliburton

IRAN
Halliburton

IRAQ
Halliburton

ISRAEL
Halliburton

JORDAN
Halliburton

KUWAIT
BJ Services
GlobalSantaFe Corp.
Halliburton

LIBYA
ConocoPhillips
Halliburton

MOROCCO
Halliburton

OMAN
GlobalSantaFe Corp.
Hunt Oil
Smith International
Halliburton

QATAR
Anadarko
BJ Services
ConocoPhillips
Exxon Mobil
GlobalSantaFe Corp.
Marathon Oil Corporation
Halliburton

SAUDI ARABIA
3D/International
Baker Botts
BJ Services

ConocoPhillips
Exxon Mobil
GlobalSantaFe Corp.
Halliburton
Hunt Oil (Hunt Refining)*
Nabors
National Oilwell

SYRIA
BJ Services
ConocoPhillips
Devon Energy

TUNISIA
Anadarko
Halliburton

TURKEY
Halliburton
Baker Botts

UNITED ARAB EMIRATES
ConocoPhillips
Halliburton
BJ Services

YEMEN
Adair International Oil and Gas
Halliburton
Hunt Oil
Nabors Drilling

Sources: Company filings with SEC, *Oil & Gas Journal, International Petroleum Finance, Petroleum Intelligence Weekly, Platts Oilgram News, Engineering News-Record,* Energy Information Administration.

*Hunt Refining is a subsidiary of Ray Hunt's Hunt Oil. Hunt Refining is a buyer of Saudi crude.

SNAPSHOT: IT'S NOT ABOUT OIL! REALLY.

Since the end of the Second Iraq War in May 2003, millions of barrels of oil have been shipped out of Iraq's main export terminal at Mina al-Bakr on the Persian Gulf. Between late June 2003 and late October 2003, about 40 tankers were loaded at Mina al-Bakr. And 25 of those tankers, more than 60 percent, were bound for the United States.

This table, showing scheduled tanker loadings, the purchaser of the crude, and the tankers' destinations, has been compiled from information published by several energy publications (see source note, below). All shipments are 2 million barrels except those marked with an asterisk, which were 1 million barrels. All destinations are in the United States unless otherwise specified. "Gulf Coast" refers to the U.S. coast of the Gulf of Mexico.

EXPORTS FROM MINA AL-BAKR

Date	Buyer	Destination	Date	Buyer	Destination
June 28	ChevronTexaco	West Coast	Oct. 7	ConocoPhillips	Gulf Coast*
Jul. 28	ChevronTexaco	Gulf Coast	Oct. 7	Petrobras	Brazil
Aug. 5	ChevronTexaco	Gulf Coast	Oct. 9	BP	Gulf Coast and
Aug. 6	Shell	Gulf Coast			West Coast
Aug. 8	Vitol	N.A.	Oct. 9	Total	N.A.
Aug. 12	Valero	Gulf Coast	Oct. 10	Exxon Mobil	N.A.
Aug. 16	Petrobras	Brazil	Oct. 10	Royal Dutch/Shell	Gulf Coast and
Aug. 23	Marathon	Gulf Coast			U.K.
Aug. 24	Exxon Mobil	Gulf Coast	Oct. 10	ChevronTexaco	Gulf Coast
Aug. 29	Total	Europe	Oct. 10	Vitol	Canada
Aug. 29	Total	Gulf Coast	Oct. 11	Vitol	Canada
Sept. 2	ChevronTexaco	Gulf Coast	Oct. 13	Valero	Gulf Coast
Sept. 8	Royal Dutch/Shell	Gulf Coast	Oct. 13	Mitsui	Japan
Sept. 9	Vitol	Canada	Oct. 14	Marathon	Gulf Coast
Sept. 16	ConocoPhillips	West Coast	Oct. 15	ConocoPhillips	Gulf Coast and
Sept. 13	ConocoPhillips	West Coast			West Coast*
Sept. 20	Koch	Gulf Coast	Oct. 16	Vadinar	India
Sept. 22	Marathon	Gulf Coast	Oct. 16	Vadinar	India
Sept. 26	Royal Dutch/Shell	U.S. and U.K.	Oct. 19	ENI	Italy*
Sept. 26	BP	U.S. and U.K.	Oct. 20	Koch	Gulf Coast
Oct. 3	Sinochem	Taiwan	Oct. 22	ChevronTexaco	Gulf Coast and
Oct. 5	Petrobras	Brazil			West Coast

Sources: *International Oil Daily, Energy Compass, Petroleum Intelligence Weekly*

Notes

Where short titles are used in the notes, complete bibliographical information on the source is given in the bibliography (starts on page 291).

Chapter 1: From Mina al-Bakr to Houston

1. James Dao, "Navy Seals Easily Seize 2 Oil Sites," *New York Times*, March 22, 2003, B1. This article provided much of the detail concerning the storming of Mina al-Bakr.
2. Bryce, *Pipe Dreams*, 270.
3. John Nance Garner, Sam Rayburn, and Jim Wright are the last three Speakers to come from Texas. Rayburn served as Speaker for three non-consecutive terms, thereby raising the total of terms to five.
4. Fehrenbach, *Lone Star*, 652.
5. *The Economist*, "The Future Is Texas: If you want to see where America is heading, start by studying the Lone Star State," December 21, 2002.
6. Richard Whittle, "Texans Star for Military," *Dallas Morning News*, January 12, 2003.
7. H. W. Brands, "The Alamo Should Have Never Happened," *Texas Monthly*, March 2003, 143.
8. *Growl* (album), 2003. Available from www.raywylie.com.
9. Ken Guggenheim, "Baker advocated Iraq loan program that amassed much of current debt to U.S.," Associated Press, January 11, 2004.
10. BP, BP Statistical Review of World Energy (London: BP, June 2002), 38.

Chapter 2: From Kilgore to Baghdad

1. Goodwyn, *Texas Oil, American Dreams*, 30, 31.
2. Hurt, *Texas Rich*, 92.

3.   Prindle, *Petroleum Politics and the Texas Railroad Commission*, 21.

4.   To avoid confusion, the modern names of these oil companies are used.

5.   Goodwyn, *Texas Oil, American Dreams*, 47.

6.   Prindle, *Petroleum Politics and the Texas Railroad Commission*, 25–26.

7.   Goodwyn, *Texas Oil, American Dreams*, 47.

8.   Economides and Oligney, *The Color of Oil*, 28.

9.   Proclamation by the Governor of the State of Texas, August 16, 1931, 3, available at www.tsl.state.tx.us/governors/personality/sterling-oil-2.html.

10. "All Wells Shut Down in East Texas Oil Field; Troops Ruling," *Austin American*, August 19, 1931, 1.

11. Ronnie Dugger, "Oil and Politics," *Atlantic*, September 1969, 76.

12. Ibid.

13. Pennington, *Coming to Texas*, 76, 77.

14. Tariki did not last as Saudi Arabia's oil minister for very long. In 1962, he was fired by the Saudi royal family. His firing came shortly after he accused the future king, Crown Prince Faisal, of profiting from an oil deal with a Japanese company.

15. Jim Tanner, interview by author, Houston, January 19, 2003.

Chapter 3: The Supercapitalists

1.   Reston, *The Lone Star*, 158.

2.   Michael Economides, interview by author (via e-mail), September 4, 2003.

3.   Carleton, *A Breed So Rare*, 298.

4.   Yergin, *The Prize*, 343.

5.   Economides and Oligney, *Color of Oil*, 76.

6.   At the time of the Aramco deal, the companies were known, respectively, as Standard Oil of New Jersey, Standard Oil of California, Socony-Vacuum, and Texaco. The companies' modern names are used here to avoid confusion.

7.   Yergin, *The Prize*, 412.

8.   Noam Chomsky, "A Modest Proposal: Let Iran 'Liberate' Iraq," *Counter-Punch*, November 18, 2002.

9.   George Strake Jr., telephone interview by author, June 18, 2003. The highest income tax rate was 70 percent or higher until 1981, the first year of Ronald Reagan's first term in office.

Chapter 4: Depleting the Federal Treasury

1.   J. Michael Kennedy, "Changing Times Doom Texas Legend," *Los Angeles Times*, January 21, 1986, 1.

2.   Carleton, *Red Scare*, 15.

3. The depletion allowance wasn't amended until 1975. Major oil companies were no longer allowed to use the allowance, but medium-sized and small independents were allowed to continue using the tax dodge.

4. Dugger, *The Politician*, 68.

5. Champagne, *Congressman Sam Rayburn*, 151.

6. Caro, *Means of Ascent*, 253.

Chapter 5: 1948: Lawyers, Airplanes, and Money—Part I

1. Hyman, *Craftsmanship and Character*, 140.

2. Pratt and Castaneda, *Builders: Herman and George R. Brown*, 104. The law firm's name at that time was Vinson, Elkins, Weems & Francis. For clarity, the modern name of the firm is used throughout the book.

3. Caro, *Path to Power*, 584.

4. Dugger, *The Politician*, 270.

5. Pratt and Casteneda, *Builders: Herman and George R. Brown*, 62.

6. Green, *The Establishment in Texas Politics*, 50.

7. Phipps, *Summer Stock*, 119–20.

8. Dugger, *The Politician*, 318.

9. Wagner, *American Combat Planes*, 296.

10. Dugger, *The Politician*, 229.

11. Caro, *Means of Ascent*, 332.

12. Ibid., 365.

13. Dugger, *The Politician*, 463.

Chapter 6: Brown & Root Cleans Up

1. Pratt and Casteneda, *Builders: Herman and George R. Brown*, 71.

2. Rodengen, *The Legend of Halliburton*, 97.

3. Johnston, *Houston: The Unknown City*, 371.

4. Dugger, *The Politician*, 285.

5. Jones, *Fifty Billion Dollars*, 344.

6. Dugger, *The Politician*, 282.

7. Pratt and Casteneda, *Builders: Herman and George R. Brown*, 118.

8. Caro, *Master of the Senate*, 248.

9. Kesselus, *Alvin Wirtz: The Senator, LBJ and LCRA*, 236.

10. Dugger, *The Politician*, 355.

11. Stone, *The War Years*, 148.

12. Carleton, *A Breed So Rare*, 312.

13. Charles J. V. Murphy, "Texas Business and McCarthy," *Fortune*, May 1954, 101.

14. Carleton, *Red Scare*, 93.

15. Ibid., 91.
16. Murphy, "Texas Business and McCarthy," 100.
17. Carleton, *Red Scare,* 227
18. Ibid., 126.

Chapter 7: Bush and Baker Join Forces

1. Letters from Zapata Oil File, Political Alpha File, Republican Party, Box 1, OAID# 25854, George Bush Presidential Library, Texas A & M University, College Station.
2. "Here's what George Bush Believes," George Bush for Senate flyer, 1964, vertical file, Center for American History, University of Texas, Austin.
3. Lawrence Lee, "Texas Republicans Analyze Their Defeat," *Houston Chronicle,* November 4, 1964, 21.
4. Bush, *Looking Forward,* 70.
5. Larry L. King, "Who's Number One in the Permian Basin?" *Texas Monthly,* February 1975.
6. Parmet, *George Bush,* 111.
7. Sedco, *Annual Report,* 1965.
8. *Texas Observer,* "The Texas Republicans' Senate Runoff," May 29, 1964, 9.
9. Freeman, *The People of Baker & Botts,* 19.
10. The firm was known as Baker & Botts through much of its history. It has since changed its name to Baker Botts LLP. For consistency, the modern name is used throughout this book.
11. Geisst, *Wall Street: A History,* 61, 62.
12. Chandler, *The Visible Hand,* 160.
13. Lipartito and Pratt, *Baker & Botts in the Development of Modern Houston,* 18.
14. Ibid., 90.
15. Freeman, *The People of Baker & Botts,* 46.
16. Lipartito and Pratt, *Baker & Botts in the Development of Modern Houston,* 164.
17. Ibid., 57.
18. Taylor Branch, "James A Baker, III, Esq., Politician," *Texas Monthly,* May 1982, 248.
19. These details were obtained from documents received from the FBI through the Freedom of Information Act.
20. Griffin Smith Jr., "Empires of Paper," *Texas Monthly,* November 1973.
21. The 1964 campaign papers are not available at the George Bush Presidential Library. A note in one of the boxes from the 1964 time period explains that Baker assumed control of those documents shortly after the campaign.
22. Amy Fantini, Daphne Eviatar, Douglas McCollam, Catherine Aman, "Plowed Under," *American Lawyer,* April 2001. Also, Moore, *Bush's War for Re-election* document insert.

Chapter 8: Bleeding Oil

1. Reston, *The Lone Star,* 197.
2. Stern, *The Great Treasury Raid,* 21, 25.
3. Ronnie Dugger, "Oil and Politics," *Atlantic,* September 1969, 86.
4. Parmet, *George Bush,* 126.
5. "Statement by Congressman George Bush on the Oil Import Program Made for the Record Today," November 12, 1969, Congressional file, General Senate Campaign Finance—1970, Box 1, OAID—25858, George Bush Presidential Library, Texas A & M University, College Station.
6. Parmet, *George Bush,* 128.
7. "Excerpts from a Speech by Congressman George Bush (R-TEX.), Before the Beaumont Gulf Coast Engineering Society, Beaumont, Texas, Friday, February 27, 1970," Congressional file, General Senate Campaign Finance—1970, Box 1, OAID—25858, George Bush Presidential Library, Texas A & M University, College Station. The second epigraph at the beginning of this chapter is from the same speech.
8. Yergin, *The Prize,* 754.

Chapter 9: Texas CREEPs for Nixon

1. Petzinger, *Oil & Honor,* 64.
2. Jeff Gerth and Robert Pear, "Files Detail Aid to Bush by Nixon White House," *New York Times,* June 11, 1972, B9.
3. Petzinger, *Oil & Honor,* 65.
4. Engler, *The Brotherhood of Oil,* 201.
5. Thomas B. Edsall, "Economic Ills Strain Alliance of Oilmen, GOP," *Washington Post,* April 25, 1983, A1.
6. Ashman, *Connally,* 180.
7. Robert Strauss, interview by author, Washington, D.C., September 22, 2003.
8. Connally and Herskowitz, *In History's Shadow,* 259.
9. Ashman, *Connally,* 85.
10. David Corn, "Who's on PFIAB—A Bush Secret . . . or Not?" *The Nation,* August 14, 2002.

Chapter 10: Brown & Root Goes to Vietnam

1. Carroll H. Dunn, "Vietnam Studies: Base Development in South Vietnam 1965–1970" (Washington, D. C.: Department of the Army, 1991), available at http://www.army.mil/CMH-PG/books/Vietnam/basedev/index.htm#contents
2. Clardy McCullar, "Army Bets on 'Copter to Endure," *Dallas Morning News,* February 9, 1958.
3. Pratt and Castaneda, *Builders: Herman and George R. Brown,* 239.

4. General Accounting Office, "Report on United States Construction Activities in the Republic of Viet Nam, 1965–1966," report 67–11159.

5. Pratt and Castaneda, *Builders: Herman and George R. Brown*, 243.

Chapter 11: All the Shah's Texans

1. John W. Finney, "Pentagon Hoping Iran Will Buy F–14's," *New York Times*, July 19, 1973, 10.

2. Michael Getler, "Clements 'Aloof' in Arms Bid," *Washington Post*, August 3, 1993, A10.

3. "Mohammad Reza Pahlavi, Shah of Iran," Associated Press, obituary, July 27, 1980.

4. Angus Deming, William E. Schmidt, Scott Sullivan, and Lloyd H. Norman, "Of Arms and the Shah," *Newsweek*, August 23, 1976, 51.

5. Pennington, *Coming to Texas*, 82.

6. Dan Balz, "The Saudi Connection: The Next Best Thing to Mecca Is Houston," *Washington Post*, April 19, 1981, C1.

7. Kinzer, *All the Shah's Men*, 50.

8. Barta, *Texian to His Toenails*, 419.

9. Export-Import Bank of the United States, "EXIMBank Supports $25 Million Sale of U.S. Drilling Rigs to Iran," press release, November 28, 1973.

10. Export-Import Bank, annual reports for the years 1968 to 1979 (figures compiled by author). During that same time period, Iraq received just $54.4 million in Ex-Im Bank funding.

11. Engler, *The Brotherhood of Oil*, 242.

12. "Mohammad Reza Pahlavi, Shah of Iran."

13. Larry Jolidon, "Clements and Shah Share Iran Oil Wealth," *Austin American-Statesman*, January 7, 1979.

14. Bill Clements, interviews by author, Dallas, April 17, 2003, and August 25, 2003 (telephone).

15. Follett, *On Wings of Eagles*, 189. In late 1978, two EDS employees were arrested and Iranian authorities demanded nearly $13 million in bail money for their release. Perot, never one to back away from a fight, decided to run his own paramilitary operation. He organized and paid for a daring rescue operation that retrieved the two men from Tehran and smuggled them over the border into Turkey. The amazing sequence of events was recounted by Follett.

16. Jim Street, "Aircraft Program Resulting from Copter Sales to Iran will Exceed $1 Billion," *Fort Worth Star-Telegram*, October 14, 1973, 30C.

17. Dan Morgan and Walter Pincus, "Iran's Ambitions Fed U.S. Strategists, Weaponeers," *Washington Post*, January 13, 1980, A1.

18. Ibid.

Chapter 12: Brown & Root and Saddam

1. *New York Times,* "U.S. Company Is Granted 117-Million Iraq Contract," September 24, 1973.
2. *New York Times,* "Iraq Nationalizes U.S. Oil Interests," October 8, 1973, 58.
3. Robert R. William, declaration in *Brown & Root International, Inc., v. State Company for Oil Projects of Iraq,* United States District Court, Southern District of Texas, 1991 (docket no. CV–91–594).
4. Parmet, *George Bush,* 292.
5. "United States Embassy in United Kingdom Cable from Charles H. Price II to the Department of State. 'Rumsfeld Mission: December 20 Meeting with Iraqi President Saddam Hussein,'" December 21, 1983, National Security Archive, George Washington University, Washington, D.C., available at http://www.gwu.edu/~nsarchiv/NSAEBB/NSAEBB82/iraq31.pdf.
6. "Shaking Hands with Saddam Hussein: The U.S. Tilts Toward Iraq, 1980–1984," Electronic Briefing Book No. 82, edited by Joyce Battle, National Security Archive, George Washington University, available at http://www.gwu.edu/~nsarchiv/NSAEBB/NSAEBB82/.
7. Lawrence Eagleburger, State Department, letter to William Draper III, December 24, 1983, available at http://www.gwu.edu/~nsarchiv/NSAEBB/NSAEBB82/iraq33.pdf.
8. Patrick E. Tyler, "U.S. Rejects 'Floating Fortress' in Kuwaiti Waters," *Washington Post,* November 29, 1987, A1.
9. David B. Crist, "Joint Special Operations in Support of Earnest Will," *Joint Force Quarterly,* Autumn–Winter, 2001–2, 18, 22.
10. Harold Bernsen, telephone interview by author, ca. June 25, 2003.
11. Williamson, declaration, *Brown & Root v. State Company,* 6.
12. *Oil & Gas Journal,* "International Briefs," May 7, 1990, 62.

Chapter 13: "America's Superstate"

1. Dubose, Reid, and Cannon, *Boy Genius,* 20.
2. National Commission on Financial Institution Reform, Recovery and Enforcement, "Origins and Causes of the S&L Debacle: A Blueprint for Reform" (Washington, D.C.: GPO, July 1993), 28.

Chapter 14: 10000 Memorial and the "Texas Strategy"

1. Walter L. Buenger and Joseph A. Pratt, *But Also Good Business: Texas Commerce Banks and the Financing of Houston and Texas, 1886–1986,* (College Station: Texas A&M University Press, 1986), 321.
2. Waldman, *Who Robbed America?,* 33, 119.

3.   George A. Akerlof and Paul M. Romer, "Looting: The Economic Under-world of Bankruptcy for Profit," unpublished paper, University of California, Berkeley, September 1993, 83.

4.   "Commonwealth Deal Will Cost $1.4 Billion," *Resolution Trust Reporter*, July 1, 1991, 10.

5.   John Hanchette, "The S&L Mess: How It Started, Where It's Going," *Arkansas Democrat-Gazette*, July 22, 1990.

6.   Pizzo, Fricker, and Muolo, *Inside Job,* 325.

7.   Bill Black, interview by author (via e-mail), June 24, 2003.

8.   "Two S&L Felons Are Leaving Prison Early," Associated Press, July 28, 1994.

9.   Waldman, *Who Robbed America?*, 33.

10. Calavita, Pontell, and Tillman, *Big Money Crime,* 97.

11. Maria Recio, "Wright's Role in S&L Crisis Questioned," *St. Louis Post-Dispatch*, March 26, 1989, 1B.

12. Jim Wright, telephone interview with author, July 3, 2003.

13. Mayer, *The Greatest-Ever Bank Robbery,* 240.

14. Pizzo, Fricker, and Muolo, *Inside Job,* 420.

15. Calavita, Pontell, and Tillman, *Big Money Crime,* 118.

16. Ibid., 120.

17. U.S. House Committee on Appropriations, *Hearings Before a Subcommittee of the Committee on Appropriations,* 100th Congress, 2nd sess., 19 April 1988, 1119.

18. Kathleen Day, "Democrats, GOP Trading Accusations in S&L Crisis; Responsibility for Fiscal Scandal Is Debated," *Washington Post,* June 24, 1990, A1.

19. Dave Skidmore, "Treasury Official Says Thrifts Should Supply Extra Cleanup Money," Associated Press, May 31, 1988.

20. Ibid.

21. Pizzo, Fricker, and Muolo, *Inside Job,* 437–38.

22. *National Mortgage News,* "Silverado Loses $245MM, Feels Deposit Outflow," September 6, 1988, 25.

23. Robert Sherrill, "The Looting Decade: S&Ls, Big Banks and Other Triumphs of Capitalism," *The Nation,* November 19, 1990, 589.

24. Ibid.

25. Anthony Harris, "FDIC Calls for Dollars 30 Bn to Liquidate Weakest S&Ls," *Financial Times,* December 1, 1988, 1.

26. For comparison, the rent on former president Bill Clinton's office in New York City in 2003 was $418,295.

Chapter 15: "It's Not About Oil"—Part I

1. Thomas B. Edsall, "Economic Ills Strain Alliance of Oilmen, GOP," *Washington Post,* April 25, 1983, A1.
2. Terence Hunt, "Bush Ends 10-Day Mideast Trip at Oil Refinery Owned by Friend," Associated Press, April 12, 1986.
3. Rick Atkinson, "In '87, U.S. Bore Brunt of Reflagging," *Washington Post,* September 7, 1990, A25.
4. Peter G. Gosselin, "Bush Taps Oil Reserve, Blasts Hikes," *Boston Globe,* September 27, 1990, 1.
5. Martin Zimmerman, "Energy Incentives Please Producers," *Dallas Morning News,* October 30, 1989.
6. President George Bush, Security Directive 54, January 15, 1991, National Security Archive, George Washington University, Washington, D.C., also available at http://www.gwu.edu/~nsarchiv/NSAEBB/NSAEBB82/index.htm. Bush's security directive was part of a raft of declassified documents pertaining to America's energy interests in the Persian Gulf that were published on the World Wide Web in early 2003.
7. Baker and DeFrank, *Politics of Diplomacy,* 336.
8. The law firm that's likely to be charged with collecting that debt is Baker Botts.
9. Letters in court file, *Brown & Root International, Inc., v. State Company for Oil Projects of Iraq,* United States District Court, Southern District of Texas, 1991 (docket no. CV–91–594).
10. "PFIAB Chairpersons," available at http://www.whitehouse.gov/pfiab/chairpersons.html.
11. Armstrong served on the board of Halliburton from 1978 through 2000.

Chapter 16: A Pit Bull on the Pant Leg of Cronyville

1. Andrew Gumbel, "Profile: George W. Bush—This Charmed Man," *The Independent,* November 4, 2000, 5.
2. George Lardner Jr., "Bush Friend Pushed for Guard Slot, Ex-Speaker Testifies," *Washington Post,* September 28, 1999, A8.
3. Thomas Petzinger Jr., Peter Truell, and Jill Abramson, "Family Ties: How Oil Firm Linked to a Son of Bush Won Bahrain Drilling Pact," *Wall Street Journal,* December 6, 1991, A1.
4. Joe Nick Patoski, "Team Player," *Texas Monthly,* June 1999.
5. Robert Bryce, "Stealing Home," *Texas Observer,* May 9, 1997, available at http://www.bushfiles.com/bushfiles/stealinghome.html.
6. Laura Vozzella, "Many Texas Officials Starred in S&L Scandals," *Fort Worth Star-Telegram,* January 1, 1996, 12.

7. Matthew Brady, "Greene Has Thrived on New Challenges," *Fort Worth Star-Telegram,* May 13, 1997, 18.

8. Peter Behr, "Bush Sold Stock After Lawyers' Warning; SEC Closed Probe Before Receiving Letter from Harken's Outside Attorneys," *Washington Post,* November 1, 2002, A4.

9. Jeff Gerth and Richard W. Stevenson, "Bush Calls for End to Loans of a Type He Once Received," *New York Times,* July 11, 2002.

10. Briody, *The Iron Triangle,* 15–16.

11. Susan Mazur, "How Bush Got Bounced from Carlyle Board," available at http://prorev.com/bushcarlyle.htm.

Chapter 17: Oil for W (and W for Oil)

1. Neil A. Lewis, "Flush Bush Turns to Soft Money," *New York Times,* July 17, 1999, A9.

Chapter 18: Halliburton Hires a Crony

1. Susan Baer, "Iraq puts Cheney in Harsh Spotlight," *Baltimore Sun,* October 1, 2003.

2. David S. Broder, "Cheney Bides His Time," *Washington Post,* June 20, 1993, C7.

3. Chalmers Johnson, "The War Business," *Harper's,* November 2003, 57.

4. General Accounting Office, "Contingency Operations: Opportunities to Improve the Logistics Civil Augmentation Program," GAO/NSIAD–97–63 (Washington, D.C.: GAO, 1997), available at http://www.gao.gov.

5. Kathleen Hennessey, "A Contract to Spend," Motherjones.com, May 23, 2002, available at http://www.motherjones.com/web_exclusives/features/news/halliburton.html.

6. Johnson, "The War Business," 57.

7. Richard B. Cheney, "Defending Liberty in a Global Economy," speech delivered at the Cato Institute, Washington, D.C., June 23, 1998.

8. Robert Bryce, "The Candidate from Brown & Root," *Austin Chronicle,* August 25, 2000.

9. "Cheney Backs Iran Investment," *Hart's Middle East Oil and Gas,* June 27, 2000.

10. "Post: Halliburton Iraq Ties More Than Cheney Said," United Press International, June 23, 2001.

11. Johnson, "The War Business," 57.

12. "Halliburton in Saudi Oilfield Logging Venture," *Gulf News,* August 2, 1999.

13. S. C. Gwynne, "Did Dick Cheney Sink Halliburton (and Will It Sink Him?)," *Texas Monthly,* October 2002.

14. Brown was fired in 2003, but thanks to the employment agreement approved by Cheney, Hunt, Baker, and the other directors, EDS was required to pay Brown more than $35 million as a going-away present. When news of Brown's compensation deal surfaced, shareholders and corporate governance experts were horrified. "Why would you design a contract that makes the chief executive fabulously wealthy if they fail?" asked Charles Elson, professor of corporate governance at the University of Delaware.

15. "New RNC Finance Chairman Named," Associated Press, May 9, 2000.

16. Bryce, "Candidate from Brown & Root."

17. Ibid.

Chapter 19: Baker Cashes In

1. David A. Vise, "Former Secretary of State Baker Joins Carlyle Group," *Washington Post*, March 11, 1993, D10.

2. Katie Fairbank, "Smart Buys, Big Names Lifted Carlyle to Success," *Dallas Morning News*, June 20, 2000, 1C.

3. Craig Unger, "Saving the Saudis," *Vanity Fair*, October 2003, 178.

4. Baer, *Sleeping with the Devil*, 48.

5. Oliver Burkeman and Julian Borger, "The Ex-presidents' Club," *The Guardian*, October 31, 2001.

6. The partners are SOCAR (the State Oil Company of Azerbaijan), BP (UK), TPAO (Turkey), Statoil (Norway), Unocal (USA), Itochu (Japan), Amerada Hess (Saudi Arabia), Eni (Italy), TotalFinaElf (France), INPEX (Japan), and ConocoPhillips (USA).

7. Daphne Eviatar, "Wildcat Lawyering," *American Lawyer*, November 2002. Pennzoil (now part of Shell Oil) later got out of the Caspian region.

8. Cited in Maria Recio, "Is Baker Too Near Pie?" Knight Ridder News Service, December 24, 2003.

9. Eviator, "Wildcat Lawyering."

10. Nofziger, *Nofziger*, 280.

11. Elsa Walsh, "How the Saudi Ambassador Became Washington's Indispensable Operator," *The New Yorker*, March 24, 2003.

12. Figures on revenue and number of lawyers from "The AM LAW 100," *American Lawyer*, June 30, 2003.

13. James V. Grimaldi, "After a Respectful Pause, Lawyers Line Up to Sue," *Washington Post*, September 9, 2002.

14. "Top 250," *Corporate Counsel*, January 2003, 1; "Who Defends Corporate America," *The National Law Journal*, October 15, 2001, C4.

Chapter 20: 2000: Lawyers, Airplanes, and Money—Part II

1. Toobin, *Too Close to Call*, 63.
2. Ibid., 7.
3. Steve Bickerstaff, "Post-election Legal Strategy in Florida: Anatomy of Defeat and Victory," *Loyola University Chicago Law Journal*, Fall 2002, 208.
4. Jason Ellenburg, Mark Murray, and Piper Fogg, "Transportation Department Profiles," *National Journal*, June 23, 2001. For further details on the work of all of the attorneys involved in the Florida recount, see American Lawyer Media, Inc., "*The National Law Journal* Lawyers of the Year 2000: Teams Bush and Gore—Boies, Ginsberg, Tribe, Richard, et al.—Exemplary Lawyers and Exemplary Lawyering," press release, December 20, 2000, available at http://www.americanlawyermedia.com/pr/122000nlj.html.
5. Toobin, *Too Close to Call*, 42.
6. Holly Bailey, "Flying High on Corporations," Capital Eye 8, no. 1 (Winter 2001), published online by the Center for Responsive Politics, available at http://www.opensecrets.org/newsletter/ce74/flying.asp. Data also from Bush campaign IRS filings, July 25, 2002.
7. Matt Bivens, "Enron's Washington," *The Nation*, January 24, 2002.
8. Holly Bailey, "Counterstrike: President Bush and the American Airlines Labor Dispute," Money In Politics Alert, Center for Responsive Politics, June 27, 2001, available at http://www.opensecrets.org/alerts/v6/alertv6_23.asp.
9. Crandall has served on the board of directors at Halliburton Co. since 1986.
10. Center for Responsive Politics, "President George W. Bush, Introduction," available at http://www.opensecrets.org/bush/index.asp.
11. These figures were obtained from Bush campaign filings with the Internal Revenue Service. Other firms who got significant checks from the Bush campaign include the Chicago law firm Bartlit Bech Herman Palenchar ($385,000) and the Fort Lauderdale firm Conrad & Scherer ($237,000).

Chapter 21: The President from Baker Botts . . . and Halliburton, and Exxon Mobil

1. James V. Grimaldi, "Texas Firms Line Up U.S. Aid in Peru," *Washington Post*, November 20, 2002, A01.
2. "Nominee for No. 2 Spot at Interior Stirs Opposition," *Seattle Post-Intelligencer*, June 20, 2001.
3. Ken Herman, "President Keeps Up Tradition with His Ambassador Choices," *Austin American-Statesman*, April 14, 2001, A1.
4. "Chevron Renames Condoleezza Rice," *Oil Daily*, May 8, 2001, 51.
5. Howard Fineman and Michael Isikoff, "Big Energy at the Table," *Newsweek*, May 14, 2001, 18.

6. Jordan served as U.S. ambassador to Saudi Arabia until October of 2003. Some news reports suggested that the Saudi government had asked for his removal. The *Washington Times* reported that Prince Sultan, a Baker Botts client, had demanded Jordan's removal.

7. White House, "National Energy Policy: Report of the National Energy Policy Development Group," May 2001, available at www.whitehouse.gov/energy.

8. General Accounting Office, "Energy Task Force: Process Used to Develop the National Energy Policy," August 2003, available at www.gao.gov/new.items/d03894.pdf.

9. William Lowther, "US Ambassador's Wealth Built on Deal with Nazis," *Mail On Sunday,* February 18, 2001, 11.

10. Michael York, "Bush and Breeder Go Way Back," *Los Angeles Times,* May 6, 1990, E16.

11. Michael Davis, "Bush Limits Florida Drilling," *Houston Chronicle,* May 30, 2002, A1.

12. John Williams, "Bush's Texas Two-Step for Cash," *Houston Chronicle,* July 18, 2003.

Chapter 22: Dreaming War

1. James A. Baker III Institute for Public Policy of Rice University and the Council on Foreign Relations, "Strategic Energy Policy Challenges for the 21st Century," report (Houston and New York City: James A. Baker III Institute for Public Policy of Rice University and the Council on Foreign Relations, April 2001), 17.

2. Ibid., 42.

3. John Diamond, "The Bribery Coast," *Chicago Tribune,* February 20, 2000, 1.

4. The full text of the letter and list of signatories is available at the web site of the Project for the New American century: http://www.newamericancentury.org/iraqclintonletter.htm.

5. Council on Foreign Relations and the James A. Baker III Institute for Public Policy of Rice University, "Guiding Principles for U.S. Post-Conflict Policy in Iraq," report (Houston and New York City: James A. Baker III Institute for Public Policy of Rice University and the Council on Foreign Relations, December 2002), 12.

6. Warren R. True, "Construction Plans Sag in Face of Stubborn Recession, War Prospects," *Oil & Gas Journal,* February 3, 2003, 62.

7. CBS, *60 Minutes,* "All in the Family," broadcast April 27, 2003.

8. Anthony Bianco and Stephanie Anderson Forest, "Outsourcing War," *Business Week,* September 15, 2003.

Chapter 23: "It's Not About Oil!"—Part II

1. Elizabeth Allen, "Elder Bush Defends Gulf War I; He Says the Coalition Indeed Did Finish the Job: Freeing Kuwait," *San Antonio Express-News*, March 26, 2003.
2. "Words on the Cost," *New York Times*, September 10, 2003, A8.
3. Council on Foreign Relations and the James A. Baker III Institute for Public Policy of Rice University, "Guiding Principles for U.S. Post-Conflict Policy in Iraq," report (Houston and New York City: James A. Baker III Institute for Public Policy of Rice University and the Council on Foreign Relations, December 2002), 12.
4. Ed Vuillamy, "Israel Seeks Pipeline for Iraqi Oil," *The Guardian*, April 19, 2003.
5. Amiram Cohen, "U.S. Checking Possibility of Pumping Oil from Northern Iraq to Haifa, via Jordan," *Haaretz Daily*, 25 August 2003.
6. Vuillamy, "Israel Seeks Pipeline for Iraqi Oil."
7. Rajiv Chandrasekaran, "'Our Heritage Is Finished': Looters Destroyed What War Did Not," *Washington Post*, April 13, 2003, A1.
8. Neela Banerjee, "Looting Leaves Iraq's Oil Industry in Ruins," *New York Times*, June 10, 2003.
9. "First Postwar Iraqi Oil Set to Load," *Energy Compass*, June 19, 2003.
10. "Ross Issues Warrants to Pay Troops," *Austin American*, August 20, 1931, 1.
11. Suzanne Goldenberg, "Up to 15,000 People Killed in Invasion, Claims Thinktank," *The Guardian*, October 29, 2003.
12. Mark Benjamin, "U.S. Casualties from Iraq War Top 9,000," UPI, November 14, 2003.
13. Dave Montgomery, "Cheney's Halliburton Ties Draw More Scrutiny in Iraq Contracting Review," *Fort Worth Star-Telegram*, September 28, 2003.
14. Information on Cheney's payments was obtained from U.S. Office of Government Ethics form 201's.
15. James K. Galbraith, "The Unbearable Costs of Empire," *The American Prospect*, November 18, 2002.

Chapter 24: Minister of Nondisclosure

1. James A. Baker III, "America's Vital Interest in the 'New Silk Road,'" *New York Times*, July 21, 1997.
2. "Georgia Situation Will Not Harm Int'l Pipeline Projects—Shevardnadze," Interfax, November 17, 2003.
3. Rob Parsons, "Even If Shevardnadze Bows to Pressure to Rerun Elections, His Troubles Will Be Far from Over," *Sunday Herald* (Glasgow, Scotland), November 16, 2003.

Chapter 25: A Black-Tie Affair

1. Allan Dodds Frank, "Creative Financing," *Forbes*, June 2, 1986, 118.
2. Craig Unger, "Saving the Saudis," *Vanity Fair*, October 2003, 164.

Chapter 26: The United States of Texas

1. "Shotgun" houses are so named because if a shotgun was fired through the front door the shot from the blast would travel straight through the house and out the backdoor.
2. Tom Kennedy, "City's 5th Ward like Third World," *Houston Post*, April 30, 1990.
3. Of course, in early 2004 there was a possibility that Rove could self-destruct. At that time Rove was one of the prime suspects in the illegal naming of Valerie Plame, the wife of former U.S. ambassador Joe Wilson, who was also a CIA operative. Plame was outed in a column written by the conservative columnist Robert Novak after Wilson criticized the Bush administration's claim that the Iraqis had tried to buy uranium in Niger in the 1990s. Leaking the names of undercover CIA agents is a violation of federal law. Rove has a history of leaking material to Novak. However, as this book goes to press, it's not clear that the Department of Justice investigation will have any success in uncovering and proving the identity of the leaker.
4. Nicholas Confessore, "Welcome to the Machine: How the GOP Disciplined K Street and Made Bush Supreme," *Washington Monthly*, July–August 2003.
5. White House, press release, July 4, 1966. The act was revised in 1974 to make it more enforceable. Some historians argue that the act was not effective until 1974.
6. "An Executive Order Hiding Presidential Papers," *San Francisco Chronicle*, November 11, 2001.
7. Harper's Index, October 2003, available at http://www.harpers.org/harpersindex2003–10.html.
8. Phyllis Schlafly, "Secrecy Is a Losing Ploy," March 6, 2002, available at http://www.eagleforum.org/column/2002/mar02/02-03-06.shtml.

Bibliography

Aburish, Said K. *The Rise, Corruption and Coming Fall of the House of Saud*. New York: St. Martin's/Griffin, 1994.

Alexander, Thomas E. *The Stars Were Big and Bright: The United States Army Air Forces and Texas During World War II*. Austin: Eakin Press, 2001.

Ashman, Charles. *Connally: The Adventures of Big Bad John*. New York: William Morrow, 1974.

BP p.l.c. *BP Statistical Review of US Energy*. June 2001.

Baer, Robert. *Sleeping with the Devil: How Washington Sold Our Soul for Saudi Crude*. New York: Crown, 2003.

Baker, James A. III, with Thomas M. DeFrank. *Politics of Diplomacy: Revolution, War, and Peace, 1989–1992*. New York: G. P. Putnam, 1995.

Barnes & Noble Books. *The Encyclopedia of Modern Warplanes: The Development and Specifications of all Active Military Aircraft*. New York: Barnes & Noble Books, 1995.

Barta, Carolyn. *Texian to His Toenails*. Austin: Eakin Press, 1996.

Briody, Dan. *The Iron Triangle: Inside the Secret World of the Carlyle Group*. Hoboken: John Wiley & Sons, 2003.

Bryce, Robert. *Pipe Dreams: Greed, Ego, and the Death of Enron*. New York: PublicAffairs, 2002.

Buenger, Walter L. and Joseph A. Pratt, *But Also Good Business: Texas Commerce Banks and the Financing of Houston and Texas, 1886–1986*. College Station: Texas A&M University Press, 1986.

Bush, George. *Looking Forward*. New York: Bantam Books, 1987.

Calavita, Kitty, Henry N. Pontell, and Robert H. Tillman. *Big Money Crime: Fraud and Politics in the Savings and Loan Crisis*. Berkeley: University of California Press, 1997.

Carleton, Don E. *A Breed So Rare: The Life of J. R. Parten, Liberal Texas Oil Man, 1896–1992.* Austin: Texas State Historical Association, 1998.

———. *Red Scare: Right-Wing Hysteria, Fifties Fanaticism, and Their Legacy in Texas.* Austin: Texas Monthly Press, 1985.

Caro, Robert A. *The Path to Power.* New York: Vintage Books, 1981.

———. *Means of Ascent.* New York: Vintage Books, 1990.

———. *Master of the Senate.* New York: Alfred A. Knopf, 2002.

Champagne, Anthony. *Congressman Sam Rayburn.* New Brunswick, N.J.: Rutgers University Press, 1984.

Chandler, Alfred D., Jr. *The Visible Hand: The Managerial Revolution in American Business.* Cambridge: Belknap Press, 1977.

Clark, Wesley K. *Winning Modern Wars: Iraq Terrorism and the American Empire.* New York: PublicAffairs, 2003.

Connally, John, and Mickey Herskowitz. *In History's Shadow: An American Odyssey.* New York: Hyperion, 1993.

Dubose, Lou, Jan Reid, and Carl Cannon. *Boy Genius.* New York: PublicAffairs, 2003.

Dugger, Ronnie. *The Politician: The Life and Times of Lyndon Johnson.* New York: W. W. Norton, 1982.

Economides, Michael, and Ronald Oligney. *The Color of Oil.* Katy, Texas: Round Oak Publishing Company, 2000.

Engler, Robert. *The Brotherhood of Oil: Energy Policy and the Public Interest.* Chicago: University of Chicago Press, 1977.

Fehrenbach, T. R. *Lone Star: A History of Texas and the Texans.* Da Capo Press, 1968.

Follett, Ken. *On Wings of Eagles.* New York: Signet, 1984.

Freeman, J. H. *The People of Baker & Botts.* Houston: Baker & Botts, 1992.

Geisst, Charles R. *Wall Street: A History.* New York: Oxford University Press, 1997.

Goodwyn, Lawrence. *Texas Oil, American Dreams: A Study of the Texas Independent Producers and Royalty Owners Association.* Austin: Texas State Historical Association, 1996.

Green, George Norris. *The Establishment in Texas Politics: The Primitive Years, 1938–1957.* Westport, Conn.: Greenwood Press, 1979.

Hurt, Harry, III. *Texas Rich: The Hunt Dynasty from the Early Oil Days Through the Silver Crash.* Bridgewater, N.J.: Replica Books, 1991.

Hyman, Harold. *Craftsmanship and Character: A History of the Vinson & Elkins Law Firm of Houston, 1917–1997.* Athens: University of Georgia Press, 1998.

Johnston, Marguerite. *Houston: The Unknown City, 1836–1946.* College Station: Texas A&M University Press, 1991.

Jones, Jesse H. *Fifty Billion Dollars: My Thirteen Years with the RFC.* New York: Macmillan, 1951.

Kesselus, Ken. *Alvin Wirtz: The Senator, LBJ and LCRA*. Austin: Eakin Press, 2002.

Kinzer, Stephen. *All the Shah's Men: An American Coup and the Roots of Middle East Terror*. Hoboken, N.J.: John Wiley, 2003.

Lee, James Ward, Carolyn N. Barnes, Kent A. Bowman, and Laura Crow. *1941: Texas Goes to War*. Denton: University of North Texas Press, 1991.

Lind, Michael. *Made in Texas: George W. Bush and the Southern Takeover of American Politics*. New York: Basic Books, 2003.

Lipartito, Kenneth J., and Joseph A. Pratt. *Baker & Botts in the Development of Modern Houston*. Austin: University of Texas Press, 1991.

Mayer, Martin. *The Greatest-Ever Bank Robbery: The Collapse of the Savings and Loan Industry*. New York: Charles Scribner's Sons, 1990.

Moore, James. *Bush's War for Re-election: Iraq, the White House, and the People*. Hoboken, N. J.: John Wiley & Sons, 2004.

Nofziger, Lyn. *Nofziger*. Washington, D.C.: Regenery Gateway, 1992.

Parmet, Herbert S. *George Bush: The Life of a Lone Star Yankee*. New York: Scribner, 1997.

Pennington, Richard. *Coming to Texas: International Students at the University of Texas*. Austin: Ex-students Association of the University of Texas, 1994.

Petzinger, Thomas Jr. *Oil and Honor: The Texaco-Pennzoil Wars*. New York: G. P. Putnam, 1987.

Phipps, Joe. *Summer Stock: Behind the Scenes with LBJ in '48*. Fort Worth: Texas Christian University Press, 1992.

Pizzo, Stephen, Mary Fricker, and Paul Muolo. *Inside Job: The Looting of America's Savings and Loans*. New York: HarperPerennial, 1989.

Pratt, Joseph A., and Christopher J. Castaneda. *Builders: Herman and George R. Brown*. College Station: Texas A&M University Press, 1999.

Prindle, David E. *Petroleum Politics and the Texas Railroad Commission*. Austin: University of Texas Press, 1981.

Reston, James, Jr. *The Lone Star: The Life of John Connally*. New York: Harper & Row, 1989.

Rodengren, Jeffrey L. *The Legend of Halliburton*. Fort Lauderdale: Write Stuff Syndicate, 1996.

Stern, Philip M. *The Great Treasury Raid*. New York: Random House, 1962.

Stone, I. F. *The War Years: A Nonconformist History of Our Times*. Boston: Little, Brown, 1988.

Toobin, Jeffrey. *Too Close to Call: The Thirty-Six-Day Battle to Decide the 2000 Election*. New York: Random House, 2001.

Wagner, Ray. *American Combat Planes*. Garden City: Doubleday, 1982.

Waldman, Michael. *Who Robbed America?* New York: Random House, 1990.

Yergin, Daniel. *The Prize: The Epic Quest for Oil, Money and Power*. New York: Simon & Schuster, 1991.

Appendix

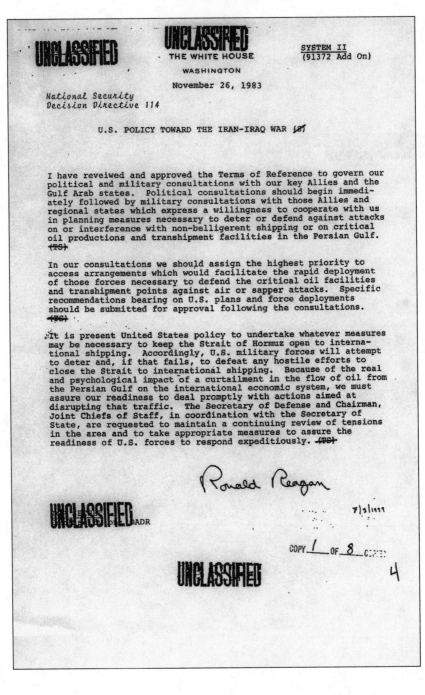

UNCLASSIFIED   UNCLASSIFIED   SYSTEM II

THE WHITE HOUSE   (91372 Add On)

WASHINGTON

November 26, 1983

National Security
Decision Directive 114

U.S. POLICY TOWARD THE IRAN-IRAQ WAR (S)

I have reveiwed and approved the Terms of Reference to govern our
political and military consultations with our key Allies and the
Gulf Arab states. Political consultations should begin immediately followed by military consultations with those Allies and
regional states which express a willingness to cooperate with us
in planning measures necessary to deter or defend against attacks
on or interference with non-belligerent shipping or on critical
oil productions and transhipment facilities in the Persian Gulf.
(TS)

In our consultations we should assign the highest priority to
access arrangements which would facilitate the rapid deployment
of those forces necessary to defend the critical oil facilities
and transhipment points against air or sapper attacks. Specific
recommendations bearing on U.S. plans and force deployments
should be submitted for approval following the consultations.
(TS)

It is present United States policy to undertake whatever measures
may be necessary to keep the Strait of Hormuz open to international shipping. Accordingly, U.S. military forces will attempt
to deter and, if that fails, to defeat any hostile efforts to
close the Strait to international shipping. Because of the real
and psychological impact of a curtailment in the flow of oil from
the Persian Gulf on the international economic system, we must
assure our readiness to deal promptly with actions aimed at
disrupting that traffic. The Secretary of Defense and Chairman,
Joint Chiefs of Staff, in coordination with the Secretary of
State, are requested to maintain a continuing review of tensions
in the area and to take appropriate measures to assure the
readiness of U.S. forces to respond expeditiously. (TS)

Ronald Reagan

UNCLASSIFIED ADR

COPY _1_ of _8_ COPIES

UNCLASSIFIED

4

THE WHITE HOUSE

WASHINGTON

January 15, 1991

NATIONAL SECURITY DIRECTIVE 54

MEMORANDUM FOR THE VICE PRESIDENT
        THE SECRETARY OF STATE
        THE SECRETARY OF THE TREASURY
        THE SECRETARY OF DEFENSE
        THE ATTORNEY GENERAL
        THE SECRETARY OF ENERGY
        DIRECTOR, OFFICE OF MANAGEMENT AND BUDGET
        THE ASSISTANT TO THE PRESIDENT FOR
            NATIONAL SECURITY AFFAIRS
        THE DIRECTOR OF CENTRAL INTELLIGENCE
        THE CHAIRMAN OF THE JOINT CHIEFS OF STAFF

SUBJECT: Responding to Iraqi Aggression in the Gulf   (U)

1.   Access to Persian Gulf oil and the security of key friendly
states in the area are vital to U.S. national security.
Consistent with NSD 26 of October 2, 1989, and NSD 45 of August
20, 1990, and as a matter of long-standing policy, the United
States remains committed to defending its vital interests in the
region, if necessary through the use of military force, against
any power with interests inimical to our own. Iraq, by virtue of
its unprovoked invasion of Kuwait on August 2, 1990, and its
subsequent brutal occupation, is clearly a power with interests
inimical to our own. Economic sanctions mandated by UN Security
Council Resolution 661 have had a measurable impact upon Iraq's
economy but have not accomplished the intended objective of
ending Iraq's occupation of Kuwait. There is no persuasive
evidence that they will do so in a timely manner. Moreover,
prolonging the current situation would be detrimental to the
United States in that it would increase the costs of eventual
military action, threaten the political cohesion of the coalition
of countries arrayed against Iraq, allow for continued
brutalization of the Kuwaiti people and destruction of their
country, and cause added damage to the U.S. and world economies.
This directive sets forth guidelines for the defense of vital
U.S. interests in the face of unacceptable Iraqi aggression and
its consequences. (S)

2.   Pursuant to my responsibilities and authority under the
Constitution as President and Commander in Chief, and under the
laws and treaties of the United States, and pursuant to H. J.
Res. 77 (1991), and in accordance with the rights and obligations
of the United States under international law, including UN
Security Council Resolutions 660, 661, 662, 664, 665, 666, 667,

669, 670, 674, 677, and 678, and consistent with the inherent
right of collective self-defense affirmed in Article 51 of the
of the United Nations Charter, I hereby authorize military
actions designed to bring about Iraq's withdrawal from Kuwait.
These actions are to be conducted against Iraq and Iraqi forces
in Kuwait by U.S. air, sea and land conventional military forces,
in coordination with the forces of our coalition partners, at a
date and time I shall determine and communicate through National
Command Authority channels. This authorization is for the
following purposes:

    a.   to effect the immediate, complete and unconditional
        withdrawal of all Iraqi forces from Kuwait;

    b.   to restore Kuwait's legitimate government;

    c.   to protect the lives of American citizens abroad; and

    d.   to promote the security and the stability of the
        Persian Gulf. (TS)

3.   To achieve the above purposes, U.S. and coalition forces
should seek to:

    a.   defend Saudi Arabia and the other GCC states against
        attack;

    b.   preclude Iraqi launch of ballistic missiles against
        neighboring states and friendly forces;

    c.   destroy Iraq's chemical, biological, and nuclear
        capabilities;

    d.   destroy Iraq's command, control, and communications
        capabilities;

    e.   eliminate the Republican Guards as an effective
        fighting force; and

    f.   conduct operations designed to drive Iraq's forces from
        Kuwait, break the will of Iraqi forces, discourage
        Iraqi use of chemical, biological or nuclear weapons,
        encourage defection of Iraqi forces, and weaken Iraqi
        popular support for the current government. (TS)

4.   While acting to achieve the purposes in paragraph 2 above
and carry out the missions in paragraph 3 above, every reasonable
effort should be taken to:

    a.   minimize U.S. and coalition casualties and

b.   reduce collateral damage incident to military attacks,
     taking special precautions to minimize civilian
     casualties and damage to non-military economic
     infrastructure, energy-related facilities, and
     religious sites. (TS)

5.   The United States shall seek the maximum participation of
its coalition partners in all aspects of operations conducted in
either Kuwait or Iraq. (S)

6.   The United States will encourage Iraq's neighbors Syria and
Turkey to increase their forces along their borders with Iraq so
as to draw off Iraqi forces from, and resources devoted to, the
Kuwait theatre of operations. (S)

7.   The United States will discourage the government of Israel
from participating in any military action. In particular, we
will seek to discourage any preemptive actions by Israel. Should
Israel be threatened with imminent attack or be attacked by Iraq,
the United States will respond with force against Iraq and will
discourage Israeli participation in hostilities. (TS)

8.   The United States will discourage any participation in
hostilities by Jordan. Similarly, the United States will
discourage any Jordanian facilitation of, or support for, Iraqi
military efforts. The United States will also discourage
violation of Jordanian territory or airspace. (TS)

9.   The United States recognizes the territorial integrity of
Iraq and will not support efforts to change current boundaries.
(S)

10. Should Iraq resort to using chemical, biological, or nuclear
weapons, be found supporting terrorist acts against U.S. or
coalition partners anywhere in the world, or destroy Kuwait's oil
fields, it shall become an explicit objective of the United
States to replace the current leadership of Iraq. I also want to
preserve the option of authorizing additional punitive actions
against Iraq. (TS)

11. All appropriate U.S. government departments and agencies are
to prepare and present to me for decision those measures
necessary for stabilizing to the extent possible energy supplies
and prices during hostilities. (C)

12. Military operations will come to an end only when I have
determined that the objectives set forth in paragraph 2 above
have been met. (S)

```
___NOV 05 '91 10:11 BROWN ROOT & ROOT HOUSTON                    P.7/8.1

  R1774                                        LEGAL ADVISE?         12

  RX-DDD 2309 CDT 05/15/91          Thanks

  B R INC HOU                       Dw Campbell -

  B R INC HOU

  TRT EXPRESS MAIL

  MESSAGE SEQUENCE NUMBER: 0016
  ORIGINATOR ANSWERBACK: 1012 PGM 3 IK
  TIME RECEIVED: 16-MAY-91 00:11
  RE:
  OCP: FKJ429
  166365 BROWN UT
  1012 PGM 3 IK


  FROME: MINISTRY OF OIL.
  TELEX: 166399 , USA.
  TO:  BROWN AND ROOT, INC.
  ATTN.: MR. THAD SMITH,
         SENIOR VICE PRESIDENT.


  REF.: 274
       M/            DTD./ 15/5/1991


  DEAR SIR.


     WITH THE SITUATION BEING BACK TO NORMAL IN OUR AREA , WE
  WOULD  LIKE TO RESUME OUR PREVIOUS RELATIONSHIP AND TO INITIATE
  WITH YOUR COMPANY DISCUSSIONS CONCERNING YOUR PARTICIPATION IN OUR
  REBUILDING AND RECONSTUCTING OUR OIL INSTALLATIONS.


  FOR THIS MATTER WE WOULD LIKE TO INVITE YOU AND YOUR
  REPRESENTATIVES TO VISIT  US IN BAGHDAD. PLEASE LET ME HAVE YOUR
  REPLY AS SOON AS POSSIBLE IN ORDER TO MAKE THE NECESSARY ARRANG-
  EMENT FOR THE VISIT.


  BEST REGARDS


  MINISTER OF STATE FOR
  PETROLEUM AFFAIRS
  OSAMA A. R. HAMADI AL- HITI
```

EXHIBIT

1

N.B.

KINDLY ADDRES ANY TELEX YOU WOULD LIKE TO SEND TO US TO ONE OF THESE
NUMBERS (UNTILL FURTHER NOTICE):(24207) (23061) THU JORDAN TELEX
CODE SHOULD BE USED WITH THE ABOVE NUMBERS INSTEAD OF THE IRAQI CODE.
TKS.

166365 BROWN UT

NNNN;012 PGM 3 IK
NNNN

B R INC HOU

THEY DISCONNECT
Elapsed time 00:00:54

PRINTED AT 2310 CDT 05/15/91

TELEX

TO: MINISTRY OF STATE FOR PETROLEUM AFFAIRS

ATTENTION: HIS EXCELLENCY OSAMA A. R. HAMADI AL-HITI, MINISTER

TELEX NO.:   24207/23061

DESTINATION: JORDAN

FROM: T. E. KNIGHT
                 EXECUTIVE VICE PRESIDENT
                 BROWN & ROOT, INC.

DATE: MAY 23, 1991

JOB CHARGE: 364-364-4243

DEAR SIR:

YOUR TELEX OF 16 MAY 91 TO MR. THAD SMITH INVITING US TO BAGHDAD
FOR DISCUSSIONS CONCERNING BROWN & ROOT'S PARTICIPATION IN IRAQ'S
REBUILDING AND RECONSTRUCTING OF ITS OIL INSTALLATIONS HAS BEEN
REFERRED TO ME FOR REPLY.

WE WERE PLEASED TO HEAR FROM YOU AS WE HAVE ALWAYS VALUED OUR
RELATIONSHIP WITH SCOP AND THE MINISTRY OF OIL. HOWEVER, AT THIS
TIME, IT IS NOT POSSIBLE FOR US TO ACCEPT YOUR INVITATION BECAUSE
OF THE LEGAL RESTRICTIONS IMPOSED BY THE U.S. GOVERNMENT. WHEN THE
RESTRICTIONS ARE REMOVED, WE WILL BE HAPPY TO MEET WITH THE
MINISTRY OF OIL FOR SUCH DISCUSSIONS.

Exhibit
2

MINISTRY OF STATE FOR PETROLEUM AFFAIRS
MAY 23, 1991
PAGE 2

AS YOU ARE UNDOUBTEDLY AWARE, APPROXIMATELY $18 MILLION U.S.

REMAINS UNPAID TO BROWN & ROOT FOR WORK PERFORMED PRIOR TO THE

IMPOSITION OF RESTRICTIONS.

WE ANTICIPATE YOUR EARLY PAYMENT OF THE OUTSTANDING SUM WHICH WILL

PROVIDE A SOUND BASIS FOR DISCUSSIONS BETWEEN US AFTER THE

RESTRICTIONS ARE REMOVED.

SINCERELY,

T. E. KNIGHT
EXECUTIVE VICE PRESIDENT
BROWN & ROOT, INC.

PWA06491.TLX

bcc: J. W. Wilson
     T. Smith, III
     M. W. Finnen

Index

PublicAffairs is a publishing house founded in 1997. It is a tribute to the standards, values, and flair of three persons who have served as mentors to countless reporters, writers, editors, and book people of all kinds, including me.

I.F. STONE, proprietor of *I. F. Stone's Weekly*, combined a commitment to the First Amendment with entrepreneurial zeal and reporting skill and became one of the great independent journalists in American history. At the age of eighty, Izzy published *The Trial of Socrates*, which was a national bestseller. He wrote the book after he taught himself ancient Greek.

BENJAMIN C. BRADLEE was for nearly thirty years the charismatic editorial leader of *The Washington Post*. It was Ben who gave the *Post* the range and courage to pursue such historic issues as Watergate. He supported his reporters with a tenacity that made them fearless and it is no accident that so many became authors of influential, best-selling books.

ROBERT L. BERNSTEIN, the chief executive of Random House for more than a quarter century, guided one of the nation's premier publishing houses. Bob was personally responsible for many books of political dissent and argument that challenged tyranny around the globe. He is also the founder and longtime chair of Human Rights Watch, one of the most respected human rights organizations in the world.

For fifty years, the banner of Public Affairs Press was carried by its owner Morris B. Schnapper, who published Gandhi, Nasser, Toynbee, Truman, and about 1,500 other authors. In 1983, Schnapper was described by *The Washington Post* as "a redoubtable gadfly." His legacy will endure in the books to come.

Peter Osnos, *Publisher*